HUMAN RIGHTS
AND THE LIBERATION OF MAN
IN THE AMERICAS

PREPARED FOR PUBLICATION UNDER THE
SPONSORSHIP OF THE CATHOLIC
INTER-AMERICAN COOPERATION PROGRAM
(CICOP) LATIN AMERICAN BUREAU, U.S.C.C.

CONTRIBUTORS

Victor Alba   Neil P. Hurley
Robert J. Alexander   François H. Lepargneur
Brian D. Beun   Jorge Mejia
Hector Borrat   George L. Metcalfe
Helder Pessoa Camara   Luis Alberto Meyer
Juan A. Casasco   Carlos Sanz de Santamaría
Louis M. Colonnese   René de León Schlotter
John F. Dearden   Juan Luis Segundo
Robert J. Fox   William N. Simonson
Paulo Freire   Glenn Smiley
Bernard Häring   Csanad Toth

HUMAN RIGHTS
AND THE
LIBERATION OF MAN
IN THE AMERICAS

LOUIS M. COLONNESE
Editor

UNIVERSITY OF NOTRE DAME PRESS
NOTRE DAME   LONDON

Library of Congress Catalog Card Number: 72-105729
Manufactured in the United States of America by
NAPCO Graphic Arts, Inc., Milwaukee, Wisconsin

Father Antonio Henrique Pereira Neto was brutally assassinated in Recife, Brazil, on May 27, 1969. An advocate of non-violence, assistant to the Archbishop of Recife and Olinda, Brazil, Dom Helder Camara, and collaborator to Brazilian and Latin American student organizations, Father Neto was a symbol of courage to each of us who believes in human rights as a means to the liberation of man in the Americas. His youthful colleagues continue to be the builders of a just and meaningful future for their peoples throughout Latin America. His dedication to the dignity of men unto death was obvious. He is one among a growing number of men committed to actual human rights for all men, even those who had harassed him in the pursuit of those rights. The torch of human liberation in Latin America may flicker under oppression. But as long as persecution produces heroic models to be emulated, the torch of human liberation will endure and prevail in the hands and hearts of other men of conviction.

If you continue in my word, you are truly my disciples, and you will know the truth and the truth will make you free.

John 8:31–32

Contributors

Victor Alba is Visiting Professor and Lecturer at the University of Kansas, American University, and Kent State University. He has written several books in Spanish and English dealing with militarism in Latin America, labor movements in Latin America, and the Spanish Civil War. Mr. Alba has been Chief of the Editorial Division of the Pan American Union (1957–62) and Director of the Center for Social Research and Documentation in Mexico 1962–65.

Robert J. Alexander is Professor of Economics at Rutgers University in Brunswick, New Jersey. An expert in labor economics he has published twelve books, including the classic *Organized Labor in Latin America* (1964) and numerous articles. Dr. Alexander has served as consultant to the International Cooperation Association, Economic Cooperation Administration, and the Office of Inter-American Affairs of the State Department.

Brian D. Beun is a Fellow of the Adlai Stevenson Institute of International Affairs in Chicago, Illinois. With field experience and an academic background in agriculture, economics, and political science, Mr. Beun has served with U.S. AID mission in

Lima, Peru, and with the State Department in Washington, D.C.
He has also served as a consultant for the National Association of
the Partners of the Alliance for Progress.

Hector Borrat received his doctorates of law and of social
sciences from the University of Montevideo, Uruguay. He is the
editor of *Vispera,* a continental publication of the International
Movement of Catholic Students, and a frequent contributor to
numerous other publications in Latin America and Europe. Dr.
Borrat is a member of the World Council of Churches' Regional
Commission for Church and Society in Latin America. Fluent in
six languages, he has travelled in the Americas and Europe, inter-
preting and relating various intellectual and social trends.

Helder Pessoa Camara is the Archbishop of Olinda and Recife,
Brazil. Archbishop Camara is a great advocate of non-violence,
and in this line he initiated a movement called Action, Justice,
and Peace, the aim of which is to apply the non-violent principles
of Gandhi to the solution of socio-economic problems in Latin
America. He participated very actively in the creation of social
development movements, throughout the northeastern section
of Brazil.

Juan A. Casasco is Associate Professor of City and Regional
Planning, Catholic University of America, Washington, D.C. He
received a Masters degree in city planning from Harvard University and a diploma in architecture from the University of
Buenos Aires. He has been a professor of urban planning and
architecture in Argentina as well as in the United States.

Louis M. Colonnese is Director, Division for Latin America,
Department of International Affairs, United States Catholic Conference. Father Colonnese performed his graduate work at
Fairfield University and the Catholic University of America. He
is the director of the Catholic Inter-American Cooperation Pro-

gram (CICOP). Father Colonnese is the author of numerous articles on Latin America in popular and scholarly journals, as well as a public lecturer.

John F. Cardinal Dearden is the Archbishop of Detroit and the president of the National Conference of Catholic Bishops of the United States. Besides holding a doctorate in sacred theology from the Gregorian University in Rome, he has taken many initiatives to organize agencies for community service in the social, educational, and welfare fields in the United States. He contributed significantly at Vatican Council II where he introduced a chapter on marriage and the family in a document entitled *The Church in the Modern World*. No stranger to international issues, Cardinal Dearden has for some time been attuned to the problems of student and professional groups in developing areas.

Robert J. Fox is Coordinator, Spanish Community Action, Archdiocese of New York. He has a Masters degree in social work from the Catholic University of America. Monsignor Fox worked in setting up language and cultural training centers for religious working with underprivileged Spanish-speaking people. He has initiated various social action programs in the slums of New York, such as "Summer in the City" and "Full Circle Associates" which aim at the self-improvement of the neighborhoods he serves.

Paulo Freire is Professor of Education and consultant to UNESCO, in Santiago, Chile. He received his law degree and doctorate in education from the University of Recife, Brazil, the country of his birth. Dr. Freire is the founder of the Paulo Freire Method of Alphabetization and "conscientization." He is the author of several books on this topic which will be published in English by the end of 1969.

Bernard Häring, C.Ss.R., is Visiting Professor at Union Theological Seminary in New York. Dr. Häring received his doctorate in theology from the University of Tubingen, Germany. He is the author of 20 books and over 400 articles. Among his publications is the book, *Law in Christ,* written originally in German and translated into ten languages.

Neil P. Hurley, S.J., is Visiting Professor, Latin American Program, University of Notre Dame. He attended Fordham University, where he received his master's degree in political science, and Bellarmine College where he received his Ph.D. in political science and a licenciate in philosophy. His postdoctoral work was done in Belgium. Father Hurley was one of the pioneers in the theory of using communication satellites to broadcast multilingual education programs throughout the world, thus making the finest educators available to all. In 1965 he founded and became director of the Institute of Social Communications, Bellarmine Center in Santiago, Chile.

François H. Lepargneur holds a doctorate in philosophy and law from the University of Paris. A French Dominican priest, Father Lepargneur was assigned to Brazil in 1958, where he taught theology at the Dominican House of Studies, and later became Director of the Pastoral Institute for Religious, as well as holding professorships at several universities. Among his books are *History's Lessons for Tomorrow's Mission, Mission et Liberte des Laics dans la Monde,* and *O Problema Sacerdotal No Brasil.*

Jorge Mejia, S.J., is Professor of Theology at the Catholic University of Argentina. He is the editor of *Criterio,* and a director of *Concilium.* He also served as a *peritus* at Vatican Council II. Father Mejia was a leading Catholic initiator of contemporary Catholic-Jewish dialogue in Latin America.

George L. Metcalfe is Director of Education of the Association for International Development, Paterson, New Jersey. As an adviser on economic affairs to several African and Latin American governments, Mr. Metcalfe has developed a sensitivity on contemporary problems of international development which he has displayed in his numerous writings and public talks in the United States.

Luis Alberto Meyer is a Professor of Engineering at the University of Paraguay. He is the vice president of the International Movement of Catholic Students. He is a member of the Latin American Council of the Laity, Director of the University Pastoral Department of CELAM, and a Fellow of the Documentation Center of Montevideo, Uruguay.

Carlos Sanz de Santamaría is the chairman of the Inter-American Committee for the Alliance for Progress (CIAP) in Washington, D.C. A native of Colombia, he has served his country as ambassador to Brazil and to the United States. One-time mayor of Bogota, he has also served as Minister of Finance and Minister of Foreign Affairs. He was elected to his current position by the members of the Organization of American States.

René de León Schlotter is the Director and General Manager of the Institute for the Socio-Economic Development of Central America (IDESAC), Guatemala City, Guatemala. He has a law degree and has studied labor law and social security at the University of Madrid and contemporary philosophy at the Mendez y Pelayo University in Santander. Mr. de León was a founder of the Christian Democratic Party of Guatemala and has served as Guatemalan ambassador-at-large and plenipotentiary to Germany, among other posts. He is a professor of agrarian and economic law.

Juan Luis Segundo, S.J., is a graduate of the Sorbonne, where he was awarded a doctorate in Philosophy and Theology. He is currently the Director of the Centro Pedro Fabro (CIAS) in

Montevideo, Uruguay. He is an expert on pastoral theology for the Latin American Bishops' Conference. He is editor of the soon-to-be-published *Available Theology for the Adult Laity*.

William N. Simonson is Director of the Inter-American Studies Center of Temple University in Philadelphia, Pennsylvania. He has served in the United States Foreign Service in Latin America, Spain, and Washington, D.C. He has lived in Brazil, Haiti, Venezuela and Colombia. He is the holder of a Ph.D. from the Fletcher School of Law and Diplomacy.

Glenn E. Smiley fulfills a special ministry to Latin America from the Mount Hollywood Congregational Church, Los Angeles, where he is minister at large. An advocate of militant, aggressive non-violence, he has worked closely with the Southern Christian Leadership Conference where he was a consultant to Dr. Martin Luther King. He has lectured and travelled in over forty countries in Europe, Africa, North and South America. He has served as associate general secretary of the Fellowship of Reconciliation.

Csanad Toth, currently President of IDEAS, Incorporated, in Washington, D.C., was formerly a Research Fellow at the Twentieth Century Fund, where he pursued studies in Caribbean development. A Ph.D. candidate at Georgetown University, Mr. Toth has served in the Agency for International Development in Bogotá, Colombia, and has traveled extensively in Latin America.

Contents

Preface

The Sixth Annual Catholic Inter-American Cooperation Program (CICOP) Conference was held in New York City January 24 to 26, 1969. The theme, "Human Rights and the Liberation of Man in the Americas," was urgent then and is more urgent today. Militarism and less obvious forms of oppression are undermining the basic dignity of man in the Americas by negating his human rights. These rights are clearly stated in the United Nations Declaration of Human Rights of 1948.

Therefore, the reader cannot help but be impressed with the quality and courage of the various points of view presented in this volume. The authors are highly qualified to speak on the issues to which they have addressed themselves. Several risked their personal security to be heard on the CICOP forum. CICOP was still free from censorship and open to an American public that has the right to listen, reflect, and respond to pleas for human progress in any region of the world. CICOP represented an openness emanating from a belief in Christian brotherhood and solidarity in the Americas. This is why the Latin Americans who came to CICOP gave their precious time to meet with American counterparts in these times of Inter-American misunderstanding, frustration, and occasional hostility.

The many participants who interacted at the 1969 CICOP conference were very important. This year a number of significant businessmen, students, and diplomats rigorously engaged in dialogue and in ad hoc working combinations with distinguished leaders from the churches, academic life, religious and professional organizations, educational movements, and representatives from the intellectual life in all of the Americas.

I am thankful to all of the above for their candor, conciseness and courage of convictions which has made this collection of articles so profound and relevant. The CICOP Planning Committee is also to be congratulated for their sensitivity in the selection of such a contemporarily significant theme. The Division for Latin America Staff accomplished the herculean task of rendering concrete the theme, the conference and the follow-up for CICOP—an ordinary task for such an extraordinarily competent team.

Finally, I would like to express my deepest appreciation to Michael J. Lenaghan of our staff who closely collaborated with me in shaping the final format of the book. He orchestrated the Division for Latin America staff preparation of final materials, while constantly providing a watchful eye on final revisions so as not to lose subtle meanings in translation or abbreviation of those documents appearing herein.

Each author's views are his own. The uniqueness and intensity of the analyses, reflections and proposals set forth herein are a product of our times, which are troubled ones in the Americas. The 1969 CICOP Conference sought to focus on a fundamental concern: "Human Rights and the Liberation of Man in the Americas." Six months later, events have sharpened that focus, as human rights have deteriorated in several countries in our hemisphere since January 1969. The reader will be left with a central problem which I must admit at the outset: What can you do to accelerate human progress and to decelerate the current dehumanizing cycles in Latin America without committing atrocities counter to those of the status quo. The problem is one of values and of their application to human dilemmas. That is why we met in the context of beliefs—in a brotherhood and solidarity which was not primarily social, economic, or political in nature, but which could not escape the overtones of shared values for human progress in the social, economic, and political order. There is no conclusion to our investigation, but rather a continuation of a process to which I would hope each reader might contribute.

Louis M. Colonnese, *Director*
Catholic Inter-American Cooperation
  Program
Division for Latin America
United States Catholic Conference
Washington, D. C.

Foreword
The Remaining Daylight

We gathered at the Sixth Annual Catholic Inter-American Cooperation Program conference to discuss the theme: "Human Rights and the Liberation of Man in the Americas."

We discussed the liberation of man because he is not free. We discussed human rights because they are denied to millions of our brothers. There are those who ask "Why does the Church speak on social and political issues?" One of the ways to answer that question is to paraphrase the explanation given to those who ask why men climb mountains: "Because they are there."

People generally recoil from simple explanations of complex questions. They feel entitled to an answer which is at least as complex as the question. One evening during one of my recent trips to Latin America, I was riding in a cab with a North American who was familiar with poverty in the abstract but was encountering it for the first time as a concrete reality. He looked out the cab window and saw real men and real suffering and he was obviously feeling the effects of culture shock. Feeling the need to say something, he asked the cab-driver why there were so many people sleeping in the streets. "Porque es de noche," the driver answered. "Because it is night."

Both the mountain climber and the cab-driver spoke volumes in only four words. Those words also provide a symbolic insight into why the church concerns itself with human rights and the liberation of man in the Americas.

Let us envision the obstacles blocking the spiritual and material liberation of man in the Americas as a mountain. They form a mountain which truly exists. But all men do not climb mountains simply because they are there. The majority of men, especially those living outside the Third World, have expressed very little desire to climb that mountain. Many of them live their lives as though it were not there.

This is a lamentable phenomenon, but understandable. The mountain is ugly. People who live, as Archbishop Camara once said, "more like a cactus than a man," present a panorama of malnutrition, disease, illiteracy, and dehumanizing poverty. It is understandable that many men living outside the Third World refuse to see that mountain. It is understandable but not tolerable.

The followers of Jesus Christ must not only see that mountain of human suffering; they must join hands with their brothers to end the bondage of underdevelopment by leveling that mountain stone by stone. It is the paradox of our times that we hesitate to tell men that it is necessary for them to tear down a mountain even when their failure to do so would bring an avalanche down upon their heads. We are counseled that men will turn from such advice because it is too hard.

It is precisely this paradox which generated the critical evaluation that Christianity was not tried and found wanting—it was found hard and not tried. Those of us gathered at CICOP have no illusions about the fact that the implementation of inter-American Christian social justice will not be easy. We know it is hard and will continue to be hard.

Christianity has never been easy. The first sentence of Vatican

II's Pastoral Constitution on *The Church in the Modern World* lists the requirements for being a Christian in this 20th century.

"The joys and the hopes, the griefs and the anxieties of the men of this age, especially those who are poor or in any way afflicted, these are the joys and the hopes, the griefs and the anxieties of the followers of Christ," the Pastoral Constitution reads.

This is a vocalization of the aggiornamento of Vatican II, but it is not the voice of a new Church. The message of Christ is living history and not a static phenomenon. Christian social justice was not forged anew in the crucible of Vatican II or newly enunciated by *Populorum Progressio*. The message has always been the same and it has always been hard.

St. James made it clear that words alone will not suffice.

"If a brother or a sister is ill-clad and in lack of daily food and one of you says to them, 'Go in peace, be warmed and filled' without giving them the things needed for the body, what does it profit?"

St. James asks "what does it profit?" It is a question asked many times in the recorded word of God. "What does it profit a man to gain the whole world if he loses his immortal soul?" The wealthy nations of this world seem intent on gaining all of the riches on this earth. Some 20 per cent of the world's inhabitants have hoarded 80 per cent of the earth's riches, leaving only the crumbs from their banquet table for their underdeveloped brothers in Christ.

The combined assistance for development on the part of all the world's wealthy nations totals some $10 billion a year. The number sounds impressive until it is viewed in its true economic perspective. Ten billion dollars amounts to approximately one-fourth of the increase of goods and services in one year in the United States. That means the U. S. commitment to development is one-half of one per cent.

That is definitely a 20th century example of a wealthy nation using the words quoted by St. James and telling the Third World to "Go in peace," while withholding the development necessary to achieve that peace. Pope Paul accurately stated that there can be no peace without development. It is also held in the broadest possible consensus that there can be no development unless wealthy nations take just action commensurate with the scope of the problem.

Dag Hammarskjold, former Secretary-General of the United Nations, was a man who recognized that there is no substitute for effective action and no excuse for not taking such action when the means are available. Hammarskjold recognized the wisdom in G. K. Chesterton's remark that Christians living during his time were disturbed about social problems, "and so," Chesterton quipped, "they sang a lot of hymns to help the unemployed."

Hammarskjold was once asked how he could reconcile the avowed good intentions of certain Christians with their refusal or inability to devote themselves to social action. Hammarskjold replied that he could not reconcile such a lack of commitment and he added:

"In our era, the road to holiness necessarily passes through the world of action."

One of the reasons we selected "Human Rights and the Liberation of Man in the Americas" as our 1969 CICOP theme was because we were in the midst of the 20th anniversary of the United Nations' Universal Declaration of the Rights of Man. That document stressed that the implementation of programs to insure the rights of the disadvantaged is dependent to a large degree upon the motivation of people who possess those advantages.

Christian social doctrine emphatically states that the advantaged owe the disadvantaged access to a more fully human life as a debt of justice and not as an act of mercy or paternalistic charity. Pope John XXIII made that emphatically clear in *Pacem in Terris* (1963) where he praised the UN Declaration of Human Rights:

An act of great importance performed by the United Nations organization was the Universal Declaration of Human Rights. For in it the dignity of the person is acknowledged. There is proclaimed as fundamental the right of free movement in search of truth and in the attainment of moral good and justice; and also the right to a dignified life with all the other subsidiary rights that this implies. It is our earnest wish that the day may come when every human being may find therein an effective safeguard for the rights which derive directly from his dignity as a person, and which are, therefore, universal, inviolable, and inalienable.

The Church recognizes the importance of the UN Declaration of Human Rights, but it also realizes that the enunciation of truths does not guarantee their implementation. Pope Paul VI summarized this problem of effective implementation in his May, 1968 letter to the International Conference on Human Rights in Teheran, Iran. Pope Paul reinforced Pope John's praise of the UN Declaration of Human Rights, but stressed that international cooperation is the road to effective implementation.

Who does not see it? (the Pope asked). There is a long road to tread in order to put into effect these declarations of intention, to translate the principles into deeds, to eliminate the numerous and constant violations of principles justly proclaimed 'universal, inviolable, and inalienable.'

The extent and urgency of the action to be accomplished requires the support of all, one with another. How can the means be found to give effect to international resolutions for all peoples? How can the fundamental rights of man be assured, when they are flouted? How, in a word, can we intervene to save the human person wherever it is threatened? How to make the leaders aware that this concerns an essential heritage of mankind which no one may harm with impunity, under any pretext, without attacking what is most sacred in a human being and without thereby ruining the very foundations of life in society?

These are all grave problems, and one cannot hide from this. It would be vain to proclaim rights, if at the same time everything was not done to ensure the duty of respecting them by all people, everywhere and for all people.

The questions raised by the Bishop of Rome are the issues we gathered to confront. We came as brothers to enter into dialogue on these inter-American issues.

We were not so presumptuous as to believe that we could solve these problems within the context of that three-day meeting, but we could establish an atmosphere of inter-American friendship and cooperation. We could establish our willingness to work together as equals in the promotion of development throughout Latin America.

We could exchange the wisdom derived from our individual efforts and distill it during that CICOP conference to remove the sediment of outdated ideas and inaccurate approaches.

But there were also things which we did not seek. We did not seek sensationalism which draws attention away from work which is essential and focuses it upon issues which are dramatic without being dynamic. Nor was CICOP an arena for confrontation between conflicting personalities or methodologies. We gathered to find our common strengths and not to criticize each other's shortcomings, whether personally or as collective entities.

We have serious work to do. We have a mountain to demolish which has stood for so long that men have wrongly come to consider it as being unassailable. We must not leave a stone upon a stone. We must level the mountain of underdevelopment which steals from our brothers their rights as men and sons of God. Let us begin immediately because the hour grows late and the work must be accomplished in the remaining daylight. The following chapters bring our tasks into focus.

PART ONE

INTRODUCTION

THE MODERN QUEST
FOR HUMAN RIGHTS

JOHN F. DEARDEN

Twenty years have passed since the General Assembly of the United Nations adopted the Universal Declaration of Human Rights. It reflected humanity's reaction to the ruthlessness of Nazi Germany. In 1948 all men had a vivid memory of the war's destruction of free institutions and associations and of the callous disregard for human life, man's dignity, freedom and equality. It was against this backdrop that the Declaration was drawn up and adopted.

Provoked as it was by the neglect of the rights of the human person, the Declaration has, nevertheless, a positive and a ringing tone that is at once timeless and yet timely. It was proclaimed as "a common standard of achievement for all people and all nations . . ." It has raised hopes and expectations. They must not be frustrated.

The thirty articles of the Declaration give expression to the rights that reside in man because of his human dignity. His rights as a person, as a member of society, as a citizen of his nation, and

of the international community, are defined. Because of his worth
and dignity as a person he is seen as the subject of rights that
affect every dimension of his existence.

The historical context into which this listing of rights is to be
placed, we leave for philosophers and historians to determine.
But without descending to particulars, we can readily agree with
the observations of former Ambassador Goldberg on this subject:
"For those of us whose religious and national traditions have long
since acknowledged the rights which all men derive from their
divine origin, the basic ideas in the Universal Declaration are by
no means new. But the effort to promote the enjoyment of such
rights among all peoples is indeed new, and it is a momentous
development in human history."[1]

Reading the Declaration of Human Rights, we are struck by
the wide range of matters with which it is concerned. Beginning
with the fundamental statement, "All human beings are born free
and equal in dignity and rights . . ." (art. 1), it asserts that,
"Everyone is entitled to all the rights and freedoms set forth in
this Declaration, without distinction of any kind, such as race,
color, sex, language, religion, political or other opinion, national or
social origin, property, birth or other status . . ." (art. 2). "The right
to life, liberty and security of person (art. 3)—"all are equal before
the law and are entitled without any discrimination to equal
protection of the law" (art. 7). "Everyone charged with a penal
offense has the right to be presumed innocent until proved
guilty . . ." (art. 11). "No one shall be subjected to arbitrary
interference with his privacy, family, home or correspondence,
nor to attacks upon his honor and reputation (art. 12). "Everyone has the right of freedom of movement . . . (art. 13), "the
right to marry and to found a family . . . (art. 16), "the right to
own property . . . (art. 17), "the right to freedom of thought,
conscience and religion . . . (art. 18), "the right to freedom of
opinion and expression . . . (art. 19), "the right to freedom of
peaceful assembly and association . . . (art. 20), "the right to

work, to free choice of employment, to just and favorable conditions of work and to protection against unemployment . . . (art. 23), "the right to equal pay for equal work . . . (art. 23).

Also, "the right to form and join trade unions . . .(art. 23), "the right to rest in leisure . . . (art. 24), "the right to a standard of living adequate for the health and well-being of himself and of his family . . . (art. 25), "the right to education . . . (art. 26), "the right freely to participate in the cultural life of the community . . . (art. 27). "Everyone is entitled to a social and international order in which the rights and freedoms set forth in this Declaration can be fully realized" (art. 28). The listing is long and full and significant.

This is not the time nor the place to trace the different currents of thought that led to the formulation of the Declaration as it now exists. It came about through the collaboration of many persons of good will. What is noteworthy is that the Declaration was accepted as a common standard for all peoples and nations, by all but eight of the member-states of the General Assembly.

It is beyond the purpose of this talk to search out the historical antecedents of the Declaration. But it should be noted that at a meeting of the Latin American states in Chapultepec early in 1945, it was declared that one of the main purposes of the new organization of the United Nations should be the elaboration of a method of protecting human rights. And the responsibility was given to the Inter-American Juridical Committee to draw up a draft resolution. This Declaration was adopted by the American states at Bogota in 1948 prior to the completion of the Universal Declaration of Human Rights. I mention this simply to reflect the particular concern that was felt in this hemisphere for a declaration such as that which was adopted in 1948.

The Declaration of Human Rights presents a pattern that is universal in scope, enabling persons from every part of the world to find a common and precise expression of rights that they can understand and accept. The very fact that this formulation exists has an impact on people and on governments. At the same time, it has made its influence felt on decisions and working programs of the United Nations and its agencies. And it has played a subtle but important role in the legislation and practice of member-states and in the formulation of the constitutions of "new" states. The Declaration is pervasive in its effects. The very fact that it exists provides a measuring stick for the definition and the realization of human rights in every part of the world.

Of itself, the Declaration of Human Rights has no legal binding force. It is, as the Declaration itself declares, simply a "common standard for all peoples and nations." To implement the Declaration, the General Assembly adopted two covenants, one on civil and political rights and the other on economic and social rights. These in turn are made up of "conventions," such as those on slavery, genocide, the political rights of women, racial discrimination, forced labor, discrimination in employment, the equitable payment of labor, and freedom of association. When ratified by a member-state, the effect is to have the convention become part of the domestic law. But even in these instances of ratification, enforcement rests upon public opinion in the international community and whatever moral pressure such opinion can generate. Parenthetically in this context, we have good reason for questioning why the United States continues to defer the ratification of at least some of these conventions.

Surely no one would question the validity of the effort to achieve full human rights for all persons. And no one would be so naive as to believe that the adoption of the Declaration on Human Rights would realize this goal of itself. The Declaration stands rather as a charter which sets a goal and at the same time will always be a standard by which we can measure progress. Its value is to a great extent educational and, to some degree, inspirational as well. It helps us to see more clearly the conditions under which the human person is entitled to live. It enables those whose eyes are dimmed by despondency, whose voices are stilled by repression, whose shoulders are bent by injustice to see a glimmer of hope. Man reaches out to his fellow man for mutual support and help. What worth and value one has achieved, another aspires to. And when we kindle the fires of hope and set them so clearly within the reach of men, we must not be surprised if they are not content until they have attained them.

And yet as our Holy Father, Pope Paul VI, noted a few months ago: "There is a long road to tread in order to put into effect these Declarations of intention." The road is long and hard. And the goal is difficult of attainment. In all candor, we can look about us and see everywhere too many instances of the violation of basic human rights. To go no farther afield than the United States, a country in which providentially many of these basic rights are part of our law and our tradition, it is evident that we have not solved the problem of poverty. As a consequence, "the economic, social, and cultural rights indispensable for his dignity and the free development of his personality" (art. 22) that are called for so explicitly in the Declaration are not realized by all of our people. Further, the right to work is not possessed by those several million Americans who are without employment. Injustices of one kind or another still are found among us. And to the degree that we tolerate their existence, we fall short of the ideals that are set before us in the Declaration of Human Rights.

And what may be said with full truth of conditions here is verified, in varying degrees, by the experience of other peoples as well. We must not gloss over the reality. We need to see it in all its stark grimness. It is only when we begin to measure the reality against the ideals which the Declaration sets before us, that there is hope of improvement. Perhaps more acutely than at any time in the past, men are fired by the desire to have that which is due to them as human beings. It is characteristic of our time. It is as if we held before them a strong and clear image and said, this is what you are entitled to be and to have. And, as is proper, they will never be content until they have achieved that goal.

There are many agencies and institutions that have a role to play in realizing for men the rights to which they are entitled. The state, the Church, economic, cultural and educational agencies all have a part in the task. And there is a role, too, that is given to the individual that he cannot shirk.

To a very notable degree in our society, it is the political structure that must accept key responsibility for the achievement of human rights. It has at its disposition the instrumentalities that ensure not only individual, but political, social and international rights as well. Unless this political structure is ordered in such a way that it works unceasingly to realize these rights for its people, it is failing in its responsibilities. And if beyond this, it ruthlessly represses and violates these rights, it is false to its trust. It would be superfluous to say that the democratic processes, for all their shortcomings, represent the truly human way through which man can achieve and hold fast to his rights. The association of many persons in the task gives a greater guarantee of freedom.

In the main, the role of the Church in trying to work for human rights will fall within the total social order. After all, human rights may be identified as they are in the Declaration of Human Rights in a very abstract fashion, but they do not exist except in the concrete. And they exist primarily within political confines. But since human rights do involve a value system and since it is the function of the Church to teach values, she has a contribution to make. And this contribution is all the more important in our time when the realization of values will be achieved in great part through the political process.

The Church, whether explicitly or not, has a role in shaping the pattern of society. The values that find expression in the life of the people owe much to the Church. Certainly many of the characteristics that distinguish the United States have religious foundations. "In this very fundamental sense, religion has helped (in Paul Ramsey's terms) provide *directions* but not *directives* to political society."[2] In a more particularized fashion, the Church exercises its influence through helping to shape the individual's value structure and in offering to the individual the inspiration and motivation to help determine the policies of his nation. In a society such as ours, individuals and groups of individuals act politically to influence policies and to shape attitudes. But they do this out of a particular kind of conviction, and not infrequently what motivates them is religious in its origin. For instance, the Catholic who out of religious convictions works toward promoting a more generous foreign aid program is giving expression to his sense of concern for his fellow men. In the process, he is inspired by religious motivation to further a political program that has in intent at least a very human goal.

In so many instances, it will be the voice of the Church that will have to censure the political structure for its failures in the area of human concern. Priorities that call for substantial outlays of military armaments when people lack basic human necessities must be protested. A disregard of the truly human concerns of people will call for strong dissent. St. Augustine reminds us that material goods are permanent occasions of discord between men, while spiritual goods tend to unite men.

And yet while the Church can do much, it will remain true that a really dynamic effort to achieve human rights will entail the collaboration of many individuals. Everyone must accept responsibility for helping to create the conditions—political, economic, social, cultural—in which all human rights can be respected and promoted. The interdependence of all members of the human community for the realization of the individual's rights, particularly in the economic and social spheres, is becoming more and more clear. We cannot evade responsibility. We are all involved.

Other papers to be presented in following chapters will focus on specific areas of concern. For this reason, it is not fitting that I address myself to them. But in the broad context of the quest for human rights, it is not possible to overlook certain basic facts that center in the theme of development. Many things are being done in its name. Much that is good, and much that is harmful. Certainly I would not attempt to justify some of the policies and the procedures of some of our business institutions which directly affect the achievement of rights for great numbers in Latin America. The great reservations that are had by so many in Latin America on the way in which these activities are conducted demand that we pause and re-examine the things that we are doing. The mistrust that has been engendered is due in great part to a concern on the part of those in Latin America that these enterprises are hostile to their legitimate human interests.

Certainly any work, any activity, any program that is undertaken in the name of development must be grounded upon the basic recognition of human rights. Unless our programs demonstrate respect of these rights and help to promote them and bring them to fuller achievement, they cannot be justified. It is for this reason that development—which is not simply an economic reality, but psychological, cultural, moral and political as well—must be grounded upon the bedrock of human rights. It must find its inspiration in a recognition of these rights. It must be pointed directly toward furthering these rights. And it must work constantly with the people involved to determine whether or not a more human existence is being attained through these efforts. This is the touchstone of the worth of development. In reality, the term "development" probably should be qualified in almost all its uses by the adjective "human." Unless it contributes to the advance and the fulfillment of the human person, it has missed its mark.

At the last meeting of the Latin American bishops joined together in CELAM in Medellin, there was evident a real sense of Christian awareness of the values that are involved in the progress of their people. A sense of Christian concern impelled them to recognize clearly the realities of the situation, to appraise strengths and weaknesses, and to propose a program of action that will help to achieve for all their people a more human existence. We applaud them for their candor, their honesty, their integrity and their pastoral zeal. And in spirit we associate ourselves with them in their efforts to bring to their people a fuller realization of their human dignity.

In the hard realities of our times, pronouncements and statements come and go in rapid succession. Sometimes they represent a faint, feeble call in the dark night of injustice and inhumanity. They are rarely heeded by those to whom they are addressed; they bring little hope to those in whose cause they are spoken. So often, they are gestures in futility.

And yet, from time to time, something is said or written that quickens the spirit of man. It buoys up his hopes. It gives direction to his strivings. It raises him as a man. Such were the great social encyclicals of Pope John XXIII, *Pacem in Terris* (Peace on Earth), and Pope Paul VI, *Populorum Progressio* (On the Development of Peoples). They have been beacons in our time, lighting the course of the Church in its effort to be of service to all mankind.

Though of different inspiration, the Universal Declaration of Human Rights is, and will continue to be, a high-water mark in human advancement. It has set a standard that we must somehow strive to attain. In comparison with its goals, some of our efforts seem puny and futile. The chasm between what is and what ought to be is so wide and so fearsome. But it must be bridged. The many strong hands and sturdy hearts that unite in trying to bring to all men what will make them more truly human are carrying forward a work of God. Many persons of good will will have a part in this task. We who share the blessings of our Christian faith bring to the task a special insight and motivation. Our very sharing in the life of God lays upon us a special duty to be involved. The achievement of human rights demands the fire and the warmth and the dynamic strength and the hope of Pentecost. We must set ourselves to the task with courage and with confidence ". . . in the power of the Holy Spirit . . ." (I. Peter, 1:12).

NOTES

1. Robert F. Drinan (ed.), *The Right to Be Educated* (Washington: Corpus Books, 1968), Foreword, p.v.
2. *Ibid.*, p. 12.

PART TWO

YESTERDAY'S LEGACY: BARRIERS TO THE LIBERATION OF MAN IN LATIN AMERICA

OBSTACLES TO
THE REALIZATION OF
HUMAN RIGHTS
IN THE AMERICAS

CSANAD TOTH

The greatest obstacle to the realization of human rights are human beings. I define human rights and their realization as the redeeming act of revolution. Revolution, I think, is a sacred word that should not be used in vain. Recently, we have been deluded by allusions to revolution: the revolution in lipsticks, the revolution in sports, the revolution in almost all walks of life. We talk about it as if it were a household word. Those of you who have ever participated in a revolution know that it is the greatest revealing act in one's life. This should be emphasized in a forum dealing with Latin America and with Americans (including ourselves here in the United States). Often there is more rhetoric about revolution than should be allowed. We talk about revolution in Latin America as if we were making a choice between alternative programs: shall we go to the movies or shall we make a revolution? I think if you want to make a revolution, you have to be mature and very disciplined. It just does not happen; *people* make the revolution.

While the rhetoric about revolution rages, we can see and fear—instead of revolution—the march of counter-revolution in the Americas.

I would like to address myself, therefore, to some of the basic causes of the emergence of counter-revolution and attempt a diagnosis of the Americas: how this counter-revolution is creeping up on us. I have no intention of launching into a defense of the United States.

I am, however, a little bit tired and worn out by the exclusive forums on American imperialism. While I don't dispute its existence, I question the motivation of those who use it as a convenient scapegoat for their own insipidity. Instead, I admit that the sheer weight of America's political, military, strategic, and commercial advocacy or opposition to revolution defines the parameter, the rate, and the direction of the revolution. I think that there are basically two major impediments to revolution in the Americas. These are those who live north of the Rio Grande, on the one hand, and on the other, those who live south of the same river.

In this context one cannot help but speak about our collective effort: the Alliance for Progress. Some (to use the words of one of the speakers at the Inter-American Forum) have approached the subject with a sense of "masochism," "nay-ism," and "witch-hunting"; others, in a narrow-minded ebullience don't want to admit any failure. Let me first, therefore, try to give a balanced view and—if it sounds more in the direction of masochist, nay-sayer, and witch-hunter—so be it.

What began some eight years ago as one of the greatest adventures of man in this hemisphere, stands today as an object of derision and a monument to frustration. After several billion dollars, aroused expectations, and voluminous statistics, the stark features of inequity and injustice, rampant illiteracy and inflation, swelling barrios and dwindling opportunities, reduced markets and increased military budgets are just as revolting as they were less than a decade ago when the Alliance for Progress was launched so that man might live for something better.

Projected against its promise, the achievement of this grandiose development scheme is far short of the anticipated result. Neither rhetorical overkill nor an assortment of gross indices can conceal the truth. What was once an exuberant testimony to man has been sacrificed at the altar of allegedly higher priorities, betrayed by our policy-makers, sabotaged by our partners, and programmed beyond recognition by the experts. I admit that success takes a long time and failures are more immediately evident. I invite you to attend Congressional hearings and listen to the statements of the executive branch of our government. You will be mesmerized by the success stories laboriously collected by droves of bureaucrats and meticulously projected on charts and tables. But walk around, if you dare in San Cristabal on the outskirts of Lima. Visit the *campesinos* in the altiplano; reflect on what made Camilo Torres join the band of guerrillas; or shed for one day—one day only—the inviolability provided to you by your U.S. passport and taste the powers of persuasion of Ongania's police or argue with the deadly accuracy of bullets in the Plaza de las Tres Culturas. Then in the shadow of success, of steadily increasing GNP's, commodity agreements, rescued balances of payments, impressive infrastructures and piddling community development projects, search for that better life and find why failures are more immediately evident.

The momentum of the Alliance has been lost, perhaps never to be recaptured and there is no single event which can be isolated or held responsible for it. Was that momentum destroyed when our State Department turned its back on the spirit of the Alliance and, at Mr. Thomas Mann's prodding, found military dictatorships quite to our taste? Or when programs aimed at utilizing the idle Latin American armies for development became, under the name of "accion civicomilitar," a euphemism for official violence and repression? Or when greater and greater portions of funds for the Alliance were poured into the rathole of balance of payment deficits, in order to shore up and support corrupt, inefficient governments? Or when we flooded the Dominican Republic with grants and loans (diverting them from other countries where they were needed), so that we might keep Balaguer's head above water and justify ex post facto, our intervention? Or did the loss of momentum occur when we realized that our so-called resource transfers to these underdeveloped Latin American countries showed a negative inflow of capital while our exports to them were promoted and subsidized with tight strings attached to aid?

The Alliance's momentum was first lost when, instead of mounting an all-out effort against entrenched privileges, it entrusted the revolutionary act of development to those very people who had done the most to block development. Instead of aiming at revolutionary change, the entire mechanism of the Alliance was constructed to produce a change that fitted into the established order. But let me say that had we stood up in time to the Latin oligarchs and juntas, with half the strength and determination used against Castro, there would not be today 135 million people under military and civilian dictatorship.

The second major cause of the failure, in my view, is the very leitmotif of the Alliance for Progress: the cherished belief that economic development alone would lead to those far-reaching structural changes in the social and political fabric of Latin American societies which modernization and humanization require. This overemphasis on economic factors was characterized by Gunnar Myrdal as an "escape from thinking."

Our infatuation with economic growth could not possibly lead to results. It has not worked and could not have worked because economic growth, to use Hannah Arendt's dictum, neither leads into, nor constitutes a proof of, the existence of freedom. In fact, our overemphasis on economic factors reinforces those very Latin American values and attitudes which are not conducive to development. In my view, development, being a revolutionary act, can

be perceived as freeing men from the shackles of brute dependence which he thinks he cannot control. Thus, the evolution of
human rights, the evolution to self-determination, is a matter of
changing values, attitudes, and behavior—a task infinitely more
difficult than bringing the Quechua Indian of the altiplano from
the burro economy to mechanized agriculture. But all these
policies of ours (and here I stop placing the blame on our government or on our collective policies) conform very well to the
type of change that harmonizes with the established-order
strategy or syndrome in Latin America. And with due deference
to our Latin American friends, let me not put the blame on the
other side, either.

There are cultural factors in Latin America, too, that are obstacles and impediments to the realization of human rights. Latin
Americans' lack of confidence in their ability to control their environment and their own affairs (along with the attendant disavowal of responsibility and reluctance to assume risks, to inno-
vate and, therefore, to change) is representative of the same
attitudes which have always raised the odds against development
in Latin America. These traits are characteristic of Latin Americans and their political culture. As individuals, when judging
their peers and their inferiors by their own standards, they see
in others the image of their own insipidity. Their betters they
view with distrust, although they accept their commands with
childish servility. Without self-respect, they cannot respect others
and they do not believe in the value of human interaction. Security, which they do not dare to look for in themselves and cannot
seek in their communion with others, is provided by the patron
or by the government and its assorted centralized agencies.

The highly centralized political institutions may be considered
an extension of the patron system based on dependence, servility,
and the disavowal of responsibility. A blind faith in the super-
natural, out of a desperate need for a firm frame of reference,
keeps them paralyzed in a blissful and feeble state.

The relative ease with which communist ideology penetrates

the universities is due mainly to the security offered by its doctrine. The often-used term "oligarchy," referring to the Latin American upper classes, is much less a definable social class than a mental state, permeating not only the upper but the other classes as well. The oligarchic mentality is only a matter of hierarchy: who stands where, so as to look down upon somebody else. Observe the oligarchic mentality of the "revolutionary" university student: his offhanded treatment of the less-educated; the patronizing attitude of the government extension agent, particularly toward a *campesino;* the union organizer's disdain for manual labor. Exceptions only prove the rule. But were this untrue, what about the so-prevalent phenomenon of co-option? How is it that a student stops being a revolutionary the day he receives his diploma? The extension agent becomes a new patron who dispenses or withholds favors, and the labor leader turns into the social climber whose certificate of acceptability is his necktie or his attaché case? Or is it not a fact that the desire of the outcast is not to change but to join society?

What about those who live neither north nor south of the Rio Grande, but from the East present still another impediment to development? Communism has never been so great a threat to the Latin American established order as it has been to movements against the established order—and why, today, would this movement be less passé in Latin America than among the radical French students, on the campus at Berkeley, or among Czechoslovakian youth?

Established and bureaucratized communist parties, if not engaged in fractricidal struggle, appear to be quite content to parade in the role of bogeyman for the classes of privilege and, in fits of dialectical idiocy, provoke and delight in the over-reaction of the establishment. Gallant and not-so-gallant bands of guerrillas have just as much difficulty in overcoming the apathy of the *campesinos* as they have in fighting the vast forces of counter-insurgency. The adulation of their heroism or vain idealism can hardly conceal the irresponsibility of their adventure, which, rather than gain a foothold for liberation in Latin America, unleashes military governments all over the continent.

But, as has been repeatedly demonstrated in other parts of the world, it always takes the extreme Left to bring out the dormant fascist of the soul.

And what have we, the Christians, done to remove the obstacle —or have we placed additional ones in the path of development? Again, with due deference to the members of the various religions here (and we all together constitute "the Church"), the time for self-criticism should come and it should go beyond the cautious word that we hear from Colombia.* I do not think it a very revolutionary doctrine to declare, as was declared in Medellín, that the people of Christ, the apostles of the Church, should defend the rights of the poor. *The poor,* by definition, *have no rights,* and it is easy to speak with comfort of defending the "rights of the poor." This is an absolutely meaningless statement! And the evenhandedness on the part of our Church in Latin America—blaming others and trying to set up straw men, discussing "liberal capitalism" as if it still existed, and speaking about "Marxist totalitarianism." I think if charity begins at home, so does revolution. The Church should stop blackballing those of its members in Latin America who fight for social justice in Christ. So let the revolution for the Church start at home!

The situation is, to an extent, almost hopeless. If I sound pessimistic, it's not without a ray of hope, however. Let's not try to put life into something that's dead and outmoded; let's start something new. The aberrations of development that we all have helped to create should be our renewed concerns. In these days that are witnessing the disintegration of the enlightened commu-

* See "Concluding Document," Second General Conference of the Latin American Roman Catholic Episcopate, Medellín, August-September, 1968.

nity which has always pressed for enlightened foreign policies and enlightened attitudes toward other countries, I still hope for the creation of a constituency of conscience among all of us. Let's not put forward some abstract ideas of uniting ourselves; then we will spend the rest of this conference and the rest of our subsequent activities in a meaningless struggle to unite everybody behind each one of us. This constituency of conscience *should* advocate the revolution; not as an act of violence (although revolution may be accompanied by violence) but as an act of human redemption that leads to the realization of human rights. Violence is not the question here, although it should be borne in mind (to paraphrase an early warning), that those who make revolutionary violence impossible also make counter-revolutionary violence inevitable.

The constituency of conscience should have one uniting slogan, not in terms of denominations but in terms of definition. Let us employ, and live up to, the words of the great Catholic priest in Colombia who gave his life to this revolutionary struggle, even if all of us here may not agree with his ways. He said, "let us be Christians, hasta las últimas consecuencias." I think his life was a testimony to this "últimas consecuencias." So I call for a total commitment, with a modicum of intelligence, to create here in the States and south of the Rio Grande a new approach, new programs, and a new spirit through which the realization of human rights can come.

WEALTH AND POVERTY
AS OBSTACLES TO DEVELOPMENT

JUAN LUIS SEGUNDO, S.J.

The word "underdeveloped" is, precisely because it is broad and vague, a useful image—if not an exact term—for considering the Latin American countries jointly and discussing the problem of their future. It is not helpful to change the expression to "developing countries," though it might have more emotional appeal. Our sensibilities are one thing; the truth quite another.

I trust this distinction will become clear through that which follows. In other words, I should like to begin by mentioning that in recent times there has evolved the *image* and consequently the *idea,* of this condition that concretely distinguishes and separates the United States from the countries south of the Rio Grande. This influence in turn has been responsible for a certain evolution of the programs devised to shorten or do away with the condition of underdevelopment.

I

The first image of underdevelopment arises from what the

word itself suggests, that is, from a comparison. Doubtless at the beginning of the nineteenth century, the Spanish-Portuguese colonies were more prosperous—or should we say more developed?—than their English counterparts. A century later the difference had increased and had taken on a new meaning. Is the trend suggested by the image not irreversible? This is precisely the question that the first image of underdevelopment does not help to raise.

Accepting the supposition that every country may pass in a shorter or longer period of time through the same path of progress regardless of the historical moment in which it begins the march, the fact of a prolonged and general underdevelopment leads to a search for causes which, though only tacitly, are assumed to be faults; in other words, causes stemming from the underdeveloped countries themselves.

Among such causes, some remained acceptable so that one might freely talk about them; others were tacitly, though efficaciously, incorporated in the image of the underdeveloped Latin American continent.

Among the first group were included a low level of popular culture, the demographic explosion, politics, incapacity for reasonable and sustained work, archaic social structures and work techniques; in short, the lack of what the English language expressed by a word untranslatable—perhaps because untransferrable—in Spanish: Achievement.

Among the second group of causes that were attached to the image of Latin American underdevelopment were the greater percentage of Indian and Negro population, the Latin temperamental deficiencies as regards the elements that foster development, such as work, prestige, money, the Catholic religion, etc.

According to this reasoning and as a result of these images, there came into being the idea of underdevelopment. What was essential was to determine the most economical stages through which, by means of self-initiative and some seed money, the road already traveled by the developed countries could also be followed by the underdeveloped ones, which would then become "developing."

The Alliance for Progress was probably the first and the last programmed attempt to accomplish, within this image and this idea of underdevelopment, the theory of the initial impulse, which, by helping those who helped themselves, would inaugurate a process basically parallel to that through which the developed countries have passed.

To be sure, the late start of the process necessitated certain readjustments, certain unpublished stages, thus giving the lie to the theory of a strict parallelism between the path traversed by other countries a century earlier. But the difference seemed minimal and hardly anyone regarded it as a serious obstacle.

Nevertheless, here was an inherent matter that would become critical and would point to a second image, to a new idea, and to a new program for the underdeveloped: the disturbing hypothesis of doubting that the point of departure on the way of development was as secondary as had been supposed. Expressed another way, it questioned whether the very fact of the earlier passage of developed countries along this route did not render it impassable to those who came later.

The image that was consequently to become decisive in order to change from one concept of underdevelopment to the other would be the vicious circle of misery. Thus, underdevelopment was no longer imagined as merely a delayed position on a common path, but as a restraint that prevented the sharing of that path.

As a matter of fact, from whatever starting point we may select the efforts to progress are frustrated by other factors. In the imaginative approach that has become classic, to increase consumption means to increase production; to increase production means to increase work; to increase work means to increase consumption (food, culture, etc.). That is, put quite simply, a vicious circle.

Innumerable analyses have shown the same circle in all the sectors of underdeveloped life, from the subject of nutrition to the cultural, from the university to agriculture, from democracy to lack of political concern. And in the field of the psycho-social it has been demonstrated that immobility as well as progress in the rural area has been transformed into urban migration with its resulting increase in needs, unemployment and critical awareness without a proportionate possibility of solutions.

As a result, in the idea of underdevelopment increasing attention is given to a unique element which many have always associated with the notion of underdevelopment. This consists not so much in a condition of relative disadvantage but in the real impossibility of beginning—with their own resources—a viable process that would lead to the fulfillment of human needs.

To this was added the mounting proof that the so-called causes or faults more or less tacitly associated with the Latin American inability for development are not necessarily such. The drain and use of a great number of Latin American technicians for important positions in North American economic development gives the lie to the myth of the "Latin temperament." And from a racial point of view, I see no more obvious proof than that of the racial struggle within the United States. The very aggressiveness of this struggle manifests the extent to which people have dismissed the belief that the supposed white superiority of itself sufficed to maintain leadership within a society otherwise the most developed on this planet.

All that has been said seems to suggest that the dominant idea of development and underdevelopment in this second stage is what is pointed up in the first social encyclical that shifts the emphasis from internal problems to international ones: the *Mater et Magistra* of John XXIII. According to this document, our times are approaching ever closer the problem presented by a mechanism that incessantly increases the world disequilibrium between rich countries and poor countries.

In the supposed common course toward development, the phenomena of wealth and poverty on the international scale, far from tending to attain a satisfactory synthesis or at least a uniform progress (though basically unequal), tend to make themselves absolute. In fact, it is false to suppose that poverty will be remedied gradually, though at a rate below that at which wealth is accumulated. Because of the growing communications and interdependence among men, it is untenable to accept as a solution even a partial one, a rhythm of betterment for a few which every day is responsible for the removal of goods desirable, and even necessary, to the life of others.

The ever-increasing understanding of underdevelopment in this second schema derives not only from the inevitable failure of the Alliance for Progress but also from its replacement, tacitly agreed to, by a new kind of assistance. This aid, without causing Latin American countries to enter the process of development, will for the moment palliate in the minds of Latin Americans the demoralizing effects of progressive estrangement and of the profound and rapid changes of the future. This condition, aside from the expressed desire of the President of the United States himself to give preference to policies of birth control rather than help in development, shows clearly a transition from one idea of underdevelopment to another.

It was inevitable that this transition should have taken a new step and that a new stage should arise in the concept of relations between development and underdevelopment. Actually, it is impossible to accept the present vicious circle, or circles, of misery without asking why they did not exist earlier in the history of the developed nations of today.

On the other hand, when one adverts, as the Christian must —not only on his own initiative but in compliance with the teachings of the Council and the papacy—to the interdependence of all the planetary processes, one suspects that underdevelopment and development should be connected more intimately than is suggested by the image of a common though unequal course.

The image that suggests itself could be described in a picturesque, though probably not physically correct, manner as follows: Let us imagine two men seated on a gigantic see-saw installed five meters above an orchard with fruit trees and plentiful food near the earth. Let us suppose the initial weight of the players to be such that the first, able to descend to the level of the first fruits of the trees, would have somewhat more than a growing advantage . . . As he eats these fruits, his weight would increase and in consequence lift his competitor above the reach of all food so that his weight would inevitably begin to diminish. With every increase in his weight, the advantaged one would come into closer contact with the more plentiful food supplies near the ground, to the final definitive destruction of equilibrium.

We may say the same thing in the words of an economist: "It is erroneous, therefore, to envision underdevelopment as an independent fact from economic development. Underdeveloped countries exist *because* developed countries exist. Development and underdevelopment are the two faces of the same coin . . . The dominant country has to acquire cheap raw materials and place its manufactured goods at a maximum price; the dominated country must produce raw materials at low cost and be in a position to acquire the greatest possible volume of manufactured goods."

Toynbee has made it commonplace in western, non-Marxist culture that all historical concentrations of power and well-being, that is, all the great empires of history, have as an indispensable ingredient the creation of proletariats.

It is a new development that does not alter the law that this proletariat today should be largely outside the national limits of the United States; that is to say, it is made up of the remainder of the continent which provides raw materials, cheap labor for highly lucrative industrial production, and even a market for the manufactured goods.

Consequently the only program compatible with the will to develop the underdeveloped in the truly supranational extension is that which this empire began without success to put to the test in the conferences on international trade at Geneva and at New Delhi.

The problem must be presented in harder terms. If development and underdevelopment are not independent phenomena, then we cannot think in terms of a revision of the Marshall Plan for Latin America. From a merely economic consideration, how to promote development and make a profit, one proceeds to a proposition I would consider radically more Christian: are we disposed to make up for, by means of a costly development that promises no return, the underdevelopment which we have produced?

From a Christian standpoint, there is no love without a gift, and the gift is not love so long as it is not a *gift of self*. The alternative has become clear. It is impossible to expect that the conditions of underdevelopment will suddenly disappear, impossible to dream that the underdeveloped countries will simply accept as good sports the difference in their rate of development. We treat no longer of merely giving but of giving oneself, because in this third concept of underdevelopment it seems clear that wealth and poverty are not results of different causes, but two aspects of the same reality indissolubly connected.

II

What would be the effect of this plan? Among the many possibilities, I shall restrict myself to those indicated in the title of this conference: wealth and poverty.

What has been said to this point shows us wealth and poverty as results of the same mechanism which leads to ever greater extremes of distance and irreversibility.

This irreversibility is immediately evident from the Christian standpoint and, actually, from the human point of view, and understandable to every man of good will as the most explosive and tragic component of the process. This is so because in the proportion that wealth increases, it feels poverty to be a threat and it discharges against it all the subconscious, if not conscious, mechanisms of aggression.

At the other extreme, as the possibility of a solution disappears from the reach of the great mass of men (in spite of having evidence of it on the movie screen, on television, and the billboard), the face of poverty acquires an even more inhuman aspect—not only that of violence which at least is proud and noble, but that of abandonment, negligence, vice, or worse yet, the unrestrained and selfish struggle to occupy the few positions of privilege that are still available in these peripheries of empire that the poor countries have become.

Every day this poor man is thrown more and more into the shadows, always further from the image of a man. On behalf of such a man, it is worth our while to recede. And recede we must; there is no other alternative.

It can no longer be truthfully said that imperialism is the result of United States foreign policy being in the hands of those whose interests make it an external cause of poverty. It is quite evident that all North Americans are solidly behind the policy because they are aware that their standard of living depends upon it.

And consistently in this inhuman process the real problems and the real options are obscured to the point that not even in the election of the governing body is this issue taken into consideration, in spite of its tragic importance; because, let us face it, for weal or for woe this power governs all the continent. We see the youthful negativism of this inhuman wealth stemming from this opulent society, not with a gift of self but in senseless rebellion or in the dead-end street of aberrations, drugs, and so on.

Both sides thus grow farther apart, increasingly delaying the achievement of a common development, the rich growing richer and the poor poorer, to the point that they no longer recognize in each other beings of the same human family. Meanwhile, for Christians, the face of Christ becomes more unrecognizable as he questions us in the persons of both the poor and the rich, because both have a desperate and urgent need for salvation.

ECONOMIC FACTORS CAN OBSTRUCT THE IMPLEMENTATION OF HUMAN RIGHTS

GEORGE L. METCALFE

What I have to say on economic factors obstructing the implementation of human rights in Latin America has been said before, but to no avail. I am referring to policies of the United States toward Latin America which postulate a primary goal of sustaining U.S. national security through the direct and indirect control of the social change and development process of Latin America, and a secondary goal of human development within the culture-value-power context we know the best, namely our own. It is a tragic cliché that we continue to demonstrate the extent to which we are victims of our own slogans, especially those about the need for stability and the potential of gradual change. But the theme of our conference is Human Rights and the Liberation of Man in the Americas. Once again, then (just for the record, as they say), we will deal with some of the barriers to the liberation process. At the outset, however, I would ask you to consider several sub-themes I shall not directly cover in my summary:

1. Liberation of man in the Americas includes North Ameri-

cans. Present policies toward Latin America, and the values and priorities which generate them, imprison us as well as our Latin brothers.

2. The prophets of gradual change in the eradication of poverty are not the prophets of the poor. Gradual change is only seen as practical and reasonable by those men who do not pay the cost—in human terms—of what it demands. Such prophets protect the values and images they have created; to the poor they are false prophets. To the leaders of the poor, they are enemies to be destroyed, and with them their myths, the systems that support them, and the values that sustain and legitimize them. The destruction of such enemies in the Americas is part of the liberation process toward the implementation of human rights; I propose that such destruction is creative violence, psychically and materially. It is essentially just and deeply Christian in its philosophy.

3. The hope for Latin American liberation is enhanced by the continuing example of Cuban survival in an austere, grass roots process of change through revolution, the revolution of will united with act through the policies of the state and the participation of the people in an authentic process of renewal with development. This example, plus the growing varieties and strength of guerrilla movements elsewhere in Latin America, form one end of a viable continuum the poor can see and experience. At the other end is the oligarchy and its allies. These polarities present the poor with something they have never had in tangible terms; namely, alternatives. Alternatives of what to believe and whom to follow. A chance for direct participation, as Richard Shaull recently put it, "in the creation of a radically different social order." To the poor of Latin America, this new process of selection and participation is what President Nixon would call "a piece of the action." Fortunately, however, the poor need not wait for private investment to begin the process.

To deal with economic factors which obstruct human rights,

one need not go further than several crucial assumptions and procedures inherent in the Western view of economic development. I shall limit my review to three concepts: (1) psychic genocide, (2) normative research traditions in economic analysis, and (3) technology and the status quo.

Psychic Genocide

The most obstructive economic factor in the implementation of human rights in Latin America is what I call the process of psychic genocide: the forced establishment of the correct mix of cultural responses to economic incentives. Simply put, psychic genocide is the value transfer process which holds as its key tenet, the establishment of a socio-political belief system which adheres to a fundamentally materialistic philosophy of the good life. All other aspects of life are subordinate to this basic tool. It is most significantly rooted in an educational process which overtly though subtly begins with the proposition that the poor must come to understand that the object of development is not them but the elimination of poverty. If they can be convinced of this reality, they can be channeled into the mechanistic programs designed essentially to solve the deficiencies in education, organization and social discipline (its real name is conformity) which, we are told, inhibit economic development at the outset. If they resist this process, economic growth is retarded and the people are relegated to the ranks of the "backward" world. A sort of "many are called but few are chosen" philosophy of social change. Involvement in this process of development, when it is made available, is mandatory and not participatory.

For those that accept the rubric of this process, and are fortunate enough to be included in its programs, the most positive gain initially is the establishment of hope, hope that the psychological transfer will lead to the reality of a better life, at least materially. Unfortunately, however, for those so involved, the process does not guarantee the fulfillment of its promises. One can become a true believer, with all the psychic ramifications in tow, only to realize that the stage is being prepared for a drama of development that is not yet written. There is no producer, no director, no benefits for having prepared oneself. There is nothing but the "promise." Eventually, for many, that, too, becomes nothing.

Mr. George Land, in a position paper prepared for the recently-held Inter-American Forum, aptly named this process psychological imperialism, "The drive to make everyone be like us." Several of his observations are particularly pertinent in Latin America-United States relations:

1. We are making massive exports of cultural ideas and accepting little or none in exchange from those we are helping. (Sen. Eugene McCarthy, at CICOP in St. Louis last year, suggested we turn U.S.I.S. around for just such reasons.)

2. Psychological imperialism has a long-term effect: The person who is never asked for his ideas ultimately stops having them, forcing him to go to someone who will show some interest in him.

3. Alienation, atrophy, resentment, even violence are the natural outgrowths of this lack of exchange. Latin Americans feel deeply that we lend a helping hand in a psychologically authoritative and exploitative manner.

The combination of this process with its promises (and with no time-space commitment to see this process through in a just egalitarian manner) tends to reshape development into a vicious, inhumane process of achievement for self, the wrenching of me and mine from the mire of the poverty-stricken masses. We have created this process around the elimination of poverty, an issue. We applaud successful individuals, products of that process, as achievers. They have successfully conquered the issue we are concerned with; they help us avoid the masses who remain—the people. Raul P. Prebisch, retiring chairman of the United Nations Committee on Trade, Aid and Development, put it this way:

Mass communication media make developing nations—even the poorest among them—aware of the high patterns of consumption in the developed countries. All this interferes very seriously with the process of development. Not only is there a tendency in the high income groups to imitate these consumption patterns but, what is still more serious, the inability of the masses to attain these standards creates in them a sense of humiliation, a tremendous sense of humiliation.*

Normative Research Traditions

In the main, analytical insight is achieved only at the natural resource level of development thinking. It is from this level that policy decisions are most often made. This situation is intellectually absurd but not conspiratorial in a conscious sense. But the format articulated definitely allows the most pragmatic, conspiratorial policies and programs imaginable. Some of its basic characteristics are as follows:

1. *People are literally treated as units of labor or entrepreneurship.* This concept is a collective instrument, modified only to separate human types—a rather interesting way of placing people on an inferior-superior continuum—and social forms of living. Urban is separated from rural, educated from noneducated, those who have from those who have not. The effects of this "methodology" is perhaps best seen in the simplistic quantitative assessments of how many people must go to school at all levels to provide something called "skilled" manpower to meet the requirements of something else called industrialization. Curiously enough, industrialization, even at the highest levels of technological advancement, has not produced a consistent demonstration of what sort of skills must be generated through education. Nor has education shown the capacity to generate them. Education, therefore, becomes the scapegoat for the non-humanistic, culturally devoid achievement of finding a place for people in the development syndrome. As you know, we are often told

* Raul P. Prebisch cited in *The Development Apocalypse*, booklet published by the National Council of Churches of Christ in the U.S.A. (New York, 1965), pp. 36–37.

Latin America is not developing largely because its people are not educated.

My point is not that education is insignificant in the development process, but that it is a major scapegoat for Western opinion as to why Latin America is not developing.

2. *Cultural diversity, representing the true heterogeneous character of man, is treated in benevolently racist class terms as part of the "backwardness" of underdeveloped nations.* This diversity, with its non-capitalist, non-Americanized style is viewed as another of the unfortunate economic factors impeding development. We are left to presume, therefore, that it also impedes the liberation of the Latin American people. The extent to which the pathology of poverty contributes to this diversity is not systematically treated. This diversity of life, then, becomes another scapegoat for the difficulty of bringing about rapid economic development. My point here is that development is deeply tied to cultural forms and norms. The ultimate meaning of social change and development, therefore, is subsumed under an incredibly superficial catch-all of behavioral "givens," or standardized concepts of what people must know and respond to in order to develop.

But make no mistake: these standards are classical only in an American-European sense, and even then only in relation to the relatively affluent classes of the Western world. To call upon such standards as the universal norms of human incentive is arbitrarily to assume that a standard of right living or the good life actually exists and is potentially meaningful to the two-thirds of mankind who are poor, including most Latin Americans. Economically and socially, this "great ascent" notion of development in an enlightened, homogeneous Third World, is functional only in the fantasy land of the intellectuals who sell it to the policy makers as though it were revealed truth.

3. *Interdisciplinary integration of knowledge in policy-oriented research is neither intellectually appreciated nor systematically considered in the mainstream of economic analysis about devel-*

opment. I know personally that some of our finest analytic economists are clearly threatened by its prospects. Nevetheless, many
economists hypnotize policy-makers with their quantitative
methods and theoretical bag of tricks, while at the same time
undercutting the psychologists, educators, ecologists and others
as not having achieved analytical methods and methodologies
worthy of their consideration. Unfortunately, policy-makers are
all too easily intimidated by such opinions from these keepers
of the development temple.

The most crucial factor in economic development research is
that it is objective in its method of anlaysis, while being incredibly subjective intellectually and irresponsible in its assessment of
behavorial and cultural factors in the process of social change.
Psychological incentives, economic motivation, technological
adaptability, educational advancement are taken as essential
static variables for development. These variables are rarely
defined in specific psychological or cultural contexts and when
they are, one finds them rooted in affluent, Anglo-Saxon images,
holistically set forth as part of a theoretically homogeneous world.
The implications of this tradition are profound in a deeply insensitive sense. Such a tradition denies in its philosophy and methodology the essential significance of the dignity of the individual
human person. It substitutes the monster creature, "Economic
Man," for this basic human right. He is a simple, logical soul—
deadly dangerous, however, to his own kind. But he is rigorously
fed by our theories of achievement and economic growth, and he
profoundly influences normative research traditions from which
the limited alternatives of Western development are generated.

Stability and the Status Quo

The most important influence of technology on the development of Latin America has been its ability to achieve economic
growth without wide participation by the masses, and in a frame-

work capable of maintaining the oligarchies of Latin America for an indefinite period. Thus it is possible through modern technology economically to exploit the physical resources of Latin America without necessarily employing proportionately greater quantities of manpower as national productivity grows. Thus, the participatory goals of development in its widest sense are subverted, and with them the widest opportunities for distributing national income. In short, human rights in the sense of sharing in greater national wealth are aborted in the very process of economic growth when modern technology is applied within the context of the status quo. The rich *do* get richer and the poor *do* get poorer.

But we must be very clear that the obstructive instrument here is the socio-political system, not technology. The impact of technology is determined by the policies and decisions of men, not machines. If social domination and the ethos toward unlimited possibilities for preserving the status quo are enhanced through the application of technology to the development process, it does not follow that machines are damning men to lesser lives in the wake of progress. Such domination is clearly the result of men's inhumanity to man and little else. Yet it is precisely this inhumane control and application of technology toward narrow economic ends that forces the revolutionary reaction of the leaders of the poor against the status quo.

Nonetheless, technology is applied in a value context which, in the Western world, includes a holistic concept of the status quo simply referred to as "stable government." This concept is neither egalitarian in character nor necessarily democratic in its foundation. It is little more than one of these characteristics we take as historically given in the development process I described earlier. Simply stated, stable government as a concept is a control feature toward the orderly indoctrination of the masses toward a particular value perspective of what life is all about, development included.

Within this concept, the platitudes of the development decade are postulated. They include all the right philosophies about human liberation from want and the establishment of human dignity through development. But the measurements of growth and human advancement are in macro terms based on the monetary value of goods and services produced, and not on the implementation of human rights within the development process. Thus, a six per cent rate of growth in gross national product in developing countries is labeled progress despite the tyranny of social injustice the development process supports within the status quo.

Conclusion

From obstructive factors such as these has grown the revolution of rising expectations, and with it, the violent clash between the status quo and modernizing forces. The issues involved in this revolution of the poor is inadequately understood when limited to the ideological combat between the forces of Capitalism and Communism. The real issues are wealth and poverty, and the potential elimination of this polarity in the material world. Clearly, development involves economic contingencies, but the process of development is not essentially economic. It is much wider and deeper than statistical assessments of progress. Development, particularly in Latin America, demands a commitment to the remaking of society in its most intimate as well as its most public attributes. In this sense, modernization is surely revolutionary, but not necessarily violent or Communist-inspired. The nature of the confrontation between the old way and the new will become more apparent as new socio-political forms and processes emerge. In Latin America, the continued co-existence of emerging forms within the structural ambivalence of the status quo creates an ambiguity which neither form can tolerate. If American foreign policy is based on such co-existence, then the violent reaction of the poor is to be expected. For such a policy will have accepted revolution as the enemy. It will have adopted a development philosophy so trapped by traditional assumptions and short-sighted reaction that the poor will be forced to resort to revolution for their liberation. So also will many of the affluent, whose own need for liberation grows increasingly significant in the struggle for human rights in Latin America today.

THE CHURCH'S ROLE AS
IT AFFECTS HUMAN RIGHTS

FRANÇOIS HOBERT LEPARGNEUR

It is a fact that in this century the Roman Catholic Church does not hold the monopoly on religion. Without even going into the more traditional sects of Protestantism, we find movements such as spiritism in Brazil and Pentecostal groups throughout Latin America which place no value on the socio-political aspects of man and still respect his individuality and conscience. Thus, they favor human rights in theory but inpede their exercise for lack of attention to the socio-structural dimension of human life. But let us dwell on the role of the Catholic Church. Given the great religious feeling in Latin American countries, channeled since the 16th century by the Roman Catholic Church, does Catholicism enhance or restrain the blossoming and exercise of man's rights?

The Present State of the Latin American Church
in the Modern World

POSITIVE ASPECTS

The Latin American Church is now embarked on a mission of awareness of Church responsibilities toward development, human

promotion, and respect for human rights. This process of awareness, however, has not taken the form of a specific ideology (perhaps it can not or should not thus commit itself to such a form
any longer). Generally, however, the stance taken by the Latin
American national Catholic hierarchies is definite; they concur in
the need for deep, urgent, and radical change, but they exclude,
more or less explicitly, the use of violence to attain these ends.[1]

Regarding the smaller-scale but specific efforts being made in
the Church, we want to discuss briefly a Brazilian non-violent
movement whose positive results are admittedly still to be seen.
Led by Dom Helder Camara, a group of 40 Brazilian prelates
signed an agreement in July, 1968, the goal of which was to exert
non-violent moral pressure on the unjust structures within the
country. The primary goal was to better implement three of man's
rights as established by the Universal Declaration which Brazil accepted in 1948: no. three (life, liberty, and personal security), no. four (freedom from slavery) and no. twenty-three
(employment).

Can moral pressure, however, be effective in abolishing unjust
elements in structures which are not Brazilian? Can moral pressure be effective and at the same time be considered legal by the
present Brazilian government? At this time, it is inconceivable
to imagine an "illegal" action being supported by a majority of
the Brazilian bishops.

REMAINING GAPS AND WEAKNESSES

A unanimous decision on these problems has not yet been
reached by Brazilian bishops. Other national hierarchies are
also arriving at the point in time where such decision may need
to be made.

Still worse, the difference between statements calling for action
and actual pastoral or socio-political work is great; this is a
difference between the theoretical stand and its exercise within
capitalist and current power structures.

There are still remnants of a "Christian" mentality which long ago was thought by some to have been overcome—a mentality which hinders the development of a truly ecumenical spirit and the tolerance which would place all religions on an equal footing in society.[2]

Although Church organizations employ generous and industrious people, there is no considerable improvement in the general picture because works and services offered by the Church are not rigorously geared toward the actual development of the population. One reason for this situation is the fact that there is a diversity of interests within the Church and each person is pursuing his own goals. In fact, in most cases, these interests do not represent either the common good or the good of the underprivileged in bringing about peaceful social revolution. These differences, indeed, are evidence of the unfaithfulness of the Church to its own values and to itself.

Generally speaking, the Church does not defend the right of individual conscience, for this weakens dependence on the hierarchy. This attitude often indirectly compromises the critical responsibility of the Christian conscience to challenge other powers such as civil or military.

There is still a rather individualistic concept of human rights in civil society, and this concept is reflected in the institutional aspects of the Church. A better developed population could see that the Church cannot struggle efficiently to defend human rights in secular society if it does not first implement them within its own structures.

After Pope Paul's visit to Bogotá, the Catholic newsletter, "Noticias da Iglesia Universal," wrote that "Reform does not and will not come. It will not come because never has a master sacrificed himself for the advancement of his slaves. It will not come because waiting around for the good will of the privileged is not the encouragement needed by the oppressed. Reform will not come because the problem is not phrased properly: instead of calling out for responsibility on the part of the rich, we must call out for responsibility on the part of the poor."[3]

Guidelines for Ecclesiastical Action Which Would Effectively Promote Human Rights

The choice between violence and non-violence is not a simple choice. The two do not balance. Violence is inconceivable on the part of the Church. The existential choice of valid resistance can and should be reflected onto an actual situation, taking into consideration its nature and consequences. This existential choice is an important factor in making a decision, and it is precisely such a decision which is the responsibility of the committed individual.

Civilly speaking, the principal choice in this socio-economic-political situation is between evolution and revolution; these are different approaches to the changing of an unjust structure which hinders human rights.[4]

Religiously, the choice lies between two concepts of the Church's role in human rights: (a) the Church should limit itself merely to presenting the idea of incorrupt purity, leaving it up to society to apply this ideal and merely delineating some lines of action which might be considered "intrinsically evil"; (b) the Church should promote a better understanding of human rights, accepting as valid all which is historically relevant.[5]

Role of the Church Leading to Better Implementation of Human Rights

What can the Church do to ensure that a larger number of Latin Americans enjoy the rights promised them by the United Nations Declaration of 1948?

(a) Give a good example by making these rights an effective part of its own institutions and those affiliated with them. Emphasize the duty of justice toward personnel and co-workers, granting freedom of worship to non-Catholics and non-practicing

Catholics. Teach that obligations to the state include that of constructive criticism.

Encourage the democratic spirit, even in non-democratic religious institutions; encourage dialogue, solidarity, fraternity, and service with special attention to the poor and weak.

Revise the Catholic system of education in terms of its relationship to the dominant classes; revise financing methods used by the Church for privileged groups and vested interests.

Acknowledge a citizen's right to the truth and unbiased information. Recognize each man's right to his own reputation and the accused man's right to be told what he is accused of and to defend himself and be heard.

(b) Struggle against individual or group selfishness is a necessary part of a realistic promotion of human rights. In this struggle we can not omit the worst and often most hidden evil in Latin America (at least in Brazil): arbitrariness. Rights are no more than words if they continue to be left to the whim of well-wishers —to the arbitrariness of those who have even the smallest amount of power.

(c) Concentrate not only on making ideal plans and inspired moral norms, but also favor (or at least do not hinder) means which will bring about the allegedly desired just society. With few exceptions, the institutional Church is not asked to choose between concrete means dealing with strategy and the *a fortiori* direct acknowledgment of the transforming elements of the situation. The Church is asked to see the possible practical consequences of its statements and actions. The Church is asked to clarify the consciences of man, to cooperate in their formation and eventual information. Concrete decisions are not the result of a simple exegesis of abstract principles; the existential context exerts an especially strong pressure in emergencies. People want a morality which is less subject to principles and more like human action dynamically in search for freedom.

The time has come for man to act on facts and not on intentions or statements of principles. This new situation demands a realistic attitude from the Church which goes over and beyond the preservation of good conscience. The accumulation of the demands for purity which could be made on the transforming elements too often dictate a preservation of the status quo, despite all the objections ot it.

(d) Examine carefully and critically the religious hierarchy's position toward the State, the preserving force of the established order. Instead of mistrust or humility, it would be more fruitful for the Church to help make the State a promoter of common good and criticize its faults from this point of view. A sign of the times is the increasing estrangement between Latin American bishops (who are unfortunately too closely tied with the current political and economic regimes) and the priests, who are more sensitive to the Latin American reality and the usurping of personal rights which takes place.

(e) Support the prophetic and charismatic role exercised in many countries by the more courageous elements of the clergy and the laity which operate despite the hierarchy's inability to assume a prophetic stand. The evolution of an entity such as the Latin American Church can not be monolithic; on the contrary, it demands the protection of such personal gifts.

NOTES

1. In May, 1967, the Seventh General Assembly of Brazilian bishops asked people to reflect on how prudently and adequately they could replace the present social structures with others which would be more just and human. "Within the capitalist system, Latin America has no chance of escaping underdevelopment—of satisfying the just and growing aspirations for broader participation in the economic, social, and political life of the country. This is why economists, sociologists, and technicians agree on the need for a radical change of struc-

tures as the only way of solving the underdevelopment problem."
Department for Social Action, CELAM, 19-5-68 SECOD 2, col. 243.
Special reference should be made to the statements and decisions of
the Medellín conference, 1968.

2. Cf. the public statements of the Protestant pastors during the
Eucharistic Congress in Bogotá, July, 1968.

3. São Paulo, January 9, 1968. Segundo Domenach, in *Le Retour
du Tragique* (Paris, 1967), pp. 79–100 says, "The weakness of the
French Revolution lies in having had an abstract projection of absolute freedom for all, of having wanted to free man before creating
a new state." C. Detrez, in *Revista Civilisação Brasieleira*, pp. 18, 103,
has written that the socio-economic-political blocs in Latin America
are not apt to allow sufficient exercise of human rights; abstract preaching of these, irrelevant to the transforming action of these blocs, brings
about slow awareness combined with aggressiveness in the face of the
inoperability of these rights. Much has been said about the resignation of the Brazilian people, and with reason. However, studies show
that underlying this "mentality of the simple man," of the "common
man," of the mass of rural workers and city laborers, there are two
constants: mysticism and violence. (Cf. Octavio Ianni, *Rev. Civ. Bras.*,
18, p. 113). The emphasis on each of these can shift from one day
to the next.

4. To reform means to review a form, to recover the shine this
form no longer has, or to perfect the splendor of an existent form.
Revolution means exactly the opposite: "To abandon the past form
for a new one. In this context, revolution means little else but the
dialectic meaning of development, of progress" [Pedro Demo, *Soci-
ollogia da Revolução, Vozes*, August, 1968, p. 693]. The sociologist,
Candido Mendes de Almeida, offers the following ideas: "Efforts will
come to a standstill unless the general blocs which condition this action
are understood; a social structure which must suffer a mutation, not
an evolution" [*Esprit* (Paris), V (May, 1968), 803]. This author's
utopia, at least in terms of Latin America, is a vision of development
in a homogenous world which corresponds to the capitalist experience
in North America: "The historic project of the Third World moves in
a homogenous atmosphere. How can we expect the end of prolonged
tyranny if the moving force of the cumulative causes of development
of this Third World can not find the ethical demands of basic change
in *Populorum Progressio?*" (p. 806). For more information on the

point, cf. Candido Mendes de Almeida, *Nacionalismo e Desenvolvimento*, chaps. 1 and 2.

5. In Latin American history, examples are not lacking of priests who opposed the established order to defend the freedom of its subjects; cf. Gustavo Perez Ramirez, "The Church and Social Revolution in Latin America," in *Concilium* (June, 1968), pp. 117–126.

THE SELECTIVE STRUCTURE OF
THE LATIN AMERICAN UNIVERSITY

LUIS ALBERTO MEYER

It is not the purpose of this presentation to give a detailed description of the present situation in Latin American higher education, and particularly not to deal with the structures related to the problem of access to higher education. On the contrary, I wish to limit myself to the principal elements of higher education in order to posit the problem and arrive at the formulation of such fundamental criteria as will prevent our taking a partial and superficial view of it.

Basic Presuppositions

It is necessary, first of all, to establish the basic presuppositions relative to the role of the university today in Latin America in order to determine the direction of our analysis. This role we shall attempt to situate according to two coordinates:

First Coordinate: condition of underdevelopment and cultural dependence.

The situation of underdevelopment is a consequences of the existence of developed countries that set themselves up as power centers on which the peripheral peoples depend.

A power center is in possession of science and technology and favors a process of evolving acceleration. The peripheral countries, on the other hand, not having the means to implement their own scientific investigation and the consequent technological development, attain only to a *historical actualization* which leads them to modernization that is merely the reflection of the proven centers. They thus remain in the position of consumers of the products of the developed countries and simultaneously become fixated in the role of foreign proletariats, as producers of raw materials.

This dependence is not limited to political and economic aspects only, but is of a cultural nature as well because it includes the cultural models of the power center.

In the process of the liberation of Latin America, which would necessarily include the severance of cultural dependence, the university as the center of scientific and applied research has an important role to play: namely, to make Latin America an active participant in scientific development.

Second Coordinate: internal colonialism and popular liberation. It is in the condition of marginality of the great masses of Latin Americans that education is of vital importance. And, as the Latin American bishops meeting in Medellin declared, present-day education from the social viewpoint is directed more toward maintaining the dominant social and economic structures than toward their transformation . . . It is directed toward the support of an economy based on eagerness to *have* more when Latin American youth is demanding *to be* more.

The role of a university subscribing to what we would call a liberating education would include the development of a work of popular *conscientization* (*toma de consciencia*) designed to bring the Latin American man to the realization that he is the subject and not the object of the historical process.

The Idea—A Determining Force

What has been said up to this point demonstrates how our interpretation of underdevelopment, as well as the kind of development sought, condition the role and, for that reason also, the kind of university desired, as well as a critical analysis of avenues of access to the university and the so-called democratization of teaching.

THE ELEMENTS

a. The consideration of access to the university cannot be made without a realization of the situation of primary and secondary education in Latin America. Selection for the university is actually begun in the lower grades. Social circumstances indicate that the educational attainment of the common people is approximately two years, whereas the minimum necessary to enter the university preparatory is eight years. Furthermore, this education, according to statistical information, is incorrectly said to be free. The fallacy of this claim is made obvious by the growth of private education which introduces economic discrimination. Consequently, university students are basically recruited from the upper classes.

b. A very important point (and one which is not always noted) is the cultural disadvantage of the youth from the lower classes who do reach the university. Modern sociology of learning has demonstrated the importance of the development of readiness resulting from being in a privileged class—libraries, travel, contacts, associations, and so forth. The experience in developed countries has shown that it is not enough to give the student the mere material possibility of entrance to the university.

c. Because of the pedagogical inadequacies in the educational structures, youth come to the university unprepared for the admissions examinations because of a lack of any kind of previous vocational guidance.

d. The so-called student mortality (that is to say, the dropping out of those who have succeeded in entering the university) reaches alarming figures in Latin America. It is estimated that 50 per cent drop out during the first year. And educational statistics show an increasing deterioration of the situation: The number of university graduates does not increase in the same proportion as the number who enter.

This dropout rate must be accounted for not only by the need for financial independence of youth, such as might be the principal motive in developed countries, but rather by the very necessity of survival itself.

e. The "democratization" of education is not to be confined to the problem of entrance to the university. The curriculum content is another significant aspect of the situation.

The university reproduces the class structure of the region where it is found. Even though this representation is statistical rather than mechanical, it certainly contributes to the fact that the content matter and the pedagogical methods do not have a liberating and democratizing result.

Challenges And Obstacles

Recalling those coordinates indicated above, the Latin American university needs to increase considerably its ability to form the technicians necessary to an autonomous development.

Some illustrative figures: While the population of Latin America and that of the United States were both roughly 200 million in 1960, the former had 600,000 university students as compared to 3,600,000 in the latter. At this rate, for a population double that of the United States by the year 2000, Latin America's students would number 3 million while those of the United States would reach 20 million.

These data indicate the impossibility of reaching an autonomous development at this rate of growth inasmuch as the industrialization process requires an accelerated increase in the number of technicians and scientists.

This points to the necessity of a total reorganization of the present university structure if it is to be able to meet this challenge. The obstacles are important, however, within the university as well as outside it. I shall not attempt to enumerate here the structural characteristics found today in the majority of the universities which complicate the realization of planning, as for example, the departmentalizing of the various faculties, etc.

Neither am I going to enumerate the internal tensions produced in the inner sanctum of the university itself as a result of it being a reproduction of the structure of society.

I shall point up two obstacles that I regard as important to the purpose of this meeting:

a. The first of these, though it may appear paradoxical, is foreign aid, particularly that by North America, to the university. This assistance, channeled through the Inter-American Development Bank and the bilateral agreements between Latin American and United States faculties, pose, among other problems, the fallacy of *quantity-quality*. It is affirmed that the universities are poor because they have too many students to be able to give them a good technical formation. This gives rise to a strong limitation policy which will impose on Latin America's development a "desarrollista" (developmental) approach and a modernization which merely reflects the power centers. This aid likewise imposes upon the university the condition of being "politically aseptic." (Students are to study and not waste time in politics and strikes.) Thus the university is denied its task of *conscientization*. And thus, indirectly, this approach also favors the elite.

b. Another obstacle is the internal situation of those countries whose regimes consider the university as a center of subversion, and exert pressure upon it to accept easy solutions; pressures that extend from economic to military intervention.

Conclusion

All this leads us to the final conclusion: To democratize the university is to seek its reform within the educational complex of the country. Isolated solutions alone will prove to be only stop-gaps that may do more damage than good.

In the face of the tension between the university and the whole of society, will it be necessary to wait until a social change is brought about by progressive forces before the university will be reformed? Or could it perhaps, dialectically, act as a super-structure in order to contribute to this social change in the countries of Latin America?

With the bishops united in Medellín, I believe in the liberating pressure of popular *conscientization* (*toma de conciencia*). The university, appealing to its perennial energies, has an important role to play in this area.

MILITARISM AS AN OBSTACLE
TO HUMAN RIGHTS

WILLIAM N. SIMONSON

We are all aware that militarism, or the predominance of the military caste in the government and political life of a country, has been a pervasive phenomenon in the history of Latin America from earliest to most recent times. It has traditionally been—and still is—one of the principal forces serving to restrict the exercise of fundamental freedom and the achievement of human rights by the masses in Latin America.

Together with the Church, the landed aristocracy, commercial interests, and so forth, the military is often depicted by observers in the United States as the dominant element in that malevolent band of oligarchical ogres that are customarily blamed for keeping the Latin American countries in a backward and unstable state. Perhaps the most that some of us are willing to concede regarding the so-called evils of militarism in Latin America is that it tends to be cyclical, seeming to be widely prevalent in the area at times and, at others, to decline in incidence.[1] There are those, however, who argue that not all military regimes in

Latin America have been repressive but that several have been benevolent in nature. It is also often asserted that the more stable, efficient, and reformist of Latin American governments have been those run by military men. Several observers point out correctly that, in any case, the military is a key element in the power structure of nearly all countries of Latin America whether we like it or not and that it is unrealistic to attribute all the ills of Latin America to militarism.[2]

In Latin America there is no major upsurge of popular opinion aimed at eradicating militarism and reducing the military's influence in political life. Students, intellectuals, politicians, and some Church elements periodically speak out against the military but have usually failed to evoke significant responses either from the masses or from the important organized groups in these societies. To many in Latin America, moreover, the military man is the hero rather than the villain on the national scene, and military presidents are often viewed by the man on the street as having taken the country to heights of glory unmatched by civilian regimes (e.g., Francisco Lolano López in Paraguay, Juan Vicente Gómez in Venezuela, Juan Domingo Perón in Argentina). Of course, spokesmen for military regimes currently in power, and often their defenders in this country, tend to assign the highest possible marks of statesmanship to the leaders of such governments. They are viewed in certain sectors of the U.S. government, business community, and news media as bulwarks against the spread of Communism and Castroism.

All in all, in looking back over Latin American history and assessing the situation as it is today, it seems only logical to conclude that militarism—either dominance of the government by the military or civilian authoritarianism backed by the armed forces—is as much a factor in the life of Latin America today as it ever was. The current exceptions to this pattern are well known —Chile, Costa Rica, Uruguay, Venezuela, Colombia—but it remains true that the major part of Latin America, both in num-

ber of countries and size of population, is today governed by
military regimes or those strongly influenced by the military.

The question, therefore, remains as to what there is about militarism in Latin America over the past 20 years that makes it a
significant study as an impediment to the achievement of human
rights. In answer, there appear to be at least four aspects to
current-day militarism in Latin America that deserve closer study
and discussion, as follows:

1. Militarism seems to be on the rise throughout Latin America;

2. The action of the military in removing civilians from power
in a number of countries in recent years seems directed at fore-
stalling efforts of populist or liberal political leaders to implement
basic reforms and promote the modernization of political, economic, and social life. Military regimes are at least as concerned
with containing these popular movements as they are with restor-
ing order and preserving government stability in these countries.

3. In several important instances, military leaders in assuming
power seem convinced that only they, and not the civilian elements of the society, are capable of governing their countries and
carrying out the basic reforms and modernization efforts essential
to the achievement of national aspirations; and

4. The U.S. government, business, the press, and other important sectors in this country concerned with developments in Latin
America seem to be swinging over (although hesitatingly) to the
position that military government is harmful to Latin America
and to the U.S. interests and policy objectives in that area,
whereas 10 to 15 years ago the opposite viewpoint seemed to
prevail.

The increased incidence of Latin American militarism is
attested to by the action of the military in overthrowing duly con-
stituted civilian governments, or tightening its existing control
in Argentina, Bolivia, Brazil, Panama, Peru, and elsewhere in
recent years. Few indeed are the countries still ruled by popu-
larly elected, constitutional governments, and in some of these
the rumblings of military discontent are ominously loud.

The most unexpected venture into militarism occurred in Brazil, where in March 1964 military leaders joined with key civilian groups in a move to overthrow the left-leaning, ineffectual government of President João Goulart and then, to the surprise of their civilian allies and the general population, broke with tradition and retained the reins of power in their own hands. One of the military leaders of the revolution, General Humberto de Alencar Castello Branco, was installed as president. He immediately embarked on a major program designed to put Brazil's chaotic economic affairs in order, to establish sanity and efficiency in government operations in general, and to reform and cleanse a corrupt and inefficient political process.

In terms of an analysis of the effect of the Brazilian military's takeover *vis-à-vis* the achievement of human rights, our attention is naturally drawn to the repressive measures adopted by the Castello Branco government to weed out so-called undesirable and subversive elements from the government and body politic. Of similar interest in the same context were the reforms it formulated in the electoral process and party system, as well as its revision of the Constitution. Thus, through a series of Institutional Acts, and related measures adopted during the first weeks of the new government, several hundred politicians and public figures of varying political hues were deprived of their political rights for ten years and/or removed from elective or administrative office. The lists of these individuals included not only a minority of those clearly identifiable as Communists or otherwise subversive enemies of the state, but several former presidents, numerous state governors, federal senators and deputies, state and local elected representatives and many other political leaders of parties and factions replaced in the government by the military and its civilian allies. Substantially larger numbers of politicians, government employees, labor and student leaders, newsmen, and others throughout Brazil were investigated, threatened, and otherwise intimidated by military commissions of inquiry on charges of corruption, malfeasance, subversive activity, and so forth, over a period of months following the advent of the new military regime. More often than not, due process of law was not followed in these investigations and, at the least, there was considerable infringement of human rights.

The Castello Branco government likewise forced through far-reaching changes in the legislative and electoral sectors. Congress' powers, as compared to those of the Executive, were correspondingly enhanced. The presidential elections, originally scheduled for October 1965, were put off a year and made indirect, so that Castello Branco's successor was chosen by Congress and not by direct popular vote. Similar alterations were made for elections of the state governors and mayors. The political party system was modified to do away with the existing proliferation of parties, 13 in all, replacing these by a government and an opposition party. These alterations and others in the Brazilian governmental and political process were codified in a new Constitution conceived by the Executive, pushed through Congress, and adopted on January 24, 1967.

The justification offered by the Castello Branco regime for such measures and reforms was essentially threefold: (1) to moralize and streamline the electoral and party system so as to avoid the excesses and corruption characteristic of the pre-Revolutionary era; (2) to provide the necessary political climate to permit the government to carry out essential reforms and stabilization measures in the economic sphere; and (3) to allow time for the new government reform measures to take effect and to insure that the revolutionary crusade embarked on by the military would not be nullified and reversed by future, perhaps civilian, governments. Although there is room for disagreement over the effectiveness of the regime's measures to put the economy back on its feet, it seems clear that Brazilians since 1964 have not enjoyed the political freedoms they experienced during the period of the open, representative government of the preceding 19 years. Although some observers had until recently judged the political situation in the country to be stabilizing and a balance of power and neutrality of respect to have been achieved among the three branches of government,[3] developments of the past few months have shown that the Brazilian situation is far from stable and gives cause for serious concern for the future. Thus, we witnessed in Brazil in December, 1968, a series of presidential-military actions (closure of Congress, stripping of congressional immunities, suspensions of the right of habeas corpus, news censorship, and so forth), which cannot but be interpreted as the foremost assertion to date of militarism in that country and as having the consequence of imposing further severe limitations on the exercise of human rights in Brazil.

Recent developments in Brazil are alarming on their own merits, as indicative of a decided shift away from eventual restoration of an open, representative political process in that country. It also probably reflects the prevailing mood of the military throughout much of Latin America and perhaps sets an example for the military to follow in other countries. Like Brazil, Peru and Panama have recently experienced military takeovers. They seemed essentially predicated on the notion that civilian politicians should not be allowed to remain in power or to assume power if they are viewed by the military as likely to alter the status quo in a drastic way, or as being incapable of governing effectively and preserving order and stability. In each country, it seemed clear that the military was no longer prepared to remain on the sidelines and to permit civilian reformers to determine the manner and the pace by which government would seek to promote basic reforms and the political, economic, and social modernization of these states.

In arriving at a judgment as to how we in the United States should react to this apparent adverse trend toward expanding militarism and the suppression of human rights in Latin America, we are confronted with serious dilemmas. This is the case whether we are speaking of a possible effective posture by the U.S. government in the face of this situation, or of steps and influence that might be exercised by the private sectors (business, news media, the Church, individuals, and others). The limits to effective governmental pressures and influence are perhaps best illustrated by the periodic soul-searching that takes place in the U.S. legislative and executive branches whenever announcements are made that one or more Latin American countries are contemplating the placement of large orders for sophisticated military equipment with European countries in the absence of U.S. willingness to provide them (rapidly and in sufficient quantity) with equipment of equal sophistication. Cries are heard in the Congress, the press, and elsewhere that should the Latin American governments and military establishments insist on going through with such extravagant expenditures, U.S. aid to those countries, which is intended for programs covered by the Alliance for Progress (and not for support of an armaments race), should be reduced by corresponding amounts or cut off altogether.

To this there is the inevitable answer that to cut aid will only exacerbate relations between the United States and the countries in question and deprive the masses of those countries of much-needed assistance (for education, health, and other reform programs), without producing a reversal of the decision to buy the military equipment demanded by the Latin American armed forces. The final argument normally advanced as the intended clincher in this never-ending argument is that to withhold aid in reprisal for purchases of military equipment in countries other than the United States would constitute "intervention," that ugliest of all sins in the inter-American firmament.[4]

Nevertheless, a realistic appraisal of the policies followed in the executive branch, particularly in the Pentagon, over the past several years, indicates that constant effort has been made to keep U.S. military assistance to Latin America to the lowest feasible level (consistent with maintaining friendly relations with these countries) and to types of equipment of a defensive nature. Within the limits of practicality, U.S. officials consistently endeavor to persuade Latin American governments and military leaders to forego the acquisition of expensive, "showcase," equipment.[5] However, it has long been clear to our government officials, and it seems finally to be sinking in with Congress, the press, academic experts, and other sectors, that there are definite limits to the ability of the United States to influence the Latin American military mind on this score. The consequence is often that the expenditures are made as insisted upon by the military, and critically short funds are expended for purposes other than programs designed to improve the lot of the Latin American common man. He is thereby deprived of a form of assistance that, if properly utilized, could add to his greater enjoyment of basic human rights.

In summary, it seems clear that militarism is on the rise throughout Latin America and that the cause of human rights is fading rather than advancing. Perhaps the most dangerous portent for the future attributable to this increased incidence of militarism is that unless by some, as yet undiscovered, magic formula, the military in Latin America is able to promote quickly and effectively the implementation of basic reforms and the modernization of Latin American countries, the military is likely to lose much of its prestige with the masses. The latter may then become more receptive to the arguments of the radical elements who advocate violent revolution as the only feasible course for these countries. Other politically active, but more moderate, elements may be forced to adopt the same viewpoint if they continue to be excluded from power by the military establishment, which in turn is failing to govern effectively with respect to the achievement of popular aspirations.

The one bright spot on the horizon seems to be the growing realization here in the United States (at the governmental and other levels), and among informed sources throughout Latin America, that the alarming rise of militarism in the area constitutes a threat of serious proportions and must be reversed if

there is to be any hope of achieving the progressive modernization of these nations and the steady improvement of the lot of the
common man by orderly, non-violent, and democratic processes.

NOTES

1. Martin C. Needler, "Political Development and Military Intervention in Latin America," *American Political Science Review*, LX
(3) (September, 1966), 616–626.
2. John J. Johnson, *The Military and Society in Latin America*
(Stanford: Stanford University Press, 1964).
3. Rollie E. Poppino, "Brazil: Second Phase of the Revolution,"
Current History, LVI (329) (January, 1969), 7–12, 52–53.
4. Simon G. Hansen, "The Alliance for Progress: The Sixth Year,"
Inter-American Economics Affairs, XXII (3) (Winter, 1968), 75–91.
5. *Ibid.*

RURAL PROBLEMS AS AN
OBSTACLE TO HUMAN RIGHTS

RENÉ DE LEÓN SCHLOTTER

A theme focusing on the basic rights of millions of Latin Americans whose liberation has been delayed is "the rigid structure of the Latin American agricultural system." We are considering wealth and poverty as impediments to human freedom. Here we shall analyze agricultural activity as an economic process, viewing it as production and distribution of farm production with special emphasis on the degree of participation of the different social groups in the agricultural field.

Economic activity is both individual and social and has as its aim the provision of goods and services that will enable each and every man to reach his human destiny. It follows then that all have the right to participate in economic development, as a means of reaching the intellectual, spiritual, and material fulfillment whose ultimate goal will be respect for his human rights.

Twenty years ago Latin American countries had the limited role of suppliers of raw materials, especially agricultural and mining products, to the industrially developed countries. In exchange

they were able to obtain basic manufactures. This role of dependent economy was by no means voluntary but was imposed by the
world economy in which the power of decision rests with the
developed countries, based on the application of the sharing of
responsibilities principle.

Since World War II a critical imbalance has arisen in this
economy because the demand for manufactured goods has increased at a much higher rate than the demand for raw materials.
The reasons for this imbalance for Latin America are too numerous to analyze completely. The introduction of synthetics, new
sources of raw materials in Asia and Africa, and the demographic
explosion in Latin America, and its corresponding demands on
the market, have precipitated the great imbalance in trade for
the countries producing raw materials.

Some Latin American countries are attempting to overcome the
unfavorable balance of trade by developing their own manufac-
turing potential. There are serious limitations to this approach
because of inadequate capital, skilled workman, technical development, and broad markets. As a result, much of the manufactur-
ing has to be restricted to articles for basic home consumption and
to easily manufactured items. This approach cannot make up the
deficit. On the contrary, it creates costly new industrial needs for
the country, as, for example, in machinery and semi-manufactured
goods for local manufacturers.

The drop in prices of agricultural exports has tended to dis-
courage farm production. Even the diversification of crops, which
could be a partial solution where the social structure would permit, has met with little encouragement. This lack of motivation
in the form of income has driven many *campesinos* to abandon
their fields and emigrate to cities where they cannot possibly be
absorbed by incipient industries. These internal migrations are
creating the new so-called "misery belts" which will constitute
one of Latin America's gravest socio-political problems in the
future. At the moment, nevertheless, approximately 50 per cent

of all Latin Americans are employed in agriculture and live in rural areas.

Developing countries on the continent have an annual population increase of 2.9 per cent. According to the Economic Commission for Latin America (CEPAL), the population of all Latin America in 1960 was 200 million and by 1975 will reach 300 million—which means a 50 per cent increase in 15 years. This means, too, that the growing human masses will need to be nourished and provided with job opportunities in a situation where undernourishment and unemployment indices are among the world's highest. By the same token, the increase in Latin American food production was only 1.1 per cent.[1]

The problem of malnutrition in Latin America is a matter of grave concern not only from a human viewpoint but also from the economic standpoint of productivity.

According to medical standards, a manual laborer requires a minimum of 3,500 calories daily. In Latin American countries, an intake of 2,000 to 2,500 calories is not unusual as a standard, and many workers subsist on far less. A case in point is found in Bolivia where a Five Year Development Plan has set as its goal to increase the 1,800 calories daily per capita consumption to 2,400 by 1971.[2] In Central America the daily urban per capita consumption is 1,762 and the rural 1,874.[3]

This brief review of some Latin American problems supports the conclusion that an increased and renewed effort is required to achieve *integral development* in these nations. Within these efforts the role of agrarian development must be given a priority role for the purpose of the following.

PRODUCING FOODS

Latin America produces only about 20 per cent of its capacity in foodstuffs.[4] By expanding this capacity it might easily become a major grain producer for several areas now suffering the effects of starvation. With adequate development, Latin America's vast territorial resources will enable it to play the rightful role anticipated by some experts in food marketing.[5]

INITIATING SOCIAL DEVELOPMENT

Starting the process of social development by means of agricultural development could provide some 150 million *campesinos* with those basic facilities that would promote not only their economic and social development but also give them the opportunity for autonomous self-development.

By and large, the efforts of governments through national and international agencies have met with a grave apathy on the part of the beneficiaries of the pilot projects because this promotion and these projects do not respond to a felt need of the people nor strike a pleasant ideological resonance. In general, it is safe to say that while the projects often meet short-term objectives by promoting irrelevant economic growth, they fail, over-all, inasmuch as they concern themselves exclusively with economic progress of the "People's Capitalism" and work in a context that tends to strengthen and reinforce rather than break with or substitute for old social structures. Again, the reasons given for mobilizing the *campesinos* correspond to the mentality and intellectual level of the promoters rather than to those of the peasants themselves.

It is necessary in this type of work that the beneficiaries become participants at every level—planning, execution, administration. To secure this involvement it will be essential that the developing action embody cultural, technical, economic, political and service areas, and that the projects be carried out by *campesino* organizations. The latter must be rendered capable of assuming representation in such a way that they may be regarded as "subjects" of promotion rather than its "objects," or mere beneficiaries on the receiving end.

Hopefully, this approach will be able to bring about the eventual integration into the main stream of society of what are now marginal sectors, resources, and services.

By providing the process of development with a secure base, this type of stimulation would have the threefold advantage of: (1) providing a better supply of foodstuffs; (2) eliminating unemployment, and (3) providing new domestic markets.

Even though it constitutes the keystone of Latin American development, this agricultural plan cannot be expected to be implemented because of the present structure of the agricultural economy. I consider this structure to be an insuperable obstacle which must be removed. Now I shall describe in outline this agricultural economic structure.

REGIMES OF LAND TENURE

". . . The rural property system is considered a fundamental element in stagnation of the agrarian sector."[6] We understand the meaning of this statement when we see on the one hand a great concentration of property in a few holdings of enormous extent and, on the other, a great number of units of extremely small size. This type of distribution is a standard characteristic in all Latin America, a condition that has created as one of its most striking consequences, the social stratification of the rural population into a rigid caste system. This system is responsible for enormous deficiencies in the living conditions of the vast majority of the rural population as well as a corresponding impairment of the socio-economic situation of all the nations. Actually the question of land is basic to most of the cultural, political, and economic levels of the continent that now impede general development. In addition to this so-called *latifundia* and *minifundia* there are also, on a smaller scale, a regime of communities and a system of colonization with characteristics relevant to the topic under consideration.

LATIFUNDIA

This institution of the great feudal estates, known in Latin America as the *latifundia,* is conceded by economists to be the number one problem. Some figures published by CEPAL, CIDA, and BID will clarify its significance.

In Guatemala, for example, 37 per cent of the agricultural lands are held by 0.15 per cent of those in agriculture: in Ecuador 17 per cent of the land is distributed in 1.69 per cent of the properties. In Bolivia, before the Agrarian Reform came into effect, 92 per cent of the land was held by 6.94 per cent of the landowners. In Nicaragua, a third of the land was in the hands of 362 landowners (a country whose total population is approximately 1.5 million). The over-all figure for Latin America is that 10 per cent of the landowners hold 90 per cent of the land—a degree of concentration unparalled by any other region of the world.

Some authors[7] distinguish two types of *latifundia,* for example, the following:

The hacienda or ranch, which concentrates on the production of cereals and/or traditional export products with extremely low yield, such as coffee or cattle, with a minimum of capital investment because of the cheap labor of farm tenants.

The plantation, a different type of economic endeavor where methods of industrial production are applied and the high capital investment brings high yields.

By and large both types operate at the expense of forced labor and furnish concrete examples of labor subjection. The owners of large estates, on the one hand, by the force of historic precedent and politics, form a politically dominant social caste. Logically, this caste opposes the demand for structural change advocated by smaller landholders, themselves middle class. This opposition on the part of the middle class is a paradox to the extent that it is the upper-class landowner who actually controls the policies on the export of agricultural products such as coffee, cotton, and bananas.

MINIFUNDIA

On the other side of the coin is the extremely small holding, which creates problems for development comparable to those brought about by the *latifundia*. These problems are social and political as much as they are economic.

Here are some data. In Guatemala 97 per cent of the "farms" are units of less than 20 hectares (or approximately 50 acres). "Farms" of this size in Ecuador and Peru total 90 per cent; in the Dominican Republic, 95 per cent; in Venezuela, 88 per cent. In Colombia, half a million plots are on the average 2.5 hectares (about 6 acres) in size, while a third of a million are less than half a hectare (or about one acre). According to the recent agrarian legislation estimates, the minimum size of a family unit farm should average between 15 and 18 hectares.

The *minifundia* presents several pressing problems, not least of which is soil exhaustion. Land cultivated excessively, particularly when crop rotation and/or fertilizer use are not possible, will soon be spent. Yields become as low, or even lower, than those of the *latifundia*.

On this subject Rene Dumont, in his book *Virgin Land,* gives some interesting comparisons. Here are a few. Meat production per hectare in Latin America: 17 kilograms; Europe, 300 to 400 kilograms. Milk per capita in Latin America: 700 to 1,000 liters per annum; Europe and the U.S.A: 4,000 liters. Corn per hectare: Central America 1,200 pounds; U.S.A. 16,000 pounds.

Closely linked with this as a logical consequence is unemployment. Taking into account the normal variations, it is estimated that the average farm worker is employed from 100 to well under 200 days annually.[8]

The situation here outlined suggests the decentralization of power in the market. As far as the small holder is concerned, he has no voice either as a producer or as a consumer of goods.

This same organization of the system deprives the large segment —in every case an overwhelming majority of the population—of the benefits of all projects organized by infrastructure to foster the development of the country. The common people lack all kinds of services and are forced to bring up their children in an ignorance equal to their own, where the most elementary education is lacking. As a result, they become objects of exploitation at the mercy of middlemen who buy their scanty products at minimal prices and sell them the staple commodities at exorbitant ones. To be concrete, cases have been reported in Central America of merchants in isolated areas charging prices for medicines 140 per cent higher than those asked in the city; money lenders who grant "subsistence" credits at the rate of 10 per cent per month. These cases of borrowing on the coming crop are found in the plateaus of Bolivia, Peru, and Guatemala.

LATIFUNDIA–MINIFUNDIA: AN ECONOMIC COMPLEXITY

It is important to be aware that these two institutions form a complementary unit. This is so not only because the *latifundia* is the direct source of the *minifundia* but especially because the system is sponsored by the large landowners who rely on the temporary labor of small farmers in harvest time. This type of employment gives rise to a whole series of social problems for the migratory *campesino* who has to move about with all his belongings and misery: to temporary famines, family separations, school absenteeism, lack of basic services, personal and social security, and a host of other problems.

THE COMMUNITY

The community as a form of land tenure is typically native in origin and is to be found especially on the Andean plateau which embraces a population of approximately six million, the Central American plateau with about the same population, and in some extensive areas of Mexico. The system consists basically in the rights of some families, with legal recognition by their governments, over determined areas of land. At first glance, one might think that this community-type holding could be a corrective for the *minifundia*, but given the inflexible internal structure of the traditionalist society and its religious and social defensive attitudes about real estate, this kind of land tenure is not capable of promoting an integrationist movement.

During its agrarian reform, Mexico established what was known as *ejidos*, or common lands. The basis of this valuable experiment was a more flexible form of the native communal structure. It proved successful in a limited way in that it was restricted to the distribution of lands and a community system of farm production where services were not established.

THE SYSTEM OF COLONIZATION OF TENANT FARMERS

There is some confusion about the system of land tenure and the tenant farmer system. Often *campesinos* work on large ranches or plantations in return for a small plot of land; in other cases they are simply sharecroppers often paying—as in parts of Central America—up to 50 per cent of their crop for use of the land. There are many different systems of payment, but the most common are the exchange of work and crop value for land tenure.

The plots held by these tenants are usually very small and subject to erosion by over-use. They yield barely enough food for the farmer and his family in spite of concentrated use and cannot be considered a means of economic production.

It is understandable that this system is inadequate for Latin America's economic development, but its defense by involved landholders has secured its continuation in the basic land distribution pattern of the countries.

INFLEXIBLE SOCIAL STRATIFICATION

The inequalities existing among the different social sectors in developing countries are well known. These inequalities call forth

diametrically opposite situations, diverse opportunities and expectations and differences in value scales with resulting dissent
and contradiction of interests. Sociologists estimate that some 2
per cent of the cosmopolitan upper class, composed of large
landowners, businessmen, and bankers, have a standard of living
comparable to that of the wealthiest social class in developed
countries; about 18 per cent are rated as middle class. This latter
group includes small businessmen, government officials, etc.,
whose interests are affected by the higher class. Then there is the
80 per cent comprising the lower class, made up of those with
very limited education, low income, and with minimal participation in government, economics, and services.

In the rural situation, the figures are even worse: 10 per cent
upper class, with 90 per cent lower class living in very marginal
conditions.[9] There are some aspects of the rural situation that
merit further clarification.

THE INDIAN PROBLEM

Social stratification is intensified in many cases by cultural or
racial differences. In the case of the Indian, there is a marked
tendency—because of tribal and local tradition—toward segregation. This segregation is not only social and economic but also
legal, and it stems from the fact that the legal system of the sur-
rounding culture appears to ignore or is otherwise inapplicable
to the Indian regime. Some countries have passed special legislation to govern Indians, but I raise the question whether these do
not smack of legal discrimination.

STRUCTURAL INFLEXIBILITY

The essential characteristic of a stratified society is the absence
of a social continuum that permits social mobility. This is particularly the case with the lowest classes where education is
scanty, work opportunities low, socio-political participation almost
non-existent, with resultant mutual hostility within the society.

UNJUST DISTRIBUTION OF INCOMES

"The average relation between per capita income of the higher class and the masses of *campesinos* may range from twenty or thirty or more against one."[10]

"One per cent of the active Chilean agricultural population receives 25 per cent of the annual income produced in the farm sector."[11] In a study of the Chilean situation, Marvin Sternberg establishes that 12 per cent of the active rural population (landlords) receive more than 65 per cent of the income, leaving 34 per cent for the 88 per cent laborers and small landholders.

These figures reflect the situation in the countries of the southern zone (Chile, Argentina and Uruguay), but it deteriorates progressively as we approach the essentially agricultural countries (Central America and the Caribbean lands) or those with predominately indigenous populations (Bolivia, Peru, Mexico, and Guatemala).

The Central American annual per capita income in rural areas is estimated at U.S. $50.00 in U.S. money. However, cases in zones of *minifundia* are common where U.S. $36.00 is the per capita income.

INSUFFICIENT AND INADEQUATE DISTRIBUTION OF
CAPITAL INVESTMENT

There has been little interest in sizable investments in plantations, probably because of the existence of more liberal policies for industrial investment. Some efforts carried out by BID in this area, offering long-term loans for crop diversifications, have stumbled because of too rigid credit regulations within the government and private banking system of Latin American countries, where it is the practice to defend hoarding rather than promote investing.

On the other hand, the private banking system usually rules on a too rigid criteria for installments and interest especially charged on agricultural loans. It is a service not accessible to the small producer. A superficial evaluation of some programs of agrarian reform in Latin America indicates that only 1 to 5 per cent of the total amount of private and governmental loans for agricultural activities is channeled to popular sectors, a statistic which explains the existence of usury.

The prices of land are too high, due to the same regime of *latifundia* (lust for retention or monopoly), or *minifundia* (shortage of land plus demographic pressure).

Low Production Yields

In *latifundia*, "ranch type" yields are much lower than normal. If an increased production is desired, a large expanse of land can be cultivated, and the operation can be kept economical because manual labor is far cheaper in increasing production than is investment in technical methods and machinery.

In *minifundia* the reasons for low yields are similar, and are compounded by the fact already mentioned, soil impoverishment.

Primitive and Exhausting Market System

The commercial promotion of agricultural food products for home consumption is in the hands of wholesalers who frequently stimulate artificial price rises by holding goods so as to create shortages. Then, in the distribution of such staples as corn, beans, wheat and rice, they can make greater profits.

The commercial promotion to international centers depends on the prices fixed by the New York and London stock exchanges or on the minimum export quotas. This condition directly affects the particular economy of each producer of agricultural export goods, and it is also subject to additional pressure in the form of existing export taxes.

Pope Paul VI in his *Populorum Progressio* makes a special reference to this point when he asks the developed countries to adopt more just commercial policies towards the developing countries by paying higher prices for raw material or agricultural goods required for their consumption and lowering the prices of their manufactured products. This point has been dramatized by milk producers in the U.S. and Europe, who have poured out their product in sewers rather than submit to price regulation, while *campesino* children in Latin America are starving.

LEGAL HINDRANCES TO THE ORGANIZATION OF CAMPESINOS

There has been great insistence on freedom of association as a natural means of solving problems and defending rights based on solidarity. Notwithstanding, many countries (notably El Salvador, Nicaragua, Haiti, and Paraguay) have laws prohibiting free unions of *campesinos*. Other nations place obstacles in their way, without publicly prohibiting social organizations of *campesinos* (Mexico, for example, does not approve any kind of cooperativism; in Central America it is legally easier and faster to organize a corporation than a union of *campesinos* or an agricultural cooperative). How can we expect social integration without organization?

LACK OF SERVICES AND SOCIAL SECURITY

Campesinos, in some cases, completely lack the most elementary public health services; in others these are partially offered, as are medical assistance, educational facilities, and housing. Social security services are not applicable to *campesinos* not receiving a salary.

The economic, social, cultural and political situation of the rural population in Latin America, as far as popular sectors are concerned (50 per cent of the total population, or around 150 million human beings), openly denies the most elementary human rights: labor, technical and professional education, and full employment (article no. 6); human working conditions and just remuneration (article no. 7); freedom for unions (article no. 8);

social security and social insurance (article no. 9); family and child protection (article no. 10); and guarantee of an adequate level of living including food, dress, and housing (article no. 11).

The existing social, economic, and political structure in rural areas is the direct source of the difficulties here observed.

The existing social, economic, and political structure of rural areas in Latin America is a direct handicap to the developmental task. The necessity of an urgent, rapid, and deep agrarian reform is therefore clear.

NOTES

1. "The Economist," January 9, 1969.

2. "Report on the World Social Situation, 1963," United Nations.

3. Marina Flores, "Patrones dieteticos en Centro América y Panamá."

4. "Agricultural Prices in Latin America." Essay by G. Dumont de Chassart in *Presencia Latinoamericana* (Brussels), Oct. 31, 1968.

5. Lecture given by James J. O'Connor, Executive Director of the Academy of Food Marketing, St. Joseph's College, Philadelphia.

6. Thomas F. Carroll, in A. O. Hirschman (ed.), *Latin American Issues* (New York: The Twentieth Century Fund, 1961), pp. 161–201.

7. Eric Wolf, Solom Barraclough, Edmundo Flores.

8. Economic Bulletin of Latin America, VII (2). A report from CEPAL on "Problems and Perspectives of Latin American Agriculture."

9. CEPAL, "Problems and Perspectives."

10. CEPAL, "Problems and Perspectives."

11. Marvin Sternberg, "Chilean Land Tenure and Land Reform," Land Tenure Center, University of Wisconsin at Madison, 1967.

THE SOCIAL FUNCTION OF THE
SLUM IN LATIN AMERICA:
SOME POSITIVE ASPECTS

JUAN A. CASASCO

Introduction

A living environment conducive to human dignity is certainly a basic human right. Our focus is the Latin American urban slum as it relates to the rights and aspirations of the poor.

The slum is a function of the rapid urbanization of our largest cities. The central city has made great contributions to society by offering the advantages of economies of agglomeration and increased opportunity for culture, higher education, government, and trade. However, city growth, due largely to rural migration, has brought about numerous negative consequences. Overcrowding and dilapidation of housing and community facilities with successive occupancy by the disinherited has given rise to the inner-city slum and the peripheral shantytown.

Slums have long been correlated with poverty, crime, and a host of other pathological urban problems. We all concur that they should either be rehabilitated or eliminated. Yet, immediate alternatives are few, and there are some positive contributions which the slum offers its dwellers.

HISTORICAL PERSPECTIVE

Latin American cities today are not as prepared to receive the steady flow of rural migrants as some of them were to receive international immigrants from Europe before and after both World Wars. The programs of the past, designed to locate entire families of immigrants in the rural hinterland, have no contemporary counterpart for the rural migrant who comes to the central city. He is pretty much on his own. Where can he go, what can he do, without money or skill?

The slums, however disturbing they may be when judged by middle class values and standards, perform a most necessary function in housing the poor.

The social fabric of the slum possesses sub-cultural values which tend to be overlooked by social planners who seek to eradicate them. An analysis of some of the positive aspects of the slum will cast light on the web of motivations, expectations, mores, attitudes, and other component elements of its sub-culture. Identification of these elements is indispensable if the human values and rights of the poor are to be considered when designing slum clearance and relocation programs. The task of identifying the positive values within the slum are more difficult and far less appealing to current bureaucratic interests than the more obvious and decried, negative aspects of the slums.

METHODOLOGY

Although Latin America shows no less evidence of discrimination towards its indigent and indigenous than the rest of our "civilized" world, the cases presented in this paper illustrate that the availability of choice spurs motivation. The study is limited to a review of selected examples of slum problems in several Latin American countries. It also offers some constructive suggestions for an action-oriented slum program.

The findings of this brief study provide supporting evidence to an obvious but nontheless generally ignored fact: in planning for the urban slums, public and private agencies and individuals must consider the great difference in socio-economic values and motivations that exist between middle, low, and very-low income groups in Latin America. These are of vital consequence in the urban development process.

In the area of research, the most crucial elements of the slum which merit examination are: (a) factors which influence the poor to remain in, or enable them to leave, the slum (such as achievement, motivation, and ability); (b) cultural mores and *modus vivendi* of the slum dweller as they apply to habitation and community organization (such as measures of privacy, types of housing design, site layouts, building materials, and general appearance). These two areas of research could provide most valuable inputs to a social program for slum improvement and/or relocation of slum dwellers in new housing.

Through research, meaningful data would be collected and analyzed and objective recommendations could be made to those responsible for planning for the poor. Plans and programs based upon such research would be responsive to the real needs, aspirations, and limitations of the poor, rather than reflecting the values of an alien sub-culture as is currently the case.

Finally some practical suggestions for action are offered. These are feasible in that they demand an ample dose of creativity within an action-oriented planning approach and only a minimum allocation of local government resources.

I. Urbanization and the Slum

All the major cities of Latin America have experienced the surge of urbanization in recent decades, notwithstanding the fact

that many of them are not considered modernized or even industrialized.[1] To a great extent their urbanization has been spurred
by rural migration.

The seminar "Urbanization in Latin America," organized by
the United Nations and UNESCO stated ". . . that many of the
more severe problems affecting mankind, especially in the underdeveloped areas, are by-products of rapid urbanization."[2]

Further, the major findings of this seminar indicated that rapid
urbanization was due largely to a transfer of poverty from the
rural areas to the large central cities, rather than to technological
change in rural activities with its consequent reduction of labor
demand. Rural migration, caused by lack of opportunities, subsistence living, and poverty was a greater force in urbanization
than the "pull" of industrialization.

Recent demographic studies show that migration represented
50 per cent of the total increase in urban population. In Venezuela the rate of urban population growth for the period 1941–
1961 was 230 per cent as compared to that of Mexico with 150
per cent for the same period.[3] Only part of the increase in urban
population was due to international migration after World War
II; the larger portion consisted of rural migrants searching for
a better life.

The index of concentration in large central cities, generally the
primate city, was 68 in Latin America as compared with 60 for
Europe and 69 for North America.[4]

The impact of this rapid urbanization process upon the large
cities resulted in an overcrowding of public services, and an
acute housing shortage evidenced by the increased number of
shantytowns and other types of slums found in most of Latin
America's large cities.

Considering the relatively low and poorly remunerated labor
market for unskilled illiterate or semi-literate rural migrants, the
"pull" of the large cities would appear to be more social than
economic.

RURAL MIGRATION

Why do the rural poor move to the cities?

The answer lies, in part, in the host of life's liabilities among the rural poor: unemployment, low wages, deficiencies in nutrition and education facilities, periodic economic depressions due to environmental factors such as drought, flood, or low market prices.

There is also the symbolism attached to urban life—opportunities for socio-economic improvement, amenities of the city, and other subjective values which the poor migrant attaches to city life. He may be well aware that life in the city with its many social and economic costs will not be easy, that his cost of living will be higher, and that his housing may be inferior to his shack in the country. When he is trading off the peaceful but subsistent rural life for the pressures and early discomforts of urban life, he is, in many cases, vaguely aware of the costs as well as the benefits involved. He accepts having to live in a slum or shantytown as the first station in his acculturation to urban society, but he hopes this will be temporary and that eventually he and his family will have the opportunity for a better life.

The city then, with all its defects and problems, "still harbors . . . hope, in an increasingly hazardous and complex society . . . (To the poor, the slum) . . . . may be the only escape from famine and stagnation, the temporary anchorage of struggling mankind slowly moving toward something better. But the prospect of something better should be there, however remote."[5]

HOUSING DEFICIT

The steady flow of migration to the central cities generates a continuously increasing demand for low-cost housing. These centers have thus been faced with the problem of providing the newly arrived with shelter, community facilities, and public services. It is therefore relevant to examine briefly the attempts of several Latin American countries to satisfy increased housing demands.

Recent studies provide statistical evidence of an acute housing deficit. Brazil currently faces a total deficit estimated at 8 million units which is growing at the rate of almost one-half million units per year. In 1966 Brazil's housing industry was able to supply approximately 120,000 units.

The statistics are no more encouraging elsewhere: Colombia has a deficit of 350,000 units which is increasing by 55,000 units per year; Chile's 1964 deficit was estimated at 360,000 units; Panama's 1966 housing needs were cited at 47,000 units.[6] These data do not take into account the hundreds of thousands of substandard houses in the peripheral shantytowns or the inner-city's overcrowded slums.

Moreover, the acuteness of this housing shortage is augmented by systematic land speculation and severe scarcity of housing mortgages. Land speculation has long been a profitable and almost uncontrolled operation in most Latin American countries. Investment in land is motivated by quick profits and has long been used by investors as a hedge against inflation. Almost all Latin American cities lack adequate government policies and implementation tools to control speculative land development. This has resulted in an endless sprawl of small-lot subdivisions, and a lack of essential municipal services, transportation, and community facilities such as schools and health centers. Entertainment is usually limited to a local movie theater or a neighborhood club with a soccer field. Such amenities as public parks or recreation centers are almost non-existent. The local town square, when it exists, often is the only place for community gatherings and social interaction.

The ineffectiveness of local municipal action is yet another important obstacle to cope adequately with the problems of housing and community services. Limited municipal budgets and lack of local autonomy, compounded by a lack of efficient land use and speculation controls, indicate the real magnitude of the housing problem.

II. The Slums

The compounded effect of urban migration and the inability of governments to provide housing for the poor inevitably results in the overcrowding of existing structures—which leads to slum formation.

DEFINITION

The slum is in general an area of physical and socio-economic decadence. From the socio-economic standpoint, the slum represents poverty, subsistence income, and social pathology. Its physical environment is one of dilapidated, substandard, and overcrowded structures, often totally lacking in municipal services.

These characteristics of the slum can be applied almost universally, to the U.S. inner-city slum or the "conventillo" of central Buenos Aires or Mexico City.

Our discussion of the slum also includes what has become an accepted mode of life among the urban poor of Latin America, the shantytown and squatter settlement located in the outlying areas of almost all of the subcontinent's large urban centers.[7] This type of slum is built almost entirely of discarded materials— wood boards, tin cans, cardboard sidings, auto battery cases. Much ingenuity is exhibited in the use of such local materials as thatch, adobe, bamboo, and cane. The sites are generally inadequate, subject to floods, on steep hillsides, on municipal or privately owned land without police vigilance and lacking minimum municipal services (e.g., running water, sewers, drainage, electricity).

THE CONCEPT OF SLUMS AS STATIONS IN THE LIFE OF THE POOR

The slum serves the social necessity of housing the poor. Slum dwellers' attitudes range from those who feel that they are in the slum to stay to those who consider the slum an area of temporary settlement. The former attitude is held by the indolent, the social outcast, and the pathologically poor, while the latter views the slum as a way station in life which allows him to adjust to urban society, find a job, seek opportunities for change.

While well-programmed relocation favors some, slum eradication destroys these opportunities for many others. If local planning agencies are to benefit slum dwellers, they should begin with a gradual and selective relocation of a few by helping them to realize their possibilities, and concurrently by trying to improve the environmental conditions of those who wish to stay or cannot move out.

TYPES OF SLUMS

Slum dwellers are provided with two options in the foregoing concept of the slum: The positive option provides the rural migrant temporary shelter and a transitional acculturation period. The negative option is the "end of the line" offering no expectations; it is the last station for the dejected, physically and mentally downcast, and the outcast. Within this positive-negative framework many types of slums have been studied, documented, and theorized.

The Urban Village and the Urban Jungle. Herbert Gans, in his study of Boston's West End, classifies two types of slums.[8] The area of first or second settlement where the migrants try "to adapt their non-urban institutions and cultures to the urban milieu" is termed the "urban village." The second, which tends to be populated by "single men and individuals who provide the more disreputable or illegal-but-demanded services to the rest of the community," is termed the "urban jungle." Gans explains that these are two "ideal" types of U.S. slums and that no existing neighborhood would necessarily fall exactly into either category.

Several other slum studies[9] show evidence that these two broad categories can be applied to Latin American cities regardless of their different stage of urbanization.

John C. Turner describes the development of squatter settlements in Lima, Peru, as offering "uniquely satisfactory opportunities for low income settlers."[10] These squatter settlements are a "spontaneous mobilization of human and material resources," characterized by a self-help type of housing built in stages to suit the immediate needs and possibilities of the squatter-builder and his family.[11] Using Gans' typology, these Lima slums would come under the "urban village" category.

The "urban jungle" slum is best described by Carolina María de Jesús in her diary of her life in the *favela* Caninde in São Paulo, Brazil.[12] Carolina moved into the *favela* from a rural town in the state of Minas Gerais, she built her own shack, lived at subsistence level, and later wrote a candid essay on the crude realities of her *favela*. Life in the "urban jungle" was characterized by hunger and its consequences—alcoholism, prostitution, violence, and crime.

As a consequence of Carolina's exposé of the *favela*, São Paulo decided to eradicate the slum.[13] Two hundred and thirty families were relocated to 75 different areas of metropolitan São Paulo. Of these a total of 140 families, or 60 per cent, either purchased or built their own homes. These were permanent structures, mainly of masonry. Other families were relocated in low-rent public housing, some were helped to return to their rural villages, and a few had to be evacuated by force. The *favela* Caninde was demolished and the land allocated to a public housing project.

The graduate students of the local Catholic University undertook a follow-up survey. The experience of the *desfavelamento* (slum clearance) of Caninde had stirred such interest that three local universities then organized the MUD, *Movimiento Universitario de Desfavelamento* (University Movements for Slum Clearance). This group subsequently worked in the clearance of Mooca, another *favela* in São Paulo which housed 100 *barracos* (shacks). The relocation process was similar to that of Caninde; private financing was added to public funding; much of the field work was done by university students acting as social workers and collaborating with lawyers and specialists in health, urban planning, housing and building.[14]

Oscar Lewis depicts other "urban jungles" in his studies of slums in Harlem and Puerto Rico.[15] His study describes the life of the Rios family in La Esmeralda, a slum of approximately 900 houses inhabited by 3,600 people, located on a steep embankment between ancient fort walls and the sea. This slum had the reputation of housing murderers, drug addicts, thieves, and prostitutes.

Other such "urban jungle" slums exist in almost any large Latin American city where the "culture of poverty" prevails. The "urban jungle" does then, in effect, perform the social function of housing those poor who do not have the opportunity to live in the "urban village" slum.

Slums of Hope and Slums of Despair. One of the most enlightening discussions on the theory of slums is offered by Charles Stokes, who differentiates between the slums of hope and the slums of despair. The positive psychological response of the dwellers to better themselves qualifies them to belong to the slums of hope. Correspondingly, the absence of upward motivation, or an expectation based upon a negative estimate of their possibilities for change relegates others to the slums of despair.

Stokes further classifies the slum dwellers into *escalator* and *non-escalator* groups, according to their ability or inability to move up through the class structure.[16]

Barriers in the Life of the Poor. Stokes has constructed a "basic matrix" depicting the social characteristics of the slums and identified income, ability, and caste as the main barriers in the life of the poor. He theorizes that:

1. *Income* barriers separate the fully employed sector of the city's population from the poor;

2. The *ability* barrier divides the poor into two groups: (a)

Those residents of the slums of hope who, when given certain over-all favorable economic conditions, can be absorbed and utilized, and (b) Those inhabitants of the slums of despair who will not be absorbed or utilized regardless of the city's economic growth.

3. The *caste* barrier separates the escalators and non-escalators according to different rates of absorption and levels of utilization. Because of this caste barrier the non-escalator class, even if fully utilized (employed) and living either in slums of hope or of despair, will have greater difficulty in becoming absorbed than the escalator class.

Slums of Hope. These slums house the rural migrant and other newcomers to the city.[17] The dwellers in the slums of hope have flocked to the large central cities searching for job opportunities, education for their children, decent housing, and the opportunity for socio-economic improvement. The slums of hope would tend to disappear as migration slows down and the majority of its dwellers would be able to move up the socio-economic class structure of the city when given the opportunity of employment.

The "Barrio de los Pobres" in Guayaquil, Ecuador, is a slum of hope. Its dwellers are mostly Indians from the jungle, *serranos* from the highland, or *costenos* from the coast. This slum, located in the marshes of the Guayas River, houses about 250,000 people or almost one-half the population of Guayaquil.[18] Its housing reflects different stages of slum development. Some older sections are located on land reclaimed from the flood marshes either by the slum dwellers themselves, or with the help of the city which provided pavement, sidewalks, and minimum sanitary services. The housing in this area is built of permanent materials, primarily of concrete. On improved land at the fringes of these permanent structures, housing is in yet another stage of development, less permanent, of bamboo, and built as high off the ground as possible on a *relleno* (fill-in).

The Barrio de los Pobres exhibits the organic vitality of continuous regeneration and growth as new shacks appear in the far edges of the slum, reclaiming new land. In Guayaquil this process of slum building is directly correlated with city growth because of the slum/non-slum population ratio. The Barrio de los Pobres with its growth cycle of temporary shelters, land reclamation, and permanent housing is a slum of hope which has the power to rehabilitate itself. If migration slows down, this vitality may show a substantial improvement of the city's slums.

Slums of Despair. The main psychological difference between hope and despair directly relates to employment possibilities. The slums of despair are often devoid of opportunity for employment. For those who cannot or do not wish to be absorbed into the employable sector of the city's population, it serves as a place of last resort. These dwellers lack the capacity to become acculturated and to overcome the ability hurdles the city erects. They are in a sense "trapped" unable to move out, and often develop a fear of the "outside." There is little feeling for one's neighbor or of community: residents may come together only occasionally in their own defense.[19]

The "tugurio" is a deep intellectual and spiritual crevice filled with constant misery and people with depressed and passive human lives. Escape is virtually impossible, and when a way out is allowed to select few, they do not understand. They suspect it, and remain in the depths.[20]

Ciudad de Dios near Lima, Peru, is an example of an Indian ghetto in partially integrated Latin America. In contrast to the Guayaquil Indians with their aggressive achievement motivation, these Peruvian Indians tend to have a passive attitude, ". . . not wanted and unaggressive, (he) sits in despair at the city's gates."[21]

The people in the slums of despair receive little sympathy from the city and have little chance of being absorbed into urban society. This slum is the only place they can go since no other choices or options are open to them. Notwithstanding the negative aspects of the slums of despair, however, an objective observer cannot help but realize that these slums also serve a necessary function in city life. Provided that efficient comprehensive social planning could break down some of the discrimination barriers, the need for this type of slum could be reduced. Education, selective welfare, and social action could contribute to the assimilation of part of the dwellers of the slum of despair into urban society. Let us now consider some of the positive functions of slums.

III. The Social Function of the Slum

Given the continuing increase in urban population due to rural migration, the inability of Latin American governments to diminish their housing deficits is evidence of the important role which the slum plays in providing shelter, however inadequate that shelter may be. The slum, in all its varied forms, also offers the unskilled, uneducated, and poor rural migrant the opportunity to be absorbed into an urban society.

Positive Functions of the Slum

It is common knowledge the most slums have a high rate of delinquency, mental deficiency, unemployment, poverty, dependence on public welfare, illiteracy, and a whole spectrum of other urban pathological conditions. However deficient and imperfect the slum is, certain positive functions tend to be overlooked not only by the casual observer, but by the overzealous bureaucrat and the emotional critic. They overlook the trade-offs between entering life in the slum as a transition period (opportunity for upward mobility) or remaining homeless.[22] Latin American governments will be unable to cope with either the problem of poverty or the acute housing shortage in the foreseeable future; it is imperative, therefore, that some of the positive contributions which the slums make to society be identified and evaluated. With these positive aspects singled out and assessed, we can then make recommendations for improvement of slum conditions.

The slum's key functions are:

1. To provide a first foothold, a way station for social transition;

2. To provide a temporary, albeit often precarious, shelter to newcomers;[23] The well-known Brazilian architect, Sergio Bernardes, views the *favelas* of Rio (and indeed all slums) as part of urban development and suggests that they should be transformed into attractive popular (low-cost) housing which actively participates in the city's growth. In his opinion slum rehabilitation is inevitable because these housing nuclei must be located within the centers of gravitation of employment. Bernardes views sanitation as the worst of the *favelas* problems. One remedy he proposes is an ingenious design for a hillside which would provide the *favelados* with a reinforced concrete platform supported by a precast concrete septic tank. Placed on a solid foundation and serving the dual function of structural and sanitary elements, the tanks would be interconnected with server lines. The *favelado* would then build his own dwelling upon this platform using modular panels and other low-cost prefabricated materials. Construction of these foundations and minimum community services would be financed by a local public agency, FINACO. The dwelling itself would then be the responsibility of the *favelado*.[24]

3. To provide to unskilled and semi-skilled labor the locational advantages of a short journey to work.

The unquestionable advantage of a slum dweller in Rio de Janeiro is clearly illustrated by the case of Pedro Mineiro, a bricklayer who lived in a *favela* overlooking Botafogo Bay, who walked to his work in Copacabana. After work Pedro could go to dig crabs on the beach. His family home had electricity but no water or sewer. His wife Rosa took in washing for rich people, and thus they were able to save a little money in a tin can for emergencies. The Mineiros were forcibly relocated to a distant housing project financed by U.S. funds through the Alliance for Progress.[25]

Now in addition to meeting house payments, Pedro has a long

and expensive journey to work, is too far away to go crabbing, and Rosa has lost her clients. The new house, roughly 12 x 18 feet, includes a bathroom and kitchen, and a small multipurpose room which the family of five overcrowds. Mortgage payments escalate with Brazil's inflation and now absorb 18 per cent of Pedro's meager income; another 12 per cent is spent on transportation. The family cannot save any more and sometimes cannot even meet their monthly payments. Some of Pedro's neighbors who continually refuse to pay were taken to an old *favela* near the city dump, a place with fetid odors and vultures. As Pedro says, "It's the end of the line." The new development has a school and a dispensary, but the teachers don't show up very often and the dispensary is usually closed. Pedro's journey to work now takes him nearly four to six hours a day; he leaves at 4 a.m. and returns at 9 p.m.[26]

The Alliance for Progress has not been able to generate enough momentum in Latin America to spur housing construction. Moreover, some of the standards it laid down were more responsive to middle-class values than to local needs, as the preceding case study illustrates.

The case of *favelado* Pedro Mineiro is comparable to countless others, not only in Latin America, but in some of Europe's large urban centers as well.[27]

Social Mobility Cycle

An examination of a hypothetical case in the urban adaptation and housing cycle will show the possibility for upward mobility of a semi-skilled rural migrant family. Attracted by the glamorized descriptions of city life by relatives or friends who preceded them to the city's slums, and by a promising employment market offering higher wages and greater health and educational opportunities for their children, such families migrate to the central city or peripheral city slum.

The following diagram, "Housing Cycle in the Acculturation of the Rural Poor in Buenos Aires," illustrates the geographic location of our hypothetical case's household and outlines the changes in housing and environment which can take place during a slow transition period (10 to 20 years) toward home ownership and residential stability.

The housing cycle is represented in the following stages:

Stage 1. Tin and wood shack, no municipal services, cooking and lighting by kerosene, outhouse only sanitary facility, no sewers, water carried in cans from communal spigot, site tends to flood during rainy season. Job opportunities: bricklayer's helper, unskilled factory worker; wife may work as domestic. Children attend local school.

Right to "squat" in choice locations is sometimes bought from previous squatter and sold when leaving the *villa Miseria.*

Stage 2. Alternative "A." Masonry tenement house (*conventillo*) in some instances 50 to 70 years old; walk-up one-room unit with communal sanitary facilities, cooking by kerosene or charcoal, electricity.

Semi-skilled job opportunities in central city: construction jobs, light industry, and in service shops. Wife is occasional domestic. Children attend local school and enjoy neighborhood street entertainment and cultural facilities.

Low-rent room or apartment is bought for "key money" from previous tenant. (Rent freezing has given rise to many illegal ways of buying and selling the "key" rights to low-rent housing in the central city.)

Alternative "B." Eligibility requirements and availability of units present problems. Semidetached, one-story public-row housing in a peripheral neighborhood within the city limits. Gas, electricity, small front and back yards, community facilities similar to Alternative "A."

Stage 3. Move to low-class suburbs. Becomes home-owner of a small unimproved lot with running water and electricity but no

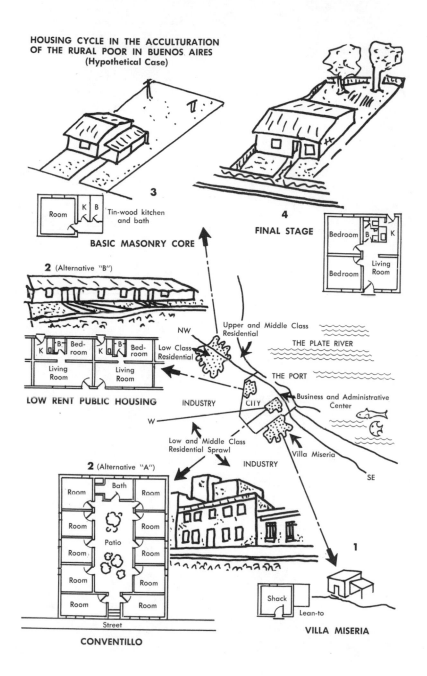

HOUSING CYCLE IN THE ACCULTURATION
OF THE RURAL POOR IN BUENOS AIRES
(Hypothetical Case)

3

Room | K | B | Tin-wood kitchen
and bath

BASIC MASONRY CORE

4

FINAL STAGE

Bedroom | B | K
Bedroom | Living Room

2 (Alternative "B")

K | B | Bedroom | K | B | Bedroom
Living Room | Living Room

LOW RENT PUBLIC HOUSING

Upper and Middle Class Residential

NW

Low Class Residential

THE PLATE RIVER

THE PORT

Business and Administrative Center

INDUSTRY

CITY

W

Low and Middle Class Residential Sprawl

INDUSTRY

Villa Miseria

SE

2 (Alternative "A")

Room | Bath | Room
Room | | Room
Room | Patio | Room
Room | | Room
Room | | Room

Street

CONVENTILLO

1

Shack | Lean-to

VILLA MISERIA

sewage, no pavement, distant school and community facilities.
House consists of one-room masonry, "basic core" with attached
sanitary and cooking facilities of corrugated metal and wood.
Materials are purchased from local lumber yard and financed
with government mortgages.

Employment opportunities for wife are limited by distance and
transportation cost to middle-class suburbs. Achievement of one
of the most important objectives in the poor's life: home-ownership.

Stage 4. Pride of ownership reflected in the improvement of the
house and successive additions.

Permanent residence is established and a sense of neighborhood
develops.

This cycle, while it may not apply to all rural migrants or slum
dwellers, does highlight the possibility for upward mobility from
a shantytown to slum tenement house or low-rent public housing
project, to home-ownership and the socio-economic status and
security connected with it. No matter how small and humble this
first owned house is, it is almost always built of masonry with
subsequent additions of permanent materials. A combination of
the achievement motive and the opportunity afforded by the
urban environment would make this transition possible in almost
all large centers of Latin America.

An example of motivation and community organization is provided in William Mangin's graphic description of the *barriadas*
in Lima, Peru.[28] Mangin dispels the notion that all the squatters
of Lima's shantytowns are illiterate Indians without ambition or
motivation, representing a socio-economic liability to the city.

These *barriadas* were set up some two decades ago by inner-
city families living in overcrowded, unhealthy, but expensive
commercial tenement houses in the inner-city slums. The families
migrated to the open-air, rent-free building sites on Lima's
periphery which offered them potential home-ownership. Students of architecture helped to plot the subdivision and showed

them how to build their brick and mortar houses. Aided by social workers and religious organizations, these *barriadas* began with a high degree of community organization. Special areas were set aside for community facilities and the settlers were organized to fight the political and legal battles to secure eventual ownership of their homes. Several attempts to eradicate these squatter settlements met with little success.

The new capital of Brasilia, with a very large slum at its doorstep, illustrates the inadequate planning on the part of agencies responsible for providing housing and community facilities to workers and ancillary service workers engaged in very large projects.

When construction of the new capital started, an area at the periphery of the city was set aside for workers' quarters; with time this area grew into a modern western town with a main street bustling with commercial facilities, saloons, banks, entertainment houses, and all kinds of legal and illegal services. Junkyards for overworked and ruined construction equipment were many. At its peak, when Brasilia was inaugurated in 1960, this area housed 60,000 construction workers.[29] The workers, the ancillary service labor force, and some of their families were accommodated in temporary housing and were legally committed to leave the area when construction terminated.

One of the gross oversights of NOVACAP, the semi-governmental corporation responsible for the construction of Brasilia, was in not taking into account that:

(a) a city is a dynamic living organism that grows and adjusts itself to changing demands (political as well as socio-economic), and (b) when a large temporary housing project transforms itself into a real town with a justifiable existence (regardless of its original status), it becomes an exercise in futility and/or it is politically unwise to attempt to eradicate it and disperse its dwellers.

This temporary town was called Cidade Livre and offered a

vivid contrast to the anonymous, regimented, and sterile structures of the new capital. It offered amenities, services, a social
fabric, and a set of sub-cultural values which could not be
ignored. The result was that Cidade Livre, a squatter settlement,
had to be incorporated as a satellite town to the pristine new
capital. Some critics give Brasilia the questionable credit for
being a new capital with its own built-in slum.

What can be learned from these actual case studies?

What action-oriented programs can be proposed to take full
advantage of the migrant's positive forces of motivation, community spirit, and social organization?

Two elements stand out strongly: opportunity and motivation.

The preceding case studies showed how the slum in Latin
America can and does offer opportunity for the rural migrant to
become urbanized. Even those members of society "on their way
down" are offered some kind of choice and opportunity. The non-
conformist, the mentally unstable, the unadjusted, the pathologically poor, the old, the marginally employed, the peddler—all
find shelter in the slum as a last resort in their declining lives. If
the slum did not exist, where would they go?

Motivation for achievement is in part responsible for economic
improvement. Latin Americans attach a high symbolic value to
home-ownership and the attainment of this goal not only satis-
fies their need for shelter and stability, but also spurs their
achievement motive and furthers their economic and social status
in other areas. Second only to home-ownership is the desire for
the *education of their children;* even the very poor in Latin
America regard education as the only hope for a better life for
their children.

IV. On Human Rights and the Slum

Human rights should be the equal endowment of all members
of society, regardless of race, creed, color, or present economic or
cultural status. Today, in the 20th century, the state owes its

people certain basic and minimal living conditions. The children of today's slum will be the citizens of tomorrow and each nation should feel itself responsible for nurturing these future citizens by assuring them a decent environment—shelter, basic nutrition, education, livelihood, socio-economic opportunity, and a full participation in community life.

Pope Paul VI, speaking to the *campesinos* of Colombia on the social injustices heaped upon the indigenous people, stated that the Catholic Church had undertaken the defense of their rights ". . . to obtain a more just distribution of economic goods and a better recognition of your members and your proper (rightful) place in society."[30]

Further on, Pope Paul referred to the rights of the poor "with particular regard to just distribution, fitting habitation, basic education, and medical assistance, and in the field of civil rights a step-by-step participation in the benefits and responsibilities of the social order."[31] This deep concern on the part of Pope Paul VI regarding human rights specifically stressed the need for a better socio-economic and physical environment for the poor.

FITTING HABITATION AS A GOAL

If fitting habitation[32] is singled out as one of the goals of human rights, the possibilities of ever achieving it should be explored. Assuming that there are no other options open to those poor who are unable to secure public housing, the slum provides the only viable solution to their shelter problem. However, this does not imply that the poor are doomed to remain forever in a substandard environment.

The case studies of Guayaquil, Rio, and Buenos Aires give evidence that opportunities for upward mobility and better housing for the poor do exist for some. The slum has not proven to be an inhibiting factor to those dwellers who became achievers (or "escalators" as Stokes would classify them). The eradication of poverty and slum conditions is a very long-range goal and could be attained by a well-designed and implemented program of continuous and massive investments during several generations.[33]

The humanitarian and subjective goal of satisfying the human right of the poor to a fitting habitation, as enunciated by Pope Paul VI, could be divided into a set of more specific objectives which:

1. Minimize the cost of housing the poor and maximize opportunities for their socio-economic improvement;

2. Channel sufficient available resources—human, financial, administrative—toward slum rehabilitation and low-cost housing for the poor;

3. Assess the socio-economic and political costs and benefits of slum rehabilitation in order to maximize benefits for society as a whole.

A Pragmatic Proposal for Slum Improvement

Slum improvement and rehabilitation could be undertaken by adopting a pragmatic and realistic planning approach. Planning in this instance would attempt to match the poor's expectations with resources made available to them by the rest of society. A possible set of planning steps to this effort would be to:

1. Develop a series of attainable specific objectives within the current administrative resources and framework and set target dates, e.g., raise the housing standards of 50 per cent of slum settlements by the next fiscal year. Resources: emergency funds, federal subsidies, private grants and the dweller's own contribution. Working framework: local housing agency and a slum dweller's cooperative.

2. Relax current building standards in order to cut down building costs. Slum dweller's needs and values are much more elementary than those established by most building codes which reflect middle-class values.

3. Adopt new subdivision regulations specifically geared to the

needs and resources of the poor, e.g., minimum lot size, cluster layouts, communal sanitary facilities, and the like.

4. Undertake a cost-benefit analysis of the slum which should include direct and indirect costs and benefits to the slum dwellers, to the local community, and to the nation as a whole. On the cost side we would have municipal improvements to the site, sanitary services, electricity, street surfacing, and drainage. Land sites would be plotted by municipal planners and leased on a long-term basis at very low cost to the slum dwellers. Leases would help to defray costs of municipal services. Housing costs would be financed by the dwellers themselves, providing labor and using low-cost materials such as corrugated tarred cardboard or panels of wood shavings compressed with cement and rough lumber structures or other locally available materials.

Landscaping, trees, and shrubbery of local species would be provided at no cost to dwellers from the regional nurseries of the Ministry of Agriculture (or equivalent local agency). The percentage of the costs of the building materials which cannot be financed by the dwellers would be loaned to them on a low-interest rate by a cooperative community organization with the assistance of the local housing agency. The accrued benefits would be:

(a) The over-all physical appearance of the rehabilitated slum would be improved;

(b) The value of the land adjacent to the slum would increase;

(c) New assessments of these lands would yield new tax revenues to help override the costs of the rehabilitation project;

(d) Community spirit and pride of ownership would be stimulated; dwellers would no longer be squatters but small proprietors;

(e) A possible reduction of crime, health and welfare costs and a decrease in illegal activities such as gambling and prostitution. This is more subjective and therefore more difficult to measure.

(f) As a whole an improved slum would have a multiplier effect by being an example to other slum dwellers and a stimulus to other communities, agencies, and organizations to undertake and support similar ventures;

(g) The result of the cost-benefit analysis would provide meaningful clues as to a possible series of alternative plans for slum rehabilitation. Sufficient supporting evidence would thus be provided to make rational planning decisions.

5. Undertake community action and social programs before, during, and after the slum rehabilitation. Physical improvement must be accomplished with programs covering the areas of health, home economics, adult education, family planning, job counseling and placement, and relocation of those willing and eligible to move out of the slum. Slum dwellers should become involved and their own leaders should be assisted by non-profit organizations, the church, the university, and local government agencies. A follow-up procedure should be devised to check on the consequences of slum improvement and on relocation of slum dwellers in other areas. Evaluation of the degree of success of the slum improvement program should then be fed back into the planning process as a corrective mechanism for future actions.

The above proposed steps for concrete action are to be considered as non-sequential general guidelines to be adopted and modified to suit every specific situation.

Realistically, if slums cannot be eradicated in our generation, would it not be wise to humanize them with a minimum investment and involve all the slum dwellers and local organizations in a community venture?

This proposed approach is action-oriented and should not be considered as a substitute for in-depth studies which would be in the realm of urban research. The approach aims also to evoke a sense of advocacy planning which is considered fundamental to help overcome the hurdles of resistance to change, bureaucratic red tape, and reaction on the part of certain segments of the more affluent.

COMPREHENSIVE PLANNING

Slum improvement should be viewed as a component element of an urban system. Cooperative team effort and comprehensive planning would be necessary to achieve "fitting habitation" for the poor. The team should be interdisciplinary and include urban planners, architects, landscape architects, social anthropologists, economists, engineers, public administrators, behavioral scientists, lawyers, health and education specialists, and social workers.

Comprehensive planning[34] should take into account the wide range of socio-economic-political and physical factors which affect urban society as a whole, and specifically affect the society of the slum. The planning team should operate under enlightened leadership capable of a good dosage of political awareness and judgment as to the feasibility of actions to be proposed, thus assuring the possibility of their implementation.

The involvement and support of local authorities and power groups, together with the participation of the slum dwellers, would give assurance of continuity of action. Finally, the problem of the slum should be viewed, not only as a local, but also as a national problem affecting the country as a whole. A share of the national budget should be allocated to slum improvement, housing the poor, and problems of urbanization due to rural migration.

RECAPITULATION

In summary, in order to achieve the humanistic goal of Pope Paul VI, the following preconditions should be met:

1. Development of a pragmatic approach to match availability of resources to possibilities and needs;

2. Comprehensive planning by an interdisciplinary team;

3. Assured continuity of action through collaborative effort of planners, public administrators, community power groups, and slum dwellers;

4. Correlation of local slum programs with national policies of housing and urbanization.

Objections are to be expected from a wide range of interested groups, ranging from the liberals[35] to the extreme conservatives who view the shantytown and marginal slum as a nuisance that must be eliminated, and its dwellers as "adverse possessors" who should be evicted and prosecuted for trespassing. Regardless of the legitimacy of these objections, the problem must be viewed in the context of society as a whole and not as an isolated issue affecting a relatively small segment of the community.

We must be aware also of the powerful resistance to change in land-tenure patterns and distribution of wealth in Latin America on the part of established ruling elites.

There is hope, however, that new generations will be more enlightened to the human rights of the poor and will follow the dictates of Christian brotherhood.

V. Research on the Urban Slum

Effective policy planning and the achievement of specific objectives depend upon knowledge acquired through research. Urban research can provide the body of knowledge necessary to the planning process in the form of data inputs, analysis, and evaluation of alternative plans.

Research efforts concerned with the problems of the slum should take into account the following considerations:

1. A high degree of ingenuity should be exercised in the site planning, design, and construction of housing for the poor with locally available materials and know-how (or low-cost, available mass-produced housing elements).

2. An assessment is needed of the degree of flexibility of the poor in their adjustment to physical environment, given either (a) hope for social mobility (improvement) or (b) no hope for housing other than the slum.

3. When planning slum improvement programs, the positive elements of local folklore, social fabric, consumer behavior, and community structure should be identified and carefully considered.

4. In-depth research into the upward mobility factors which influence the successful "escalators" should be undertaken. Meaningful insights to be gained from community-attitude surveys could then be applied to develop urban policy.

5. Effective programs of guidance and assistance should be undertaken by public agencies with the participation of the poor. This would require a radical change from the current paternalistic attitudes of government bureaucrats toward slum dwellers.

6. More support could be given to self-help housing and other pump-priming programs aimed at stimulating the slum dweller's pride and achievement motivation. Current welfare and charity views should be turned into assistance for self-improvement of the poor. The slum dweller has a potential which, properly channeled and supported, could almost, *per se* (or with a minimum investment of public resources), improve the environmental conditions of the slum.

7. Policy formulation for relocation and rehabilitation should take into account the above points. Most slum eradication programs have failed both in their socio-economic efforts on the dwellers and in the cost-effectiveness of government action because of inability to relate slum dwellers' real needs and expectations to the programs drawn up with reference to middle-class professional values.[36]

8. Programs for low-cost, low-rent, temporary housing should be developed to allow the poor migrants to become acquainted with the opportunities and problems of city life. While living in these (locally, state, or federally operated) settlements, the newcomers would receive medical attention, education for their children, basic home economics instruction for the housewives, and assistance in securing employment.

9. A conscious policy for housing the poor should be correlated

to the social consequences of urbanization and national development policies. The crucial issue would be the allocation of necessary human resources to the various tasks of the development programs.[37]

10. Community organization and citizen participation should be considered as basic factors in any slum program. By involving the poor in the studies, formulation of policies, and program design, both the members of the interdisciplinary planning team (as advocacy planners) and the poor could gain meaningful insights into the other's problems and tasks. Above all, a communication linkage based on mutual trust would establish a solid foundation for program effectuation and would increase the probability of success.

11. Interdisciplinary university research institutes for urban studies could be encouraged and given full support by the local administration. These institutes could provide non-political, unbiased views of the real magnitude of the component elements of the slum problem and could suggest viable alternative courses of action.

Urban planners, architects, social anthropologists, urban ecologists, economists, lawyers, public health and public administration specialists organized under the large interdisciplinary "umbrella" of local institutes for urban studies could contribute toward the understanding of the slum problem and feed back research findings into the policy planning process.

12. The mobilization of currently under-utilized resources such as the slum dwellers under self-help programs and other groups such as the military should be promoted.[38]

The preceding sections of this paper have brought to light some key issues involved in the process of slum improvement. The need to undertake some of these specific research studies is apparent, and private organizations, government agencies, university-centered research institutes and religious organizations would do well to focus their attention on the areas of study outlined above.

NOTES

1. Gideon Sjoberg considers that urbanization can precede industrialization and that there may be industrialization without heavy urbanization and that both could conceivably occur without modernization . . . as summarized by H. Wentworth Eldredge (ed.), *Taming Megalopolis*, vol. 2, *How to Manage an Urbanized World*, Chap. 21, "The Urbanization of Developing Nations," (New York: Anchor Books-Doubleday, 1967), p. 1002.

2. Philip Hauser (ed.), *Urbanization in Latin America* (Paris: UNESCO, 1961).

3. Hauser, *ibid.* "Demographic Aspects of Urbanization in Latin America," pp. 91–117.

4. *Ibid.*

5. Charles Abrams, *Man's Struggle for Shelter in an Urbanizing World* (Cambridge, Mass.: M.I.T. Press, 1964), pp. 9, 10.

6. U.S. Congress, House Committee on Government Operations, *U.S. AID Operations in Latin America Under the Alliance for Progress*, 90th Cong., 2nd Session, Aug. 5, 1968. House of Representatives, 1849, "Housing," pp. 28–29.

7. These settlements have been given such indigenous names as "barriada" in Lima, "Villa miseria" in Buenos Aires, "favela" in Rio and Sao Paulo, "mucambo" in Recife, "maloca" in Porto Alegre, "jacales" in Mexico, "ranchos" in Caracas, "arrabal" in Puerto Rico, "tugurio" in Bogota, to mention only a few.

8. Herbert Gans, *The Urban Villagers* (New York: The Free Press, 1962).

9. Oscar Lewis, *Five Families: Mexican Case Studies in the Culture of Poverty* (New York: Mentor, 1959).

10. John C. Turner, "Housing Priorities, Settlement Patterns, and Urban Development in Modernizing Countries," *AIP Journal* (November, 1968), pp. 354–363.

11. John C. Turner, "Barriers and Channels for Housing Development in Modernizing Countries," *AIP Journal* (May, 1967), pp. 167–181. Turner discusses the "Pampas de Cuevas" settlement near Lima, Peru.

12. Carolina Maria de Jesus, *Cuarto de Despejo* (Sao Paulo: Livraria Francisco Alves, 1960).

13. Divisao de Servico Social, Prefeitura do Municipio de Sao

Paulo, *Desfavelamento de Canindo* (Sao Paulo: Prefeitura do Municipio de Sao Paulo, July, 1962).

14. *Ibid.*, p. 47.

15. Oscar Lewis, *La Vida: A Puerto Rican Family in the Culture of Poverty*, San Juan and New York (New York: Random House, 1965).

16. Charles J. Stokes, "A Theory of Slums," *Land Economics* (August, 1962), pp. 187–197.

17. Rio's *favelas* include the newly arrived Portuguese immigrants.

18. Stokes, *op. cit.* Population data is from 1961.

19. Sam Schulman, "Latin American Shantytown," in Eldredge, *op. cit.*, pp. 1002–1011. Schulman depicts the Colombian *tugurio* or squatter slum, barrio 65, where dignity is buried in the abyss of urban poverty.

20. *Ibid.*, p. 1010.

21. Stokes, *op. cit.*, p. 193.

22. In Calcutta 600,000 people sleep in the streets and an estimated 30,000 families have never had a roof over their heads.

23. Rio de Janeiro's *favelados* rate their dwellings higher "in most respects than the conditions prevailing in the rural areas from which the greater number of them have come." Hauser, *op. cit.*, p. 196.

24. "O Que Disse Sergio Bernardes," *Agente* (Rio de Janeiro), Jan.-Feb., 1968. p. 34. Free translation of an interview in this Brazilian publication.

25. The Alliance for Progress has not been able to generate enough momentum in Latin America to spur housing construction. Moreover, some of the standards it laid down were more responsive to middle-class values than to local needs as the preceding case study illustrates.

26. Lance Belville, "Alliance a Failure to Pedro," *Syracuse Herald*, November 21, 1965, as summarized by Turner, *op. cit.*, p. 355.

27. In Paris' slums approximately 40,000 journeymen (Portuguese, Algerians, and Spaniards) and their families live in *bindonvilles* on the periphery of the city. At one point the city government decided to move 60 Portuguese families to a new housing development; on the scheduled moving day only six families volunteered to move, the other 54 families preferring to remain with their kin and save rent money rather than acquire advantages of sanitary facilities and electricity. Also very obvious was the locational advantage of their housing related to place of employment as well as the values they assigned to the various components of urban life. *New York Times*, March 27, 1966, as cited in Turner, *op. cit.*

28. William Mangin, "Squatter Settlements" *Scientific American* (October, 1967), pp. 21–29.

29. Divisao de Servico Social, Sao Paulo, *op. cit.*, p. 10.

30. Address by Pope Paul VI to an assembly of *campesinos* (rural workers) near Bogota in San Jose, Colombia, on August 23, 1968.

31. *Ibid.*

32. Habitation (habitat) is interpreted here as including not only housing *per se*, but the necessary community facilities, services, and organization.

33. Gunnar Myrdal estimates that to eradicate poverty in the U.S. will take several generations and trillions of dollars. The reader may draw his own conclusions regarding the possibility of achieving this goal by Latin American countries in the light of the magnitude of their poverty problems, socio-economic and applicable environmental standards, target expectations, and financial feasibility.

34. The planning process includes: systematic analysis of problems, evaluation of alternatives and their consequences, plan formulation, and implementation procedures.

35. Professed liberals, well-intentioned but unrealistic, who would advocate adequate housing to *all poor* regardless of the socio-economic and political feasibility of ever achieving this goal.

36. From different points of view, both Herbert Gans in the *Urban Villagers* and Martin Anderson in *The Federal Bulldozer* (Cambridge: M.I.T. Press, 1964), give supporting evidence that this also applies to U.S. projects.

37. E.g. Housing the poor could be considered a social overhead project when connected with industrial or agricultural development. Under such an approach, if national policy were aimed at decentralizing its basic industry into several regional "growth poles," the housing of the low-income labor force of these new industries would come under the responsibility of industrial development planning, rather than of local governments. Under such a policy a certain percentage of slum dwellers could be induced to relocate in newly developed industrial towns. The costs of relocation could be subsidized by the national government while the cost of local low-cost housing could be financed as a social-overhead project connected with the capital investment of the industrial plants. Local municipalities would provide the adequate infrastructure of street pavements, sewers, drainage, water supply, electricity, schools, transportation, health and community facil-

ities. These investments could be financed in part by bond issues and the balance through federal assistance programs.

38. In 1961 the writer proposed to the Argentine Army Corps of Engineers a program whereby noncommissioned officers would be trained to act as community building supervisors, enlisted men would supply part of the skilled labor, and local garrisons would supply management know-how and the logistics of transporting building material, tools, and heavy earth-moving equipment to the site and in general manage the whole project. It is most unfortunate that the high ideals professed by the young military officers in Latin America who consider themselves the saviors and protectors of their countries' well-being, have not been channeled toward programs of community development such as low-cost housing and slum rehabilitation. (The response to this proposal was polite interest with no action.)

More recently the Colombian Army established labor batallions to help construct low-cost homes for *tugurio* dwellers. In Peru and Brazil the armed forces are now engaged in certain strategic road-building projects. (See Schulman, in H. Wentworth Eldredge (ed.), *op. cit.*, p. 1011.)

THE MOST SIGNIFICANT
OBSTACLE TO THE LIBERATION
OF MAN—ME

ROBERT J. FOX

When we talk about the liberation of man, whose liberation are we talking about? While I am most anxious to talk about everybody's liberation, and while I would like to think I am concerned about my own liberation, I feel very much like a hypocrite because I do not know how much I really want to be free. I do not know how much *I can afford to be* free. I'd like to feel that there are structures—that there are people: archbishops and governors and mayors and a host of other people that are holding up my freedom. But I know so frequently I cannot bear to be free from my own fears; to be free enough to be myself. I recall an experience not too long ago in which the subject of my own freedom glared at me: . . . and I came up not so free.

I work here in New York City in areas like Black Harlem, East Harlem, and the Lower East Side. We have a program that's been called the Poverty Program. We're supposed to be involved with the people of the neighborhoods, seeking our own liberation and so forth. Well, about a week or two ago, in a white enclave here in the Bronx, my mother was mugged by a black man. She came home from work and was about to get on the elevator when a man came through the hall. She turned around and before she could say "take my pocketbook," he hit her and knocked her unconscious. I was called, and when I saw my mother, her face swollen twice its normal size with bumps on her head, I looked at her and I was so tempted to think about law and order; to think about the man who did this thing. The fear of facing myself and facing my mother made me want to think about this man and the structures, the laws, all the rest of these things. But, do you know the experience that really offered itself to me? The revelation that suggested itself to me, that I was so afraid to admit to myself? The fact was that as I looked at her, I realized that I have left her that way so many times—dozens of times. I've never hit her, but in so many different ways I've been insensitive to her; I've been kind of numb, I have labeled her, with her age, her white Irish background and all the rest of it, and I have not been sensitive to what she's tried to say to me. In a very real way I have left her like that. But you see, I wanted to think about this black man and his problem; our own city, poverty, and justice, and all these other things. I didn't want to be free enough to let this experience put me in touch with myself.

Everybody's Liberation or Mine

I want to talk about "everybody's liberation"; I don't want to talk about *my* liberation. I want to talk about peace, and think in terms of myths and fantasies, and not have to come to understand that peace means being in touch with myself. Sure, I want to believe in the Lord who comes to bring peace to men, but I don't want that Lord to come at the price of putting me in touch with myself. I want to talk about love, but I don't want to talk about love if it comes down to a concrete instance of your looking me in the eyes and telling me that you love me. I don't even want

to hear about it with regard to other people. Let it come down to
a reality, let it come into flesh, let it be real and we all run away
from it. It's so much easier to come together in the workshops and
team meetings and neighborhood organizations we talk about.
We are so glad to talk about liberation and about peace, about
love, and about how committed we are to bringing this to all men;
but when the opportunity presents itself to me, the individual
me, to really put some flesh on what I'm talking about—well then,
I'm not always there to embrace the possibility of making it real.
So I have this question for myself—not for you, for myself—as
I sit at a meeting like this and participate in the sessions. To what
extent do I mean it? To what extent do *I* want it?

I guess the question really boils down to this: "To what extent
do I really want to see God?" I wear a collar; I like to think about
saving people, I like to think about bringing the good news to
people, about bringing Christ to people, but the real question for
me is not: "Can I bring Christ?" Where am I going to bring Christ
that He isn't? This man who has taken all things to Himself and
has redeemed all human experience so that all human experience
now is a vehicle and a means of meeting Him. Where am I going
to bring Him? The question is much more radical: "Can I 'take'
Him?" Can I 'take' this living Christ who is surging and coming
up through everything that's going on? Can I be fool enough to
walk every street and into every situation on my toes, with my
eyes wide open, vulnerable to what's there, seeking to be in touch
with the mystery that's written deeply into every piece of reality?
Can I afford to be such a fool? Can I afford to walk through the
streets of the so-called slums where the big planners have all
kinds of programs to eradicate all of this? Can I walk down those
streets again, like some fool, when prophets, sociologists, journalists, and everybody says "No, never mind not walking it; the whole
thing should be destroyed and annihilated so that we can construct circumstances in which a man can be a man." Can I walk
down those streets? Why not? And anticipate meeting something
or someone significant, alive, vital, and challenging to me?

Alienation From Self

We have seen and read so much in this nation about alienation, and we've made the mistake of thinking that alienation for the poor man means that they are cut off from the middle and upper classes. That's not the problem that the poor are facing in our nation; in this city! It may be their chief advantage: that they are cut off from the middle and upper class in our society! The problem of alienation is that what the poor people are facing is an *alienation from self* and in this problem they—rather than being "other" than the rest of society—are such graphic reflections to the whole of our society, because our whole society reeks of alienation!

How does this cutting off from one's self come about? If you live on a street like 117th Street and Lexington Avenue (or down on the Lower East Side on 6th Street), you wake up in the morning, you pull up the shade, and you look out at the street. What do you see? You see garbage, maybe, and a gutted building and a couple of addicts sitting in one doorway and a prostitute in another and a cop taking graft down at the corner. Your immediate temptation is to pull the shade down quickly . . . . because we all believe that what we don't know won't hurt us. But when you pull the shade down, it just gets worse. Besides, when you pull the shade down on *it*, you're pulling the shade down on yourself, because the only way that we have of being alive or in touch with ourselves is as a result of looking at, listening to, smelling, touching, tasting, and experiencing that which is before us. If it all comes to be too ambiguous or contradictory or painful or asking too much of me, so that I decide to shut it all out—well then, I shut myself out from myself. Alienation is the result of my taking the action of shutting off, and this really means shutting off the living God.

Alienation Shared

Some people think of alienation in terms of the poor, but alienation is not the exclusive property of the poor. We have another street in this city which is a little bit more famous than 117th Street, a street called Wall Street. You could walk up and down Wall Street every day of the year and you'd never see egg shells, orange peels, empty beer cans and that kind of garbage, and yet Wall Street is full of garbage every day. Every working day of the year, there are shady deals and unjust contracts and there are very respectable men, impeccably dressed, who walk into that street and wallow around in that kind of garbage for seven hours every day. They are vaguely aware of it in the back of their minds, but they are afraid to look at it, afraid to be vulnerable to it, afraid to let themselves believe that there is vitality and significance and challenge written into their experience there on Wall Street, if they'd only let themselves be tantalized by it.

Or the media! ABC and NBC and CBS and the men who have master's degrees and doctoral degrees in creativity, who walk into those buildings every day and wallow around in the garbage of what we call the "boob-tube," again vaguely aware of it but afraid to be really vulnerable to it. Afraid to take it really seriously, respect it, and get themselves into it, let themselves be chewed up by it. And they are alienated men!

Or the suburbs in this nation where you can walk up and down the streets with the lawns, the flowers, and the trees, and the people. There are so many millions of people in this nation walking up and down these streets numb to this boring reality of the suburbs, afraid to dig in a little bit and chew it up a little bit and let it really put them in touch with themselves.

So, this problem of alienation is so real in every segment of our society; perhaps no more real than in the Church, where somebody, several years ago, began to say: "Let's open the windows and let the light and the sun in. Sure there will be all kinds of dust, and people will see the fact that we have dirty linen, but let's be believing enough in reality, let's believe enough in the redemption, that we're willing to look at the living Christ in reality, and let ourselves be vulnerable to Him." Ever since then the turmoil and the challenges have been so great that we have been hanging on to those windows and trying to push them closed again, because of the way that we've been shaken and shattered and challenged by the vitality of that whole process.

And so I am not asking: "Do I want the liberation of man?" I am asking about my own liberation. I know that that liberation can only come at the hands of God, but I know that that God is a living God; He's a coming-to-be-God; He's not the God He was yesterday, He's unfolding all the time, and He's challenging me to keep on my toes and be fool enough and vulnerable enough to keep seeking Him in the most unlikely kinds of places and experiences. And if I'm going to be a priest or I'm going to be a Christian, then my first responsibility is to be faithful to that challenge and to be looking for Him myself. But we can't look for Him in any ongoing process; we can't really be vulnerable to any street, no matter where we live; we cannot continue to look at any piece of reality without filters and shades and all the rest of it, unless we are developing our own capacity to be expressive: to put a name into this God we are seeking, to say who we are becoming as we look at this street which is ours. We can't look at the street every day unless we can afford to cry, because if we're looking at the street every day, as often as not it's going to ask us to cry! But if we are going to believe in our basic American value system (which says you belong insofar as you're on top of the situation; which says you can afford to believe in love insofar as you've got the goods to prove that you're lovable), then we can't afford to cry; it's very unrespectable to cry in our society. If we come to the point of being so complete in ourselves as priests or sisters (or Christians or educators or politicians or whatever) that we cannot afford to cry, well then, we have no alternative than to draw the shade on this living God or the shade on the street. It's a painful kind of a thing to cry, but maybe it's even more painful to laugh—to kind of dance. If we're looking at our street vulnerably every day, that street is going to bring us to want to dance with joy and when I say with joy, I don't mean in the kind of a ballroom like this, with tickets and the right kind of dress. I'm talking about Zorba dancing, where our whole being gets into an expression of joy and celebration! Such a threatening thing, to dance; to allow ourselves to experience ourselves as joyous and celebrative of ourselves!

Of course the street will also ask us on such an on-going basis and with such frequency to experience frustration and fear and, experiencing fear, maybe to sweat, when in our society (with our value system) it's a very unrespectable thing to sweat. (We have a major industry in this country that produces products to help you if you have to sweat, not to let anybody know that you are sweating.)

Compassion Reverses Alienation

The process of alienation can be reversed only insofar as people, all of us, are developing this capacity to be expressive, and to be expressive of who we are, and to be proclaiming who we are becoming, at the hands of this living God who is written into all of reality. But we cannot do either one of these—I mean we cannot really look at life and be expressive and respondent to it unless we are at the same time developing our capacity to relate, to love, or perhaps more precisely, to be compassionate. Compassionate, not in the sense of pity which we so often make that word out to be. Compassion doesn't mean pity at all. Take its Latin roots: com-passion. It means to experience with or to experience in, so that I allow myself to experience myself in the other, rather than making the other, "other."

I thought of this during Father Häring's talk last night, where he began with the whole question of the relationship between man and woman and how it has come, in so many cases, to be a question of domination and submission, either man versus woman or woman versus man. And I thought, in our society (and I guess in every society, but I know mine better) to what an extent we make the masculine thing a question of being "other than woman": i.e., if a man is really a man, he mustn't have any of the qualities of a woman. And yet, it's so the reverse; if a man is going to be a man, if a man is going to be a human being, how can he *not* experience the woman in him as a result of relating to women and loving women, really allowing himself to be involved in a relationship of love? How can he possibly be a human being?

Making Latin America "Other"

The common characteristics that we ordinarily associate with a woman: what are they? Receptivity, let's say. Well, if a man is not developing his capacity to be receptive, is it possible that he's growing as a man or as a human being? Think of a woman and how she nails down big concepts into concrete, nitty-gritty realities. If a man is not experiencing that same capacity within himself as a result of relating to women, well then, he's not growing as a human being. The fantastic need that we have—if we are to grow and be liberated as men—to experience ourselves in the other! And yet at the same time we find a tremendous drive within us to make the other, "other." The groanings of Latin America for such a long time now, against this whole posture that we've had of making Latin America "other": the under-developed, and we the developed! What a laugh! The pains and rampant social ills that are in the city areas because teachers go into these areas without any sense of the teacher in their students—because priests and sisters go into these areas without any sense of the priest and the Christian in the people! The extent to which we're in a crisis in this country at this time, because people watch television sets and see violence erupt in Detroit or Newark and talk about "the violence of those poor people" and "what are we going to do about the violence of those poor people?"!

A year ago, when all this came out about Detroit and Newark and the riots, all America looked at it and immediately labeled the ghetto people as "other." America divided up into two possible responses to this reality of "other" people, this violence. Some people said, "Well, let's get out tanks and the state troops and the federal troops and the world troops and buy them mace and dogs and guns and helmets and control and put the lid on those peoples' violence." And the rest of America said, "No, that's kind of archaic; it's conservative. We've got to get a lot of money and we've got to pay for social workers and educators, and get them into these areas to solve these peoples' problems so that we can diminish these peoples' violence." Very few people in America looked at all that evidence and said, "My God, are *we* violent!" You know, I'm sure there's violence in the inner city and in the ghetto. Nobody's going to phantasize and say there's no violence. There's violence there! But when there's violence, there's a knife and there's blood and it stinks; you can take a picture of it right out there. But is there any connection between that kind of violence and the violence which reeks in every sector of our society? Is there any connection between the violence in Harlem and the violence in our corporate offices where very respectable men sit at desks, smiling like Dale Carnegie tells them to, while in the back of their minds they're trying to figure out how to get the legs out from under the guy in the inner office (and keep their legs from the guy in the outer office)? Is there any connection between the violence in East Harlem and the violence in our universities, covered with ivy, and gentlemanly, learned men spending at least part of their time under-cutting and undermining one another in pursuit of the desired chair?

Lawlessness Is Unsophisticated

And then there is the issue of "lawlessness." America looks at the lawlessness of the poor people who are looting and they say,

"Oh my God, these people are going to undermine and destroy our whole society with their lawlessness." During the riots, America watched as people came out of stores with cases of beer and suits on their backs and boxes of food; many said, "Shoot those niggers! They're lawless; they're undermining our whole society." Hardly anyone made the connection between that kind of lawlessness which is graphic and concrete, and the lawlessness which is to be found in every sector of our society. In the *New York Times* a couple of weeks ago there was an article about 14 of our major publishers, the most respectable of them, being brought up on charges of price-fixing over the past five years. A couple of years ago three major milk companies here in New York were found to have been price-fixing and thereby fleecing New York out of a million dollars a year. When one of these corporations, which is about a $50 million corporation, was finally brought to trial, it was fined $5,000 and the corporate officers went home that night as respectable as they left their homes that morning. And nobody said, "Shoot those guys; they're undermining our whole society!"

There is lawlessness in the Church. We have synod laws that say you cannot charge anybody to get into church, and yet we have so many pastors who lock every door except the main entrance and put a table there and a big man behind the table, so that anybody who tries to get in without putting a quarter on the table knows he's gotten away with something. Yet if you ever stopped that pastor and said, "See, you know, you're a looter," he would say, "What do you mean a looter?"

Or prostitution, which is such a sensational thing among the poor. Again the middle and upper classes have conventions about people with "social problems" and they have designed great new plans and new structures as a way of serving them, a new way of helping them with their problems. Do you know what happens with prostitutes in some of the streets where we work? You'd be down the street and sometimes a little group comes through, from a convention or from a college. They walk down the street in this kind of zoo, looking all around at this strange reality and they make no connection between it and their lives. As they walk through the street, maybe their guide or their teacher stops them at one point and says, "You see that lady there over by the doorway? She's a prostitute," and they say "Wow! a real live prostitute." Some people say, "Well, should we get a cop? They're kind of detrimental to the society." Another would say, "No, not a cop; get a social worker. She'll solve her problems." And other people like to be Christians, like to be religious, and they say, "There but for the grace of God go I!" The fact of the matter is, *there go I!* Sure this lady sells her body for $10.00, I sell my *mind* a dozen times a week; I sell my *convictions* to buy a little bit of belonging. I have strange ideas about our society. I think we have real, deep problems. I have strange ideas about Vietnam and about the war on poverty and strange ideas about the Church. As often as not, I find myself with my family or some classmate or some people I feel a part of, and I know if I say what I'm thinking, they're going to reject me. So I make myself what-they-need-me-to-be, and buy a little bit of belonging. When I see this lady with her fleshy revelation of what it means to be a prostitute, what is being asked of me in a context of liberation is that I be liberated from the fantasy and the myth of Robert Fox and come to taste in my mouth Robert Fox, the prostitute. Then let me talk about celebration and baptism and people loving you and what I'm going to do for the rest of the world—with that taste of me as prostitute in my mouth.

Self Liberation Toward Action

Addicts. There are world-wide studies about what to do about narcotics addicts. As I watch that man on the corner, with his head rolling around and his eyes rolling around in his head looking like something less than a man, I'd like to tell myself the priest: "What am I going to do to save this man?" I'd like to feel myself the teacher, the educator: "What am I going to do to educate him?" I'd like to feel myself on top of the situation and on top of him, because I'm the social worker and I'm going to solve his problem. But before any problem can be solved, there has to be this experience of compassion—there has to be a liberation of me through experiencing this man as he is, to come in touch with myself the addict. No, I don't use heroin and I don't smoke marijuana but I have a whole bag of psychological tricks that I carry around with me everywhere to coat my nerve endings so that I'm not in touch with what is challenging, embarrassing, painful or shameful to me. And so, as I look at this addict, I have an experience, I have the opportunity of being liberated to experience another part of myself. I have the opportunity of being wrenched away from that little static, idealized, phantasized me that I'm comfortable with and maybe come in touch with the rest of me. But I don't want to be alive to myself! I don't want to take the risk of living! I don't want to be vulnerable in that way, and so I walk through life, pulling shades down here and there and protecting myself and getting involved in all kinds of sessions about world-wide problems—and I never let it all touch me! In so many different ways this happens.

Liberation to Risk Vulnerability

The other day we had an incident right here in New York. The *New York Times* carried a story about Monsignor Illich, and you may have noticed that in that newspaper, "a diocesan official" was quoted. After about a half-hour conversation with a reporter on the telephone, I was asked "Do you mind if I quote you?" I said, "I'm not so sure it would be a good idea to quote me." Now here's a man (Monsignor Illich) whom most of you know. He has had a tremendous impact on the Church, on this hemisphere. You may agree with many things he does, you may disagree, but I'm a personal friend of his. I've known him for years. And when this reporter asked me on the phone for permission to link my name with his, I chickened out. I wasn't free enough. Talking about freeing all the black people and all the Puerto Rican people and all the poor people in New York City, and here's this great big unfree, tied down, scared man. You know, as it turned out, "a diocesan official"—everybody knew who the diocesan official was. (I wasn't even an efficient self-protector!). But I was afraid, and I'd much rather deal in big types of things, big issues, and big struggles.

Yesterday we had a celebration here. It was, I thought, a fantastic celebration. I didn't have a thing to do with it. We had a staff of neighborhood people, and Angel Perez, who works with us, planned this whole thing. Yesterday he came to me with an innovation—a new idea. He said, "You know, instead of just ending up the program here on the stage singing, wouldn't it be terrific if we all had flowers and went out among the people and just simply presented them with flowers and tried to embrace them? You know, I got kind of panicky. It was risky. It was such an unsophisticated thing to do: Come off the stage and go over and kiss somebody and give them flowers! And so I fought with him for about half an hour. You know, the great big creative director of Full Circle! But Angel is a very strong person, a very great believer, and so he fought with me and we did the flower thing and embracing. And it meant so much!

I don't know what all this means, except that we have so many people here and very few people have spoken. The rest of us have listened, and we have thought about it: the whole question of structures and politics and economics and education and all the rest. But unless you and I allow ourselves to be liberated to the point where we come in touch with the *impact* of what has been said and where we begin to believe in these lights that pass through our minds and be unsophisticated and foolish enough really to be liberated to come in touch with ourselves . . . . well then, the necessary reforms in education and politics and housing and economics and all the rest are never going to mean anything. The reason why it's so difficult for me to be liberated or for me to approach my own liberation is that I know it requires so much vulnerability. It requires so much my letting myself be up for definition, day after day after day. It asks me to live with a name for myself rather than a label. It asks for me to read the Gospel and understand that this is the account of a man in encounter and confrontation with life's circumstances, just as you and I. It asks me to understand that Christ was this kind of a man, who wasn't an alienated man. He didn't insist on "big issues in the kingdom" to the point where He couldn't stop and look at a kook who got up into a tree to see him close by! He was the kind of a man who, even when His followers were trying to push him down the street and away from looking at this kook, insisted on being in touch with this man. Again, he insisted on being in touch with the lady who had had five husbands and not a shred of formal education. Whereas we'd be so concerned about planning for her, and getting her into one of our institutions and one of our programs, Christ spends I-don't-know-how-much time dialoguing with her about grace. (We know theologians have knocked their heads together for centuries trying to figure out what grace means.) But Christ is so anticipatory as He approaches this woman, that He causes to come in her something that other people would say isn't even there. He was a man so willing to cry up on that hill with his followers around, looking at this small little town, of Jerusalem. (And we're talking about a whole hemisphere here!) He had this little town of Jerusalem, and it bothered him so much that he wasn't able to communicate and He was so frustrated and so allowed Himself to be frustrated, that He cried. And He was willing to sweat and He was willing to fail, and He was willing to laugh and dance, and He was willing to go through the adolescent crisis, and He was willing to endure every human experience ... because He so deeply believed that it's a man who can make the difference, if a man will but believe what is in him. He believed that if a man will but allow himself to make of his life a call to the living God to come, then whatever the circumstances are, God *is* there to come. A man like Martin Luther King, who so invested himself in unbelievably ambiguous circumstances and, like some fool, continued to make of his life a call to come. In the process, he flushed out 50 times the evidence that you and I have that there's no Lord to come. He had 50 times the evidence that you and I have to turn off the light and be invulnerable, and the more the evidence multiplied, the more he dug in. And the more he became for this entire nation a call.

I'd like to end with just one final experience that maybe in a certain sense sums up the whole question of liberation. Last summer we had a riot in the Lower East Side and during the course of this riot there were many New York City policemen with plastic masks and steel helmets in one street. The people in the area were very resentful of the presence of these policemen because, by their presence the policemen were saying, "This is a jungle, and you're the animals and we're the keepers and we gotta stay here." The people were trying to say in many different ways, "This is not a jungle and we're not animals and we don't need any keepers here." So there were all kinds of taunts going on.

At one point I looked across the street and I saw a man standing on the corner. He was a Puerto Rican, a young man, a strong-looking man. He had a tee shirt on with the sleeves cut off. He had a handkerchief around his head, a grimace on his face, and a big bottle in his hand. And as I watched, he took that bottle and he threw it at a policeman. It just missed the policeman and it crashed on the street. Nobody else saw who did it, so he wasn't arrested, and as I looked at him, I was tempted to conclude that this man was "a bottle-thrower." I felt I had enough evidence to sustain that conclusion. Something else in me was telling me that there was more than a bottle-thrower in the man, but the more I thought of the person of the Puerto Rican in this man, the more the evidence of this mad "bottle-thrower" crashed in on me and I was in a kind of conflict.

Somehow I got up enough courage to walk across the street and place myself in front of him. I said to him, "I know why you threw that bottle; I'm angry, too, that we have the cops here, but if we keep throwing bottles, then they'll have more of an excuse to stay. Maybe you ought to think about not throwing the bottles." At this, the guy looked at me in such a way that he gave me ten times the evidence that I originally had for calling him a bottle thrower! He didn't say a word, but his whole face screwed up and the expression was telling me, "You're a real fool; you're a jerk; what the hell are you doing here; get outta here." Any number of phrases like that he was telling me with his face. And I was tempted at that moment—because I wasn't able or free enough to experience myself as this fool, to experience myself as this failure, to experience myself in a questionable posture, all of which he was offering me—I wasn't that free, and so I was tempted to walk away and say, "I have the evidence now and I can withdraw." But somehow or other I didn't. I stayed there and we talked and we talked, for about 20 minutes. In that time he put me in touch with dozens of me's that I had long since refused to be in touch with. But somehow or other, in the process of this conversation, the man literally said to me (and these are his textual words), "No, I'm not a bottle thrower." He said, "I came home from work, I was sitting on the stoop, and all these police came running through the street. I just grabbed a bottle and went, and here I am throwing bottles, but I'm not a bottle thrower."

Liberation . . . to Challenge Me

The point of this is that the question of the liberation of others is the question of the liberation of me. Can I, in my relationship with others, allow them to challenge me—to come in touch with me? Can I really come to understand that I'm incomplete—that there's a vast degree of riches within me that I haven't even begun to be in touch with? And that there's a vast degree of poverty and garbage within me that I don't even begin to be conscious of? Can I so believe in love (and again, not some Pollyanna thing)—*can* I so believe in love that I allow myself to be loved? Can I allow myself to be alive to me, to take the risk of looking at life and looking into reality, to take the risk of coming up with my response to it? And can I do this in a context with other people in which I allow them to write in my flesh the revelation of who they are, and I write in their flesh a revelation of who I am? That's the kind of fool we have to be, the kind of fool that any black man is, in this country, if he even comes near a white man. Because any black man has so much evidence to sustain his conclusion that it's crazy for him to go near a white man, because he knows that the white man reeks of prejudice. It's true of all of us; it's as true of me as anybody. It's true of every white man in this country. Can we afford to experience ourselves as cripples and sick and needing redemption, and can the black man be fool enough to let himself come near us and believe so in love that even in the coming years when he flushes out all the evidence that there is no such thing as love, he continues to believe in it like Martin Luther King? Can young people be fools enough to be vulnerable to old people and vice versa? Can all of us so radically believe in love, that we will allow ourselves to get into the developing solution which human experience is, and come more and more to be conscious of who we are? This is what it seems liberation is about.

PART THREE

TODAY'S CRISIS: HUMAN RIGHTS IN THE LATIN AMERICAN REALITY

POLITICAL FREEDOM
IN LATIN AMERICA

VICTOR ALBA

Political freedom in Latin America is usually discussed with a wealth of data, statistics, projections and a great variety of charts and graphs. The result is to give the impression that the matter is extremely complex, and that it is therefore impossible to arrive at any conclusion. In politics things are not simple, but they are direct and clear. In politics the fundamental issue is power; being in a position to take part in the decision of how to distribute wealth, a situation so clear and tangible that we refer to it colloquially as "dividing the pie." Political liberty is an aggregate of guarantees held by the citizens so as to give assurance that the path to this power is open to them in keeping with certain conventional rules: that the majority cannot close the path to the minorities, and that the minorities cannot block it for the majority.

All this is elementary. Yet because of its simplicity we seem to forget the ground-rules of political liberty. Thus I consider it appropriate to remind ourselves of a few fundamental definitions inasmuch as our discussion is to be based on these understandings.

We might speak with academic air of the 178 violent changes of power that Bolivia has suffered; of the 70 governments Mexico had during a 53-year period before the Revolution; of the 60 successful military coups in Latin America between 1930 and 1960; and of the 120 unsuccessful ones, which would be an average of six attempts annually (of which two were successful), or of the nine attempts per country (of which three were successful). We might attempt to relate the political instability to the percentage of one or another racial group in the population, to the degree of economic development or even to the extent of illiteracy. We might arrive at the conclusion that none of these factors appears to influence the condition of civil liberties in Latin America. The condition of civil liberties is not merely precarious, but actually non-existent, because wherever civil liberties are not secure for all, they do not exist, and no one may presume to enjoy them without fear of future reprisal.

But all of this has been said and repeated frequently and it can be found in the numerous textbooks on the politics and government of Latin America. Our concern is to propose those questions which diplomats obscure, academicians shun, political leaders silence; some because they have not found the answers, others because they fear the answers they might find.

It has been said that within the last few years Latin American political stability has progressed, that there have been fewer military coups, fewer rebellions and disorders. However, the deeds cited as proof of these statements indicate they are merely expressions of wishful thinking. It is becoming increasingly difficult therefore, to shun these dangerous questions. Fortunately they are controversial questions which permit, indeed they require, that they be discussed with a certain passion and without the hypocritical pretense of impartiality.

If I shared the North American obsession for an unbiased approach to these questions, I might launch forth on an easy and safe path by means of stereotypes, speaking of the "vocation of

freedom" in Latin America. There would be no dearth of cases
in point. For example, a legislator in El Salvador in 1950, upon
discussion of a new constitution said: "First the light of freedom
must shine in the minds of our youth; only later, the light of
truth." I might point out that those called "Fathers of Their
Country" in the United States are called "Liberators" in Latin
America, and add the opinion of the Chilean positivist, José
Victorino Lastorria: "The emancipation of the mind of man is the
true purpose of the Spanish American Revolution." Or those
words written in our own day by the Argentine philosopher
Franco Romero: "The Latin American experiment is above all an
experiment in freedom."

But this array of quotations would be misleading because
words do not mean the same thing to the north and to the south
of the Rio Grande. In Latin America there is almost never har-
mony between the word and the act.

Under the most favorable circumstances in Latin America,
freedom is comparable to Rousseau's "general will," the liberty
of the majority to crush or silence the minority. It hardly ever
implies the freedom of the minority to become a majority. When
it is known how the majorities can be manufactured within the
framework of Latin American politics, it is understandable why
we say that the so-called vocation of Latin American liberty is
simply a rhetorical figure.

How could there be a vocation of freedom in a continent which
has not yet experienced liberty? From what source could this
vocation spring, when Latin Americans have really never enjoyed
authentic political liberty? In a society like that which they suffer,
what would be the source of a desire for freedom? It happens that
we are aware of a small minority of Latin Americans. Their songs
of liberty make us overlook the fact that the word "liberty" means
absolutely nothing to the great majority. There are millions of
Latin Americans in whose vocabulary the word liberty does not
so much as appear—and this literally, for I refer to the lan-

guages still spoken by the Indians of Mexico, Peru, Ecuador and Guatemala.

In the pre-Columbian theocratic societies, it is obvious that the idea of political liberty did not exist. It did exist on a municipal level in colonial society, but only for the colonizers and the creoles—never for the Indian masses. After the independence, there was much talk of it, but in what context? The societies of 1825, of 1900, and of 1968 are not fundamentally different except in two or three countries. There is at the top a thin stratum of landholders and hierarchy who by tradition, and thanks to their possession of the land, control political power. Beneath this is the ever-widening layer (which I call "public opinion") of people who are more or less involved and who participate, even if only fictitiously, in political life—bankers, industrialists, merchants, professionals, the military, churchmen, bureaucrats, intellectuals, students, owners of small estates, organized laborers. And beneath this, an enormous submerged mass. In no country (let us not deceive ourselves!) does this group comprise less than 50 per cent of the population, and in many as much as 80 or 90 per cent. This layer is composed of unorganized laborers, of rootless shantytown dwellers, of peasants without land, of sharecroppers and farm laborers. These masses have not the least political participation, nor do they so much as know that they possess rights that could be defended, nor are they informed about anything at all, never having enjoyed the least spark of political liberty.

It is merely academic, to characterize as oligarchical the society where the political power is always found in the hands of a minority, where political decisions are adopted by a minority, and that (in many countries) without even the facade of democracy; in others with a false democracy; and in some few, with democracy for the group of "public opinion." In all cases the marginal masses are completely excluded. There could be political liberty, in the sense of respect and guarantees, for the greater part of this privileged minority that forms the "public opinion." Indeed there has been, though only rarely. There has never been political liberty in the sense of respect for the authentic majority because they have never been consulted—nor are there channels for such consultation. Much less is there respect for the minorities or for their right to aspire to become a majority. A brief glimpse at the political history of Latin America would suffice to prove this point.

The first condition for the enjoyment of political liberty is organization. Without organization there is no way to express collective aspirations. There is no opportunity to be aware of rights, much less to defend them. But the submerged masses have never been organized. In many countries it is forbidden by law for peasant farmers to organize. In other countries the law permits organization, but in practice makes it impossible. In all Latin American countries, it is not only the law, but the conditions of life, education, and the political traditions which prohibit the organization of these submerged masses.

If there is to be political liberty, power must be strong. Strong power is not hard power, but rather power independent of a minority group. And this kind of power has scarcely ever existed in Latin America—not even when it resulted from free elections —because the elected always feel threatened by a coup if they make themselves independent of the oligarchy.

Political Stability and Social Instability

Goethe once said he would prefer order to justice. In Latin America—and in the United States' attitude toward Latin America—there are many who prefer stability to liberty.

There are still many in Latin America (also in the U.S., as was evident during the last elections) who seem unaware that there can be no order without justice. Order is not simply the absence of physical disorder. Order is the result of a balance between man and his society, a balance that can result only from man's conviction that his society treats him, generally, with justice or at the very least, without injustice.

There are many who have not even begun to realize that there can be no stability without liberty.

Let us consider one country—the United States—which has great political stability, which has had only one constitution, has never changed its political system, has never seen its legitimate authorities deposed, has its elections always on the appointed days, and whose elected officers have always been able to take possession and complete their legal terms of office, or when an assassin prevented it, were succeeded without problem by their legitimate successors. All this doubtlessly indicates political stability. This political stability has been possible because, not only have the fundamental liberties been respected, but they have been extended, have become broader and more complex, encompassing constantly larger groups.

But this situation, at the same time, indicates that the North American society is a society in which no one has remained long "in his place." (And when it has been attempted to keep a group for a long time "in its place," as with the Negroes, a situation has been created that threatens the political stability of the country.) It is a highly mobile society, and it is this quality that gives it the capacity to adapt to new situations, to make the necessary adjustments for the solution of problems that arise. It is a changing society. The United States has great political stability but little or no social stability. If it had the latter, the political life would be unstable, because there would be no pressure groups, or at least they could not express themselves. These groups promote political liberty by opposing vested interests, and the resulting political interplay constitutes precisely that basis for a democratic system which makes political liberty possible.

The worshippers of stability consider that it is a panacea; sometimes it is seen in the strong hand of the military; other times under the influence of false democrats, or in the demagogues that make the trains arrive on time. In spite of the obvious example of all the history of Latin America—repeated 20 times in its 20 countries—they have not yet observed that where there is social stability there is no political stability, that the two types of stability are incompatible, that political stability can be had only where a sound social instability exists, but that the price of a pernicious social stability cannot but produce a permanent political instability.

The United States is unstable socially and stable politically; it has experienced a growing affirmation of the civil liberties that have at the same time accelerated social instability. Latin America has coldly rigid social stability, so much so that present-day society could be represented by the same graph used to represent society at the time of the independence, or 100 years ago or 50 years ago. But it has also had an uninterrupted political instability. Social stability has not permitted the formation of interest and pressure groups aware of their interests and the interests of society in general, nor has it permitted the expression of what might be called the germ of such groups. At best those who could express their views are identified with the oligarchical system or were willing to support it. Different interests do exist, but they are not allowed to express themselves nor to exert pressure. Consequently the minimal conditions for the development of civil liberties have not been created. Because of this defect, Latin American politics lacks the fundamental stabilizing factor: the exercise of civil liberties that results from social instability.

It follows that whoever fights for civil liberties will be persecuted, not so much because the liberties are disliked in themselves, but because the fight for these liberties implicitly brings in its wake, consciously or unconsciously, the battle for social instability. A society as socially stable as that of Latin America prefers stability and immobility to liberty and, in the present set-up, order to justice.

In Latin America every social reform must be measured not

only in terms of what it can contribute to the improvement of living conditions, but also in terms of what those conditions can contribute to the continuing existence of civil liberties. There is something suspicious about any social reform that does not have as one of its consequences an increase in viable options for political freedom.

An agrarian reform need not necessarily provide more civil liberty. There have been agrarian reforms in various places in Latin America—in Communist countries, in Cuba—that have contributed nothing to civil liberty. But I suspect that when this happens, it is proof that the agrarian reform was only a parody and not authentic. In summary, every social reform always has three objectives: one social, one political and one economic. In the case of the lands in Latin America, the social objective is the formation of a rural middle class. The economic objective is the improvement of the living conditions of the peasantry, their transformation into industrial consumers, and as a result, the promotion of industrialization (and indirectly, the long-haul increase in farm productivity). The political objective can be no other than the destruction of those conditions that make possible the monopoly of political power on the part of the landed oligarchy. These are precisely the conditions that have deprived Latin America of authentic and lasting political freedom. Therefore, no agrarian reform will be a true one if it is limited to distributing lands, without taking lands from those who use them as a means to monopolize power. This must not be done, of course, for the pleasure of expropriating lands or of expropriating from the rich; it must be done because of the necessity of extending political power to all who have been excluded from it by a monopoly of power exercised by the landed oligarchy.

Furthermore, all social change in Latin America needs to be defended. We can hardly imagine a social change, however modest in scale, that will not call forth immediate reactions of anger, hatred and aggression, and which will not lead some social group or some of the elite to attempt to annul it. But how can a social change be defended if it does not represent a greater freedom to defend it than there was to impose or acquire it?

It is possible that an agrarian reform might be initiated by the pressures of urban forces, through the interests of these forces, and on behalf of a disorganized, sleeping peasantry. But it is impossible to imagine that this reform could be defended by its immediate beneficiaries, the peasants, unless it bring first of all, the freedom—so completely denied in Latin America—for the farmers to organize.

Economic Reform and Political Liberty

In Latin America, whatever may be the case in other places, the possibilities of political liberty are in inverse proportion to what has been called economic freedom. This, in an oligarchic society, is liberty only for the oligarchy and for those whom it favors. In the least offensive of the cases, it is liberty only for those who take part in decision-making. But it is the absence of freedom for those who find themselves outside the system; that is to say, the vast majority.

So-called economic freedom has served during many centuries to capitalize on labor, that is, on underconsumption and overwork, a method of capitalization that characterizes equally the totalitarian regimes and the oligarchies of the Latin American type.

The simple fact that the rate of increase of production and that of population run parallel and that at the same time there is an increase in the number of persons who are part of those intermediate groups (that I have labeled public opinion) and that the welfare of these groups and the income of the oligarchy increases, indicate that this prosperity is concentrated in certain social sectors and obtained by means of underconsumption and over-exploitation of the submerged masses.

This is possible precisely because this so-called freedom exists, though in Latin America it is a freedom limited by the tradition of economic management. The economic freedom of the oligarchy and of the public opinion group is incompatible with the economic freedom of the submerged masses in the case of Latin America. This situation can continue to exist only because there are no authentic and permanently guaranteed civil liberties. If these did indeed exist, the economic freedom of the minority would have been modified by the exertion of power by the pressure groups which are to be found only where civil liberties are enjoyed. In this context, more governmental action against the monopolies and political manipulation, more control of foreign and national investment and more planning, are elements of political freedom. So long as economic freedom can be used to marginate the political life of the submerged masses, there can be no authentic political freedom for all, and that which exists for the minority will never be assured or capable of being extended.

All the enemies of these reforms have stimulated our contempt by repeating year after year: "Agrarian reform, yes, but first the peasant must be educated." Although they mouth these words, they have done nothing to educate them. And logically, they will not do it in the future, for no regime prepares its undertakers. In the same way the legions of enemies of political freedom repeat: Freedom is essentially related to education. They educate by resorting to dictatorships, so that afterward the young will have no experience, not even theoretical, of freedom; so that they will be disposed to accept in good faith, believing they serve the cause of freedom, to create new dictatorships as we have seen in Cuba: in this Cuba where the Castroites and the anti-Castroites forgot—and we along with them!—that there would never have been a Castro had there not been a Batista. Permit me to say in passing that one of the peoples with the most solid political education, and with no illiterate voters, the Germans, placed Hitler in power, supported him, died for him and allowed the most horrendous crimes to be committed in his name.

History teaches us that one does not learn to govern well except by governing badly, that one does not learn to be an efficient proprietor except by being an inefficient one, that one does not learn the value of liberty except by committing errors and even abuses in the use of liberty. There is no reason why Latin America should suddenly have to be an exception to the universal law and place education before reform. Are there reasons? I see one very powerful reason: The convenience of those who do not desire reform and know that the most efficacious manner of preventing it is requiring education—which they will neither give nor permit to be given, because it is a prerequisite for social change.[1]

Authentic Political Liberty

It is impossible to overlook how often the word "authentic" is used in every study on the Latin American political life; authentic agrarian reform, authentic planning, authentic democracy, authentic political freedom. It appears to be a redundancy inasmuch as any of these things, to exist at all, would have to be authentic. Still, it is a necessary redundancy in speaking of Latin America, because all this and much more has been systematically falsified, altered, disguised, with the special talent of the oligarchical system of serving cat for rabbit. "Authentic" attempts to say it is not a formality empty of content used to conceal damaged merchandise; the idea conveys that the name and the thing are identical.

Civil liberty granted as a privilege and not recognized as a right is not authentic. Civil liberty designed to prevent mass participation rather than develop it is not authentic. Civil liberty that serves as a disguise for dictatorship is not authentic. Civil liberty intended to perpetuate the enjoyment of a minority is not authentic. Civil liberty that is not guaranteed, that appears in the Constitution but is not found in daily life, is not authentic.

Authentic democracy always implies the alliance of different pressure groups, for no one is the majority. But in Latin America, who cán ally himself with whom?

If the elements of the middle class wish to be allied, they will have to create their own alliances. They must go to the masses to awaken and organize them. The same holds for the elements of the organized working class, the labor unions. An alliance between the middle class and the labor unions would not be strong enough to replace the oligarchical system. It would, however, be strong enough to awaken the submerged masses, to organize them and subsequently to become allied with them. This alliance could then lead to a replacement of the oligarchical system.

But every time there appears to be even a remote possibility of an alliance of this kind, there is a military attack. If the situation appears threatening to the oligarchy, an accusation of Communism or pro-North Americanism is made against those seeking the alliance.

Terminate Minority Privilege

The only right—for lack of a more exact name—that seems to be guaranteed as legitimate, is precisely one which is in no sense legitimate: the *right* of the oligarchy to hold the power to manipulate the different minorities and the submerged majority in such a way as to perpetuate their own rule and prevent social change.

That right is guaranteed, not by the force of law or the authority of the constitution, but by the force of arms. Without military coups the oligarchical system in Latin America would long since have disappeared.

Even though the crucial problem of political liberty is rooted in the oligarchical social structure itself, it appears in practice to be a problem of violence of a minority against a majority.

It is truly a problem of violence. This violence which in the United States seems to terrorize diplomats and academicians is with us in Latin America at all times and in all places, yet no one is shocked by it. It is the fear of military force and of the reality of military coups.

It appears that the military, year after year and from one country to another, is devoted to the demonstration of the thesis that simple economic development alone would change conditions in Latin America favoring the gradual establishment of a democracy. Basically, it is the same thesis that led to the affirmation that a surfeited Communist is preferable to a hungry Communist (a thesis which the Russian Communists, less hungry now than previously, seem to be undertaking to disprove in Czechoslovakia).

Argentina has continued to make economic progress, but what is lacking is financial status due precisely to the mistrust created by thirty-nine years of governments under military control. Nevertheless, there is very little political freedom in Argentina. It is said that Brazil is progressing, but there, political freedom is diminishing.

Peru has had, during the past five years, the highest indices of economic growth in its history and in that of all of Latin America, and today has a dictatorial government established to obscure the complicity of the military in its illegality, shielding itself behind the flag in the supposed nationalism related to the petroleum question. This should be a good lesson for North American businessmen who feel a sense of peace and security when the military "protects" their investments.

Almost everything has been tried to prevent military violence and the feeling common to most Latin Americans is that the military is a political party with an advantage, the advantage of being armed. The "education" of the soldiers has been attempted: training in the United States; keeping them in barracks by constitutional provisions; pacifying them by the government giving them every imaginable privilege; buying them every kind of deadly and expensive toy; even by dissolving the army and reforming it (as in Bolivia after 1952). To date none of these has succeeded in most countries. Only four countries have not had at least one military coup since World War II.

The only thing that has not been tried is to use the only language they apparently understand: their own language. That is to say that the only recourse remaining is to create conditions that would convince the oligarchy that any attempt at a coup would bring on an armed conflict . . . Up to the present whenever there is a crisis, and a president faces his generals, the president allows himself to be imprisoned, exiled or deposed.

In one country during the past few years the military has not been able to effect a coup, but not for lack of desire to do so. That is Venezuela. In Venezuela whenever there was a rash military attempt, the peasants, workers, the militant members of various parties and the police, went out into the streets. And the military accustomed to coups by telephone without physical danger, did an about face. The only manner, I believe, of finishing with military coups is by making them dangerous for the military.

Naturally, this is not easy. It is necessary that there be one or various parties and labor unions prepared to fight, presidents disposed not to allow themselves to be imprisoned, nor to make fine phrases, but to shoulder the responsibility of asking their people to fight. And it is necessary that the people know that the president and those parties will not abandon them. Moreover, it would be necessary that these parties arouse and organize the people and give them the means of fighting; that is, they must trust the people.

This cannot be accomplished through promises and programs. It can be done only by giving land to the peasant and participation in real power to the middle class and the workers. It can be done by making the people feel that freedom is not merely a phrase for politicians but is something tangible, something that can be captured. It is done by linking freedom to the land, to power, to salaries, to the daily life of the people . . . And then, as in the case of Venezuela, the people will oppose not only the unruly military, but also the guerrillas that try to bring on attacks, and anyone else who endangers the prize won by the people.

Up to now we have always feared that the people should make a conquest and so we have given them things. Instead of allowing them the exercise of a right, which is the basis of the concept of political liberty, we have given them a privilege, which is actually the negation of political liberty.

As long as there remains the strong hand that prompts the military, the military will rebel. The same action is needed for the replacement of the oligarchy by the citizen as is needed to prevent military coups: to arouse the masses and organize them so that they may freely choose and gain their victories. Only then can authentic political liberty be obtained, authentic because it is a right and not a privilege granted by some oligarchy, authentic because it cannot be taken away or suspended. When these conditions are established, we will have reached the end of what seems an interminable series of military coups. Minority privilege will terminate.

Replacing the Oligarchy and Military

The first condition for finding the answers is to admit with frankness that today in Latin America violence is almost omnipresent: open violence at times, at times dissimulated; often disguised as legality, though illegitimate; at times insolently illegal. Military coups are violent; the fact that those who effect them wear a uniform, have appointments as government employees and receive government salaries, does not make them legal. Indeed all this makes them more illegal.

Falsified elections, herding of voters, false vote counts, the elimination of illiterate voters, impossibility of the organization of the peasants—these elections are also a type of violence: the rule by fear. And let us not plead that frequently electors know that if such and such a candidate wins, there will be a military coup. Is this not a form of blackmail based on the fear of violence of the military? Let us not deceive ourselves, if the military can establish themselves in power, it is not because they charm us by their uniforms, nor inspire our respect by their inefficiency, nor convince us by their commands and screams, nor do they seem to us necessary. It is simply because we are afraid of their guns, because, plainly stated, we fear those arms might be directed against us.

As long as this fear exists, we cannot speak about political liberty in Latin America, not even when there is a semblance of it, because we are always conditioned by fear of the military, because we cannot do what we believe necessary but only what we believe will prevent the soldier from raising his finger to the trigger. And even in this, we are often wrong, for nothing is more fickle than the convictions of the Latin American military.

We thus arrive at an unbiased question that may take various forms but always means the same thing. Without agrarian reform there can be no political liberty, but without political liberty the agrarian reform cannot be accomplished. With militarism there can be no political liberty, but without political liberty it is impossible to create conditions that make militarism unnecessary or impossible. Without planning there can be no political liberty, but without political liberty, the planning carried out is not authentic but farcical. So long as there are enormous submerged masses of population, political liberty will be for a minority—a privilege, rather than a right—but so long as there is no political liberty as a right, it will be impossible to bring these submerged masses to the surface. How shall we escape the contradictions that present themselves at every step in Latin American political life, that appear every time a problem arises?

This syllogism must be insisted upon: Without the possibility of full participation there is no authentic political liberty; without organization there is no possibility of total participation; therefore, without organization there is no political liberty.

Then it is necessary to dare to go on to the following syllogism: With the oligarchical system, organization is not possible; without organization there is no political liberty; therefore, with the oligarchical system there is no political liberty.

Whoever, then, believes that political liberty is essential to his life, to his dignity and also to the development of Latin America, must accept the idea that it is necessary to destroy the oligarchical system.

This presents a question which writers shun for fear of the conclusions to which it would inevitably lead. It is this: can a democracy be established by democratic procedures? Or stated in another way: Can democratic methods exist in a country prior to the establishment of the democracy? Or are these methods consequent upon the existence of democracy?

Bear in mind that undemocratic methods do not necessarily indicate actual violence. But bear in mind also in the light of history, that the advocates of change have never chosen their arms. These arms have always been determined by the adversaries of change. If those opposed used legal means, they were fought by legal means; if legal channels were closed, they fought by means of counterplots, conspiracies, maneuverings; if the adversaries have recourse to violence, it is perfectly legitimate to fight through violent means. (In Latin America, however, the latter has been done rarely but always with success as in Venezuela in 1958, in Cuba before 1959.) The Latin American peasant —so patient and passive, so broad-shouldered, so persecuted— can never be thought of as violent. Whenever he has become so, it has not been without sufficient cause. Theologians tell us that there are just wars and unjust ones. They speak also, I suppose, of just and unjust violence . . .

And here let us pause. A violence of the elite, paternalistic, not supported by the will of the submerged masses, a violence that is only a strategy and not a popular outbreak . . . in summary, the artificial violence of the guerrillas of the paternalistic middle class which we see today, is only a different form—though its consequences are the same—of the military violence of coups. Fundamentally, the guerrillas represent attempts at a coup from outside the barracks.

The common people have never been interested in violence, because even when they conquer, they pay for it more heavily than their enemies. Hence, the advocates of democratization, of modernization, of social change, or whatever one wishes to call it—those who consider civil liberties a fundamental element of development, that aspect without which there is no development as such—these do not desire violence. But the hour is approaching in which we all realize (the diplomats in the first place) that the only way in 20th-century Latin America to prevent actual violence is to dispose beforehand of a greater potential violence. To deny this right to the people would be like asking unilateral disarmament of the Western powers. Yet what we refuse to accept in international politics, we have tried systematically to impose in every one of the Latin American countries.

Potential violence is precisely that which seeks not to arrive at violence. It operates by convincing those who actually exercise effective violence (that is, the oligarchy and the military) that their violence will meet not with simple verbal protest, but that it will set off a violence that will sweep them out of power. In the long run, this knowledge alone could prevent civil wars, popular uprisings, guerrilla raids and also the old familiar military coup.

But this potential violence, this innoculation against the systematic violence of the defenders of the status quo, is possible only if the masses are aroused and organized, if the people are involved. If this were the action of minorities, of the elite, of abject classes, it would differ in no way from the raids of the guerrillas on the military. And should it triumph, it would not lead to more freedom or more equality, but to a picturesque totalitarianism of the Castro style, to a cold technocracy, or to a mixture of both types of denial of freedoms. This potential violence obviously does not consist in arms. Who would be able to overcome the military with arms? It consists in organization, in the ability to exert pressure, and to make resistance to this pressure more costly than compliance.

It is for this reason that the liberty most frequently denied to Latin Americans (and not by coincidence) is the one most necessary to establish a democracy, the freedom to organize. Not simply to organize parties, but to organize the masses and create a series of popular organizations, labor unions, farm brotherhoods, cooperatives . . . and a hundred other such that their needs would suggest. But bear in mind that in most of the countries, the organization of peasants is prohibited, sometimes by law, sometimes by police action. And here recall the case in Guatemala where three years ago a priest was expelled from the country because he had organized a cooperative with the Indians in an abandoned and isolated village.

To be in favor of political liberty is a thing we take for granted. But whoever is in favor of the means—the only means possible— to establish political liberty, apparently devotes himself to the exercise of insults (dirty words, much more so because they are longer than the simple-minded traditional four-letter words). It is, notwithstanding, a necessary exercise. Without favoring the means required, it is mere frivolity to profess to further political liberty.

The conclusion seems obvious to North Americans: the justice of an identification of their own national interest with the interests of the Latin American submerged masses, according to the pattern—timid and wavering though it was—set for the first time by President Kennedy. The Latin American policy of the United States should, then, direct itself to the submerged masses. Title 9 of the foreign aid bill, passed by the United States Congress in 1967, permits this orientation (and even seems to impose it), although the State Department and the technicians of AID appear reluctant to apply it. The official organisms can do much in this way. But in order to eliminate scepticism about their willingness to do it, there should be encouragement of private organizations and institutions—labor unions, cooperatives, foundations, churches—to show themselves more courageous and go directly to the people, not to be afraid of the people. And do all this without paternalism. If there is one thing that North Americans should have learned—and one wonders whether they have—from their experience in Latin America, it is that aside from the strictly technical aspects, no one knows better than Latin Americans what Latin America needs. To deal with the governments, but work with the people might be the formula. And naturally, to cease to fear social change and begin to desire it and be disposed to accept it with openness and sympathy, realizing that what can be done from the outside is little compared with what has to be done from within.

What has to be done in every country from within is evident: Go to the people; arouse them; organize them in such a way that they will have a potential violence superior to the actual violence employed day after day by the oligarchical system. Use the capacity to destroy the oligarchical system and to approach a typically capitalistic social structure that will be open to other future transformations.

One must have the courage to see things as they are, to accept the fact that taken as they stand, things are uglier than whatever action would be needed to change them. It must be realized in advance that any action marked by paternalism or aristocracy would result in the perpetuation of the system of oligarchy, the only change being in the personnel who compose it.

There is a vacuum in Latin American politics, not for lack of power but for lack of opposition. The anti-oligarchy forces have weakened during the past 20 or 30 years. The middle class, which before World War II advocated change, ceased agitating when the oligarchy allowed them to take part in the benefits of their systematic oppression of the submerged masses. They may possibly again become revolutionaries when it is no longer possible to extract more from the masses. But so long as the pie increases in size and is divided (even with great inequality) among the oligarchy and the middle class, this group will remain passive even while they continue to use the vocabulary of revolution. This passivity, more than the indecision of Washington bureaucrats and more than the trickery of oligarchical Latin American governments, is the explanation of the failure of the Alliance for Progress.

Must it be required of the submerged masses, harassed by the demographic explosion, by the voracity of the rising middle class and of an oligarchy sure of its power, that they be utterly exhausted, completely spent in order that changes can begin, changes not only in the economic and political facade, but also in the social structure?

No one can answer this question. The answer will have to be given, not by the reforming parties, which today are worn out and tired, spent by so much failure in the face of military coups, but rather by the young elements of these parties and, in general, the youth of the middle and working classes. If these elements continue to devote themselves to the sterile romanticism of the guerrillas, which serve as a springboard for the military, we shall have to wait a long time. If they can discard their aristocratic and paternalistic attitudes, learn to trust and respect the people, go to them, arouse and organize them, and then allow them to decide for themselves. . . . If they do these things, then possibly it will not be necessary to wait any longer, until not another crop can be pressed from the submerged masses.[2]

NOTES

1. "Thorough" studies have become another stalling technique, like education, in order to prevent reforms. In the face of these evasions one must dare to say: Reforms with studies, yes; but if one is to

choose between studies without reforms or reforms without studies, it is better to have reforms without studies.

2. I imagine that I hear you telling me that all this is very emotional, not at all academic. I beg to differ. It is my experience that the only possible way to be academic, documentary, solid and responsible, when treating Latin American problems, consists in pouring into it the greatest possible emotion. To use the traditional cold, objective, impartial approach to Latin American affairs is simply a way of avoiding the problems, of preventing that they be raised with all their crudeness, and of dissimulating by saying that no answers are found or that one prefers not to seek them for fear they should appear a little . . . academic. How could there be a solution worthy of the name that would not be academic by the simple fact of being a solution?

Although at times it may appear so, this is not a political exhortation. I have attempted to indicate the real causes for the deficiency of political freedom and the means open to Latin Americans to remedy the situation. In doing so, however, I have borne in mind that treatises written in the academic world exert influence—more than their authors believe on the diplomats' and politicians' views of questions. For this reason I have endeavored to avoid clichés which at one time expressed new ideas, but today are commonplace, and I have attempted to foresee—to guess, if you will—what may very well be the reaction of the Latin Americans of tomorrow. It would be well if at that time, those of the academic world would not find themselves influenced toward misunderstanding and reprobation. Because if this should happen, we would make ourselves one more of the factors responsible for the lack of political liberty in Latin America, in the same way that a doctor, who, through mental laziness, lack of imagination, or deficient information, gives a wrong diagnosis, becomes an accomplice of the virus.

ECONOMIC FREEDOM
IN LATIN AMERICA

BRIAN D. BEUN

I. The Declaration of Human Rights versus Reality

As is true for the Declaration's general pronouncements on social, political, cultural and religious freedoms, as well as its provision for other basic human rights, the meaning of its reference to economic freedom is clear. The ideal of freedom from want is proclaimed: "Everyone . . . is entitled to realization . . . of the economic . . . rights indispensable for his dignity and the free development of his personality." The right to own private property is proclaimed, along with the proviso: "No one shall be arbitrarily deprived of his property." In essence, the Declaration links property ownership with "indispensable economic rights" as necessary for realizing man's dignity and well-being.

During the 15 years after the Declaration was originally proclaimed, the many new states that had become members of the United Nations pressed their demands for more specificity in order to protect their national sovereignty from the dangers of economic colonialism. As a result, an International Covenant on Economic, Social, and Cultural Rights was incorporated into the Declaration in December, 1966. This new Covenant, among other things, reflects the more specific demands of developing countries to maintain economic rights concerning international aid as well as the sovereign rights of nations to determine the privileges of non-nationals in their national economies:

Article 1.2: All peoples may, for their own ends, freely dispose of their natural wealth and resources without prejudice to any obligations arising out of international economic cooperation, based on the principle of mutual benefit, and international law. In no case may a people be deprived of its own means of subsistence.

Article 2.3: Developing countries, with due regard to human rights and their national economy, may determine to what extent they would guarantee the economic rights recognized in the present Covenant to non-nationals.

The Covenant also recognized "the fundamental right of everyone to be free from hunger" and suggested, for the first time, the inherent responsibility of all nation states to take steps to promote economic development, including measures "to improve methods of production . . . and distribution of food . . . and by developing or reforming agrarian systems in such a way as to achieve the most efficient development and utilization of natural resources."

I need not point out the outrageous discrepancies that exist between the Declaration's stated hopes for mankind and the reality of the human condition in Latin America today. Likewise, I need not undertake a descriptive analysis of the economic impoverishment of the majority who are poor, for God knows they have been described *ad nauseam*, by others who mean well, but don't live with it.

II. Slavery versus Economic Freedom

From the dawn of history certain societies divided human beings into two distinct classes. The propertied classes were the owners of property, i.e., land, slaves, animals, tools, and machines. As masters, they were economically free men. In sharp contrast, the toiling classes were propertyless. They were the slaves, men without economic freedom.

According to Aristotle, there were two kinds of slavery. He defined chattel slavery as consisting of a system where some human beings were the absolute property of other human beings, as in the American South before 1865. Chattel slaves are completely deprived of property, even the property represented by their own labor power. The second type of slavery can best be illustrated by the example of the American Negro after the Emancipation Proclamation: a slave who is no longer the property of another man, but who has no property beyond his own toiling capability and is thus forced to live a servile life.

Adopting Aristotle's definition of slavery to cover both the condition of men owned by other men as their private chattels, and also those who are forced by lack of property to lead servile lives, we must conclude that there are tens of millions of slaves living in Latin America today. How many of the hemisphere's 120 million *campesinos* can logically be termed slaves? Likewise, how many of the tens of millions of ex-*campesinos* who fill the rotten *barriadas* that surround most of the major cities can also be called slaves?

Economic freedom must provide the basis of man's opportunity to lead a human as opposed to a sub-human life. The primary difference between an economically free man and a slave is the former's freedom from toil, an indispensable condition for leading a free as opposed to a servile life. As a consequence of lacking freedom from toil, the slave also lacks economic independence and personal security, without which political liberty cannot flourish.

In most of the countries of Latin America today, there is a multitude of people whose servile lives consist of nothing but toil in order to subsist. These Latin Americans have the misfortune of being chattels or of being propertyless and hence are forced to lead a servile life of toil, insecurity and dependence, and as a consequence, one that is devoid of political liberty.

In contrast to slavery, economic freedom means that every man, having a natural birthright to life, must necessarily have the right to participate in the production of wealth. All men who participate in this production are rightfully entitled to receive a proportionate share, equivalent in value to the contribution each man makes to the production of that wealth. Since free men can participate in the production of wealth only with the use of their own productive property (their labor or capital or both), the freedom to earn a living is a natural right to property in the means of production.

While all men must possess this economic right in order to be free, no one has the right to an inordinate ownership of the means of production, to the degree that others are precluded from a like opportunity to participate in production of the wealth necessary for deriving an equitable livelihood.

The imprecise process of economic development is likewise concerned with the production of wealth. It must also be concerned with the elimination of slavery. For economic freedom to displace slavery, the process of modernization must ensure that efforts to increase the production of wealth harmonize with the principles outlined above. If the quest for modernization is to succeed in a manner consistent with the prerequisites of economic freedom, it is clear that Latin America rests on the horns of a dilemma not easily reconcilable. For neither of the two approaches to development most commonly employed in the world today provide much opportunity to expand the horizons of economic freedom for the broad masses of the people. On the contrary, both methods circumscribe the opportunity for attaining development with economic freedom.

III. The Quest for Development
Without Economic Freedom

THE TOTALITARIAN METHOD

There are those who believe economic freedom is a luxury only the rich nations can afford. By combining ownership of land and capital with political power, the totalitarian method creates a centralized authority strong enough to force raw materials, land, and manpower into the priorities that comprise development. This method provides a deceptive ideology around which energies can be regimented; it can enforce austerity; and it may persuade a desperate nation that it is able to bring about modernization faster than other means.

All of these apparent advantages are short term and bought at the price of economic freedom. If men are dependent for their livelihood upon the arbitrary will of the state, or on that of its bureaucrats who manage the state-owned means of production, they are as unfree economically as when they are dependent upon the arbitrary will of private owners. Furthermore, "the equal liability of all to labor," which is a basic principle in the totalitarian program, impedes rather than promotes economic freedom. This approach to "development" also forecloses any hope of democratic institutions.

EXCLUSIVE CAPITALISM

It is difficult for most comfortable Americans to realize that capitalism in the Third World represents a very exclusive system. As such, it contributes little to the growth of economic freedom. Indeed, the more exclusive this system in any one country the less relevance it has to the process of development and modernization.

Perpetuation of the tradition of exclusive capitalism is accomplished by various methods of financing capital formation. For most of Latin America, there are essentially three alternative approaches currently being used as the basis for financing "development." All three alternatives are based on the indispensable truth that development requires capital. One characteristic of capital is that it has a price tag that must be paid in some fashion, i.e., in monetary terms, in political terms, or both.

Capital to finance development can be derived from external sources, including (1) long-term government loans through foreign aid, or (2) direct investment through foreign capital, or (3) from internal sources by financing through indigenous capital owned by the wealthy elite. For the broad masses of the people, however, each of these three alternatives generally ends in disappointment and frustration because it is capital that is the primary producer of wealth while labor produces only subsistence.

This results from the fact that there are two basic factors involved in the production of wealth. The first, the human factor, is represented by labor in all its forms, while the second, the non-human factor, represents capital, defined as machines, structures, productive land. The role of each of these two factors in the production of wealth is determined by the current state and application of technology and by management practice. Technology is the primary agent of economic change. As such, technology represents the process by which man harnesses nature through the use of his capital instruments and makes nature work for him. Hence, technology acts only upon the capital (non-human) factors of production. The result is the increase in the productiveness of capital at an accelerating rate which in turn paves the way for putting more of the non-human factor into production. If capital and technology produce the bulk of an economy's wealth and income is distributed on the basis of productive input, the individual can hardly reach his goal—an affluent level of income— solely by means of his labor. Wealth, in short, is the product of capital.

Since the production of wealth is the product of capital, foreign

investment ordinarily leads to foreign ownership. Foreign ownership may or may not be consistent with the respective development goals of the host country. Some jobs are created, and this is
better than nothing. However, the universal objective of modernization is to make the poor nations richer, not simply to provide
some people with jobs while making the foreign-owned enterprises of the rich nations richer.

The use of indigenous capital (where it exists) results in the
same consequences as foreign investment. The only difference
results from the fact that capital-produced wealth need not be
exported, but instead becomes increasingly concentrated in the
hands of those who already own capital—not more than one-half
of one percent of the total population of Latin America. Again,
one by-product of this indigenous process of financing capital
formation for "development" is the creation of some jobs that
provide a fortunate fraction of the population with work opportunities.

The problem is further compounded by the fact that most
government loans to private enterprise in Latin America have an
effect identical to reliance on use of concentrated domestic capital. Government loans simply further concentrate the capital
ownership of the wealthy elite who already own the great bulk
of the productive capital in the hemisphere. And the concentration of capital ownership in a narrow segment of the population
grows apace with technological advance.

Myth has it that all of these financing techniques are good
because they create jobs: "Say a mass, Father, for the success of
the new flour mill. It will provide work for your parishioners,"
says the foreign businessman to the Latin American priest. The
fact is that the new flour mill, a golden goose for its capital
owners, will provide a few jobs for the padre's parishioners. And
the fewer jobs it provides, the greater success it is, because the
logic of technology is not to make work, but to save it.

Modernizing an underdeveloped economy in this technological

age is not analogous to the industrial revolution America experienced during the 18th and 19th centuries. The basic distinctions evolve around the fact that the major limitations to economic growth at that time were primarily technological in character. Unlike Latin America today, the problem was not so much one of financing technology as it was one of creating the principal basis by which to achieve modernization. Most countries in Latin America want the latest in technology. Capital rather than labor produces technology. It is the multiple application of packages of technology and capital that produces wealth and hence modernization in a developing industrial society. During the American Industral Revolution it was the gradual development of the flourishing technology that offered liberation. But in Latin America, the ownership of new capital (including technology, home grown or imported) automatically goes to the people whose money is used to finance it. While total concentration of political and economic power may be avoided in part, ownership of economic power necessarily is forced to concentrate in the hands of a stationary or even shrinking proportion of the population, depending on the rate of population growth.

As "development" proceeds, this process continues in an accelerating spiral. Since labor produces only subsistence, the purchasing power of the broad population remains limited. Consumption, as a consequence, cannot keep up with production. In order to establish some temporary balance, a forced redistribution of income is undertaken by artificially elevating the price of labor, through legislation or coercive bargaining, usually to many times its competitive market value. This in turn brings on inflation and provides additional incentive to use more and more capital-intensive, labor-saving technology.

In an age when technology will increasingly play the dominant role in the development process, the already huge but ever growing labor force is not a resource (as it was during the Industrial Revolution in England and America) but a liability. This again underscores the basic truth that in the less economically developed countries of Latin America, wealth (i.e., technology and capital), to the extent it is generated, is and will remain the product of capital while subsistence is and will remain the product of labor.

For all of the interrelated reasons discussed above, it is apparent that new forms of economic organization and systems to finance the growth of such organizations must be devised if modernization is to benefit the lives of the broad masses of the people and, in so doing, provide some measure of increased economic freedom as the basis of their economic livelihood.

IV. On Economic Democracy: A Few Thoughts on Modernization with Freedom

Evidence suggests that political democracy cannot take root and flourish under all economic conditions. A democratic tradition requires an economic system that supports the political ideals of liberty and equality for all. Men cannot exercise freedom in the political sphere when they are deprived of it in the economic sphere. And so it follows through history that political enfranchisement of the working classes came on the heels of their economic emancipation from slavery and serfdom or from adject dependence on their employers or patrons. If this is essentially true, then some potentially important but unanswered questions present themselves:

What is the economic counterpart of political democracy?

What correlations can be drawn between the economic substructure of a society and its political substructure, and how might these relationships be harmonized to maximize economic freedom and the possibility for rapid modernization?

What types of economic organization must be devised to support the institutions of a politically free society, and how can development programs help facilitate the free growth of such institutions?

In order to support free political institutions, an economic substructure must rest on two things: economic liberty, or the elimination of all economic slavery, servitude, or dependence; and economic equality, the enjoyment by all men of the same economic opportunities to earn a decent livelihood. Add to this the technological revolution that will continue to shift the burden of production from the workers (the human factor) to capital instruments, and the central issue can be described as follows: If we are to make the individual more productive we must devise new institutional means for enabling him to acquire ownership of the non-human factor of production, capital.

Assuming the goal is rapid modernization consistent with maximizing economic freedom, then the task must be to devise new institutionalized arrangements whereby it will be possible to broaden the capital ownership to include millions on millions of new capitalists into what eventually over time would become an economically classless society. In order to move in this direction, contemporary forms of exclusive capitalism would need to be supplemented by new forms of inclusive capitalism. By possessing a broad base of ownership, these wealth-producing institutional forms would automatically maximize economic freedom. Devoted to modernization, these institutions would provide the basis for "development capitalism" as a system of production and distribution of wealth through which economic democracy could eventually be achieved, i.e., the ever-increasing number of owners of capital would permit an automatic and direct distribution of wealth through participation in production.

In essence, the problem of private enterprise in Latin America is that the private part of it (ownership) is much too private. Being restricted, it cannot—in its present form—contribute much to economic freedom and development. Alternatively, to create a functional basis for economic democracy, specifically designed corporate prototypes need to be established to demonstrate the feasibility of a "development capitalism." We may find support for economic democracy in *Mater et Magistra,* where John XXIII has said that, "It is not enough to assert the natural character of the right of private property, productive included, but its effective distribution among all social classes is to be insisted upon," including that of "shares in middle-size and large firms." There are new initiatives now being undertaken to create corporate prototypes with these objectives in mind.

CULTURAL FREEDOM
IN LATIN AMERICA

PAULO FREIRE

As I face the words written on this almost-empty sheet of paper, I know that I am called upon to perform an act of cognition. Because this act requires my understanding, it will not be limited to the relations it sets up between myself as the subject and the knowable object which I am seeking to analyze. It will reach out to include other subjects who are likewise called to reflect critically and who will join with me in dialogue. The mediator of the dialogue between us will be the topic which we are seeking to explore together.

Introductory Reflections

Since I am initiating an act of cognition, the first thing I need to do is to limit the knowable object wrapped in the linguistic context: "Diagnosis of cultural freedom in Latin America—meaning access to education in the general sense." I therefore have to begin my reflection directly upon the given text, looking for the meaning of its parts as interrelated dimensions of the whole structure.

Therefore, I will first take the linguistic structure as a whole, and as a knowable object. Then, after "breaking it up," I will be able to "see" the whole from within and behold the "contextual sense"[1] of its words. The first operation will give me the central theme, isolated for my analysis, and the other operation will follow, namely, my attempt to reach into the subject itself in order to unveil it.

In the process of analyzing the linguistic context, I perceive that the word "diagnosis" is related to the restrictive expression "cultural freedom" and that it is bound to it through the preposition *of*. For this reason, too, the diagnosis is not an unqualified diagnosis but the one determined by the restrictive character of "cultural freedom" in which the adjective "cultural" modifies the word "freedom." On the other hand, the phrase "Latin America" tied to the linguistic entity "Diagnosis of Cultural Freedom" by the preposition *in* designates the time-space relationship within which we must study cultural freedom, which is the central subject of our analysis.

The subheading "meaning access to education in the general sense" constitutes the second linguistic whole whose role it is to further define the first entity and reinforce the answer given to the main topic. Moreover, the subheading, while fixing a meaningful relation between education and culture, avoids the possible restriction of the thematic nucleus through the expression: "in the general sense." In this way we not only investigate the "meaning access to education" in a restrictive sense, but rather access to activities of a cultural nature.

Nevertheless, despite the use of statistics and percentage indices revealing quantitative failures in the field of systematic education, the diagnosis of cultural freedom in Latin America is not possible without a previous analysis of what is understood by "cultural freedom." But the moment I ask about the sense of "cultural freedom" itself, I discover that I face even more radical requirements which bring me back to the concept of culture and consequently to the dialectic relation man-world. In this deeper dimension, implied within the linguistic structure being studied, lies the starting point for one of the operations previously mentioned: namely, the study of this subject which will lead to its unveiling. Nevertheless, I can reach this insight only to the extent that when I write, think, and talk I do not allow any dichotomy between my thought-language and the reality upon which I act, talk, and think.

At this moment, when writing—which includes thinking and talking—I am apparently wrapped up within the cultural world, surrounded by cultural objects in the mysterious company of the authors of the books in my library. The "theoretical context" which is fundamental and needful in order to allow me to think and speak about the "real context" is, also, a cultural context. It is not possible to think "culture," unless it be done culturally. This is the reason why the theoretical context that is now my library, at the moment I vitalize it with my inquisitive presence, allows me to perform a double operation of reflection: on one hand, I can "admire" my cultural activity as I accomplish it, and, on the other, I can bring to this context the "real" given facts which I call the "real context," in order to "re-admire" them. Both operations will lead me to the roots of culture as a product of man's transforming activity (praxis) upon the world. If I make an effort to "ad-mire" the occupation in which I am engaged, if I am able to objectify it at the very moment when it happens—which implies reflecting on my own thought and perceiving myself perceiving— I discover that my action-language-thought finds itself within the same original structure which frames the potentiality of men, likewise cultural, to "ad-mire" the world. If on the other hand, I consciously reflect on the facts occurred and occurring in the social context in order to, in a certain way, "re-admire" them, I reach the same conclusion.

Culture: Effect of Transforming Acts of Man

Culture arises as an effect of the transforming action of man, of his work, which acquires this meaning through the dialectic operation of the world's "ad-miration," by means of which he "separates" himself from it in order to remain *in* and *with* the world. This is the reason why man, a cultural being, is unique among the becoming ones. He is able to have not only his own activity but himself as object of his own consciousness. This fact makes him different from animals which are unable to separate their "self" from their activities. In this apparently superficial distinction, we will find the lines which separate man from the point of view of his actions within the space in which he is placed.

Because of its inability to separate itself from its actions, upon which it is incapable of reflecting, the animal is not able to instill into the transformation which it brings about, a meaning beyond itself. In the measure that its action is a "part" of the animal, the results of the transformation it has brought about do not go beyond it. The results do not become separate since the latter's locus of decision is to be found outside the animal, in the species to which it belongs.

As it does not have a locus of decision within itself, as it cannot objectify either itself or things, as it lacks purposes to propose to others and to itself, as it lives immersed in a world to which it cannot give meaning, as it has no yesterday, no tomorrow, and lives an oppressive present, the animal is not a historical being. His ahistorical life is lived in a world which is not a "non-self" which might change him into a "self" and, in this way, allow him to be conscious of himself and of the world. The human world, a historical one, is for the "being in itself" a mere support. Its shape is not a problem but a stimulus. The life of the ahistorical being is not a running of risks inasmuch as it does not realize it is running them. Due to the fact that these challenges are not perceived in a reflected way, but merely "noted" by the signs which denote them, neither do they require a response implying decisive action.

Animals, for this reason, cannot be committed. Conditioned as ahistorical beings, they cannot "assume" life, and as they cannot assume life, neither can they "build it." At the same time they cannot realize that they are being destroyed alive because they are not able to transform the support where their life flourishes into a meaningful and symbolic world, the comprehensive world of culture and history. This is the reason why the animal does not animalize its environment in order to animalize itself; neither does it become de-animalized.[2]

In the forest as well as in the zoo the animal continues to be a "being in itself," an animal in both places.[3] Man, on the contrary, is conscious of his activity and of the world in which he lives. He acts in terms of the fulfillment of purposes he proposes to himself and others. Because he has his decisional locus within himself, in his relations[4] with the world he is able to "separate" himself from the world, and in "separating" he is able to remain within it. Man, unlike an animal, not only *lives* but *exists* and his existence is historical. If the life of the animal elapses in an a-temporal, heavy, dull, support-environment, man's existence occurs in a world he constantly recreates.

If in the life of the animal the expression "here" denotes nothing but a "habitat" which he simply contacts, in man's existence the expression "here" denotes not merely a physical space, but a historical-cultural space as well. Strictly speaking, there is no here, now, tomorrow, or yesterday for the animal, as he lacks a consciousness of self and his being alive is a complete determination. On the contrary, man, being the world's consciousness and as such a "knowing body," lives a dialectic relationship between the restrictions set by certain boundaries and his freedom.

Because of his ability to step back and look objectively at the world upon which he acts, man overcomes the "limit situations" which should not be considered as something beyond which nothing exists.[5] At the very time when man recognizes them as barriers, when they appear as obstacles to freedom, they become "outstanding perceptions" in the "depth of their vision." In this way they appear in their real dimension: concrete and historical dimensions of a given fact. The "limit situations" themselves do not generate a hopeless climate. The perception men have of them in a given historical moment does. Concomitant with the genesis of critical perception, which is never separated from action, there develops a climate of faith and confidence which pushes men to struggle in order to overcome the "limit situations" which crush them. Once these have been overcome by the transformation of reality, new situations arise which elicit new actions from men and these are actions which Vieira Pinto calls "limit deeds." Therefore what is proper to men as beings conscious of themselves and their world, is to adopt a permanent posture *vis à vis* reality where the "limit situations" appear historically. And this confrontation with reality to overcome the obstacles which they face may only be effected historically as the "limit situations" become historically objective.

In the animal world, which is not strictly speaking a world but *support* of it, there are not "limit situations" because of the ahistorical character of each in relation to the other. Therefore, instead of the historical "limit situations," the limit is the *support* itself. What characterizes the animal, then, is that it is not *in relation* to its support, but *adapted* to it. Consequently, as a "being in itself" in producing a nest, a beehive, a hole in which to live, it is not really creating products as a result of "limit deeds." Its productive activity is subservient to the satisfaction of a physical need, merely stimulating but not challenging. For this reason, their products, undoubtedly, "belong directly to their physical bodies, while man is free before his product."[6] Only inasmuch as the products that come from the activity of a being itself "do not belong to his physical body," will they give rise to the meaningful dimension of the context, which, in this way, becomes *world*.

The main difference between the animal, whose activity goes no

further than mere production, and man, who creates the domain
of culture and history through his action on the world, is that
the latter only is a being of praxis. He is a being who creates
and knows it as changer and creator. That man, in his permanent
relationship with reality, produces not only material goods, sen-
sible things, and objects but also social institutions, ideologies,
art, religions, science, and technology. While the animal, as we
have seen, is limited by his *support,* man is conditioned by the
products of his own activity which, through the "inversion of
praxis" turn back on him. In this way, culture, the creation of
man, in a certain way creates him. Affected by his own praxis, he
conditions it through the dialectical movement between culture
itself as a superstructure and the intrastructure.[7] It is through creating and being conditioned by his own creation, by creating an
object and becoming an object, that he finds the great challenge
of freedom. Only those beings who live this paradox of creating
and being conditioned by their creation are capable of achieving freedom. Alienated, they are able to surpass alienation;
oppressed, they are able to struggle for freedom.[8]

Latin American Opportunities in History

Now if culture has such a conditioning effect on its own creat-
ors, cultural freedom as well as cultural oppression are directly
conditioned by culture itself. Freedom of culture as well as the
lack of it are expressed not only by limiting access to culture to
certain social classes but also by curtailing the right to re-create
it. For this reason the center of the discussion is now shifted
towards the inquiry about whether the Latin American cultural
framework does or does not provide an opportunity for the participation of the popular classes in the existing culture, as well as
whether they do or do not feel free to create and re-create their
own values.

While avoiding a detailed analysis of this question, we may

assume that since the conquest, Latin America has been a subjugated land. Its colonization consisted of transplantation by the invaders.[9] Its population was crushed; its economy was based upon slave labor (particularly that of Negroes brought from Africa as objects); it was dependent upon foreign markets, and usually followed a cyclic pattern. Moreover, its economic structures, biased from the beginning in favor of the conquerors, were based on natural resources which were systematically exploited and directed towards European markets.[10] The economic, social, political and cultural control of the colonizing centers—Spain and Portugal—molded the Latin American societies into both agrarian and exporting societies, subject to a rural oligarchy, initially transplanted and always dependent upon foreign interests. They were oligarchies superimposed on the people referred to as "natives" (in the pejorative sense), who had their origin in the race mixtures which emerged as a result of miscegenation.

During the colonial period we were "closed societies": slaveowning, without a constituency, mere "reflections." The keynote of our formation seems undeniably to have been the exaggeration of power which brought about what was almost a masochistic desire to remain subject to it. This had as its corresponding pleasure that of being related to a power which could be relied on as almighty.

The prevailing kind of economic domination determined a culture of domination which once internalized, meant the conditioning of submissive behaviour. "Nobody dared to pass a soldier on guard without a show of respect," says Luecock when speaking of his observations during visits to Brazil. Another distinguished visitor, Saint Hilaire, adds: "It may be said that respect was imbibed with the milk they suckled," referring ironically to the internalization of the ruling culture.

Rugenda's observations, in his "Viajem Pinturesca a traves de Brasil," are also to the point: "Truly, there are laws that impose certain limits to the will and rage of masters: an example is the one which determines the number of lashes allowed at one time without the intervention of the authorities; while these laws are not enforced . . . the punishment for slaves due to either a real or an imaginary fault, the bad treatment due to the landlord's cruelty and arbitrariness, are only limited by the fear of losing the slave, either due to his death, to his escape, or to human respect for public opinion."[11] The latter limit should of course be the weakest of all. . . .

From the point of view of systematic education,[12] which is characterized by elitism, there is a difference between Spanish America and Brazil. While in Spanish America universities began to rise about 1551 (poor copies of the metropolitan universities though they were), in Brazil during the first two hundred years of colonial life, the Jesuits were the only educators, engaged in catechizing the natives. Their activities were aimed mainly at "conquering souls" for the Catholic faith, to which they added the teaching of Latin. Nevertheless, we must acknowledge the great effort made by these first educators in Brazil and the fact that some, like Nobrega and Anchieta, were the forerunners of valuable pedagogical methods.

It was only with the migration of the "royal family" in 1808 and the consequent renewal of the metropolitan government in Rio de Janeiro, that the first changes in educational policy became evident in Brazil with the rise of schools, libraries, press, etc. It is important to note, however, that the school of higher learning created during this period was a fine arts school. . . . This difference in educational policy between the Spanish and Portuguese conquerors might give the naive impression that the former were better colonizers than the latter, more eager for education and culture. However, it was simply due to the fact that the Portuguese did not find in Brazil the challenge to their conquest that the Spaniards had to face within the area of their domain. While the Portuguese found in Brazil more geography than history, the Spaniards faced highly developed cultures.

Culture of Silence

The above-mentioned culture of domination, which lives on in "the culture of silence," was forged during a colonial past of kings and viceroys, Crown representatives, oppression and reproof, of an elitist education not able to free men but able to forbid them the possibility of personal expression. In Brazil the only voice one could hear amid the silence was the one issuing from the pulpit. Quoting a Latin phrase that ended with the word *infans* from a homily honoring the arrival of the Marquis de Montalvo, Viceroy of Brazil, Rev. Antonio Vieira says: "Let's begin with this last word, *infans; infans* is the one who does not speak. This was the situation of the Baptist when Our Lady visited him, and this was the situation of Brazil for many years, and this, in my opinion, was the main cause of all its ills. The fact that the sick man cannot speak forces the doctor to guess, which makes it even more difficult to prescribe. For this reason nothing was more difficult for Christ than the cure of a dumb man possessed. On this miracle He expended more time than on any other. The worst crisis faced by Brazil during its illness was the silencing of its speech."[13]

This "culture of silence" survived the colonial period and experienced in some countries a formal lull during the wars of independence. It endures today, especially in the extensive Latin American rural areas. It is important to emphasize that although under these historical circumstances the oppressed conscience "hosts" the oppressive conscience,[14] the "culture of silence" is predisposed to be "reactivated" in its manifestations under more favorable circumstances, even though this would mean a change in the structures that support it.

The phenomenon of emergence—stronger in some societies than others—through which the popular classes in Latin America announce their intention to break with this culture and demand an active participation in the political process, is quite recent among us. It had its beginning in the dislocations suffered by the "closed societies" during the first decades of this century. "A period of crisis," says Weffort, "born either of the deep rupture produced by the 1914–1918 World War or the great depression of 1929, depending on the country, undermined the foundations of the old Latin American society.[15] This crisis characterizes the historical-sociological transition Latin American societies are undergoing as dependent societies, a condition which aggravates their internal and external contradictions. Nevertheless, it is important to point out that the transition to which I am referring does not have, at least for me, the connotation which some sociologists give it. They speak of it as the mechanical passage from a traditional society to a modernized one. This kind of transition, identified with the passage from underdevelopment to development, constitutes one of the dimensions of the dominant ideology. There is no way to identify development with modernization. Although development implies modernization, modernization is not, in itself, development.

Development is achieved only when the locus of decision for the transformations suffered by a being is found within and not outside of him. And this does not happen with dependent societies, which are alienated and, as such, are "object societies." When the source of decision-making, including the political, economic, and cultural aspects, continues to be outside, in the metropolitan society upon which the common people depend, only a modernization process is achieved. For this reason, the historical-sociological transition of Latin American societies must either be channeled into overcoming their dependent condition and thereby assuming their role as subjects and achieving development or they will be prevented from discovering their historical destiny.

Obviously, this means much more than the breaking down of an obsolete structure in order to set up a modern one; it means the overcoming of its condition of "existing for others." The first option can be induced from the outside without involving the people, and ordinarily with the purpose of sooner or later plunging them back into their initial immersion; the second one may only be achieved with the people as the subject of the process.

Modernization Not Enough

The option for modernization as against development implies the restriction of cultural freedom as well as the use of methods and of techniques through which the access to culture would apparently be controlled. It implies an education for the maintenance of the status quo, preserving the non-participation of the people in whatever the process in any field; an education which, instead of unfolding reality, mythifies it and, consequently, domesticates and adapts man.

For this reason, too, modernization may be seen as an objective reply given by the elites in power to the growing grievances expressed by the submerged popular classes. Such an emergence as we have seen is recent among us and "means," says Weffort, "on the one hand, a double pressure on the ruling structures: pressure on the state structures in order to broaden popular participation in politics (especially through the vote), as well as in social life (social rights, education, etc.), and pressure on the marketing structures (through pressure on the state), particularly with reference to the broadening of participation in the fashioning of employment and consumer policies." On the other hand, continues Weffort, "The political emergence of the popular classes meant, in a certain degree, their effective incorporation into the institutionalized political framework, thus becoming a popular pressure within the existing political regime. . . . And typical populist movements and governments may be observed in countries such as Brazil and Argentina where they have found fulfillment."[16]

Inasmuch as these popular classes emerge within certain specific historical conditions, they create a new style of political action, populism. In our opinion the following statements are legitimate: The emergence in itself, even when it means, as mentioned above (Weffort), double pressure, does not imply the automatic expulsion of the mythical specters which were internalized during the period of immersion; and populism, as a new style of political life, characterized by the manipulation of popular emerging classes and a kind of leadership which mediates between them and the power elites, is not capable of accomplishing the necessary "exteriorization" of such myths.[17]

The more the rise of the masses is emphasized in Latin America, the more the elite holding power, committed to foreign interests, will polarize against them. In this way, to the extent that the populist phase seems to indicate its goal by the intensification of popular pressures and an attempt to organize, the power elites, feeling ever more threatened, have no alternative but to end the process. By doing it repressively, denying the popular classes the right to express themselves and offering them a mythical education, they reactivate the old tradition of the "culture of silence." It seems to me that we can find here an explanation for the apathy of the popular classes (especially the rural, but also the urban) which follows upon the closure of the political process. Their "fear of freedom," which had not disappeared during the emergence, is restored in a stronger way through the "failure" of their first endeavors at participation. Once again they tend to live their former fatalist posture before the world, a position characteristic of oppressed awareness. Again they feel unable for the most part to face their "limit situations," not perceiving beyond them the so-called "unedited viable," understood as the future to be built by men.

For these reasons, cultural freedom in Latin America is the freedom of the leading classes to approach their culture, while using it as an instrument to forbid the popular classes the right of expression. On the basic level, and in some cases on other levels as well, a small number from the popular classes is able to attain an alienating culture which by its very nature prevents their liberation. Insofar as they are "closed societies" predominantly dependent, going through a process of modernization but not of development, their power elite, separated from the masses and afraid of structural changes, does nothing but invade the value frame of the popular classes in order to impose its options and frustrate their action. And under these circumstances it is not possible to speak about cultural freedom.

"Freedom Restored"—Beings for Themselves

In order to have freedom restored as a right, and not as a privilege through access to a false culture, it would be necessary for Latin American societies to become "beings for themselves." Moreover, a deep and intense effort in behalf of cultural action would be necessary in order to face up culturally to the "culture of silence." A fundamental step would be the unfolding of this culture, placed as a knowable object before the popular classes who, perceiving it critically, could then "exteriorize" their myths. Through this liberating cultural action, inasmuch as it involves dialogue instead of cultural invasion, a cultural synthesis is accomplished. For this reason *the program for such action cannot be chosen exclusively by those who initiate it* but must also be chosen by the popular groups who, as much as the others, must be subjects in the act of knowing reality. It is because of this that this style of action has its starting point in objective reality and on the perception of it held by the popular classes. To the extent that these masses, through *conscientization*, become aware, bit by bit, of their becoming and their reality (which is also becoming), they are preparing themselves for insertion in the historic process. They are no longer dual beings, "hosts" of the oppressors, but beings in the process of freeing themselves. And this is possible because this cultural action is not merely an intellectual dilettante's pastime, a useless combination of words, but rather a reflective and positive task—a real knowing of reality in order to transform it consciously and, by transforming, to know it. Thus, true cultural freedom does not exist within the concrete situations of domination where, in the best of cases, even a disguised power elite assumes a paternalistic role, thinking for and by the popular classes, which means against them. Cultural freedom is not a gift but the conquered right of the popular classes to express themselves, an act which enables them to "pronounce the world" and to live a continuous re-creation of it.

Freeing cultural action, previous to and concomitant with any truly revolutionary process, is the basis of cultural freedom itself because it is the revolution in the superstructure in a dialectic process with the infrastructure. Under these conditions, to attempt a diagnosis of cultural freedom is to arrive at the diagnosis of the lack of freedom. It is not possible to have cultural freedom while the "culture of silence" prevails in Latin America.

NOTES

1. On "basic and contextual sense" of words, see Pierre Giraud, *Semantics* (Mexico City: Fondo de Cultura, 1965).

2. As Ortega y Gasset said in one of his books: "The tiger does not 'de-tigerize' itself."

3. This does not happen to men who, in re-creating the world with their work, "humanize it." It is in this sense that culture, as a product of this re-creation, is already humanization, which is to say that it is the transforming presence of men in the world; and from the fact that men can "humanize" the world, it follows that they can also dehumanize and humanize themselves, be alienated, integrated, be less or more, be slaves or free men. It follows from this that all "humanization" of the world, in the sense of transformation effected by men, does not always mean humanization of men. Never has humanity reached such a high level of technological and scientific progress as today. This advancement, nevertheless, militating as it does against the naive theses of uninterrupted progress which identify scientific advance

with human betterment, does not appear to be an established fact. "Il semble," Marcuse says, "que la société industrielle advancée prive la critique de sa véritable base. Le progrés technique renforce tout un systéme de domination et de coordination qui, á son tour, dirige le progrés et crée des formes de vie (et de pouvoir) qui semblent réconcilier avec le systéme les forces opposantes, et de ce fait rendre vaine toute protestation au nom des perspectives historiques, au nom de la libération de l'homme." And even more, "la société industrielle qui s'approprie la technologie et la science s'est organizée pour dominer toujours plus efficacement l'homme et la nature, pour utiliser ses ressources toujours plus efficacement." Herbert Marcuse, *L'Homme Unidimensionel* (Paris: Les editions de Minuit, 1968), pp. 18–42.

4. Regarding differences between "relations" and "contacts," the first ones belong to the human domain and the second merely to the animal orbit. See Paulo Freire, *Educaçao Como Practica de la Liberdade* (Rio de Janeiro: Ed. Paz e Terra, 1967).

5. The Brazilian, Professor Alvaro Vieira Pinto, analyzes quite clearly the problem concerning the "limit situation," going beyond and exhausting the pessimistic dimension which we originally find in Jaspers. Vieira Pinto says that the "limit situations" are not "the unavoidable barrier where all possibilities end, but the real margin where all possibilities begin"; they are not "the frontier between being or not being but the frontier between being and being more." Alvaro Vieira Pinto, *Consciencia e Realidade Nacional* (Rio de Janeiro: Institute Superior de Estudos Brasileiros—ISEB, 1960), vol. II, p. 284.

6. Karl Marx, *Economic and Philosophical Manuscripts* (New York: International Publisher, 1964).

7. "According to the materialistic view of history, the fact which in the long run determines history is the production and reproduction of real life. Neither Marx nor I have ever affirmed more than this. If someone distorts it, by saying that the economic fact is the only determinant, he will turn this thesis into an empty expression, abstract and absurd. The economic situation is the foundation but the elements of the superstructure . . . also exercise their influence in the course of historical struggles and often shape their course." Letter from Friedrich Engels to J. Bloch, London, September, 1890, in *Marx-Engles, Selected Works* (Moscow: Ed. Progreso, 1966), vol. II, pp. 491–493. See also Louis Althusser, *Pour Marx* (Paris: F. Maspeso, 1965).

8. On this subject there is an excellent essay by the Brazilian,

Professor Ernani M. Fiori, "Culture and Alienation," to be published soon by the Instituto Latinoamericano de Estudios Sociales, ILADES, Santiago, Chile.

9. If economically the action of the laymen during the colonization period effected the destruction of the natives' traditional system of production, the Church completed this process with the destruction of the pre-Columbian cultural system. It is based upon this action that the "Europeanization" of Latin America will slowly erase all the characteristics of an aboriginal culture which from this time onward will only survive under the form of regional habits and peasant subcultures." Tomas Vasconi, *Educacion y Cambio Social* (Santiago: Universidad de Chile, Centro de Estudios Socio-Económicos, Facultad de Ciencias Económicas, 1967), pp. 39–40.

10. "The economic structure in Latin America is deeply deformed in the sense that the distribution of both income and population is very inequitable. Such a deformation has its origin in the impact of the conquest over a non-monetary, primitive economy, where the income (standard of living) was fundamentally determined by both the availability of natural resources and the socio-cultural level. Therefore, the distribution coincides with that of the population. With colonization, the products coming from the mines and other extractive industries, and later those coming from agriculture and animal raising, were almost completely channeled towards the metropolis. In most areas, especially in mining regions, which used slave labor, the local income may be said to have been negative. The aggregate value in the colonies was limited to the centers which serve as intermediaries for the metropolis. The best areas were then appropriated and the remaining and rebellious workers were pushed towards marginal areas where they remained on the level of subsistence allowed by the natural resources available.

"Such an economic structure was then deeply deformed. Moreover, centuries later, the effects of this deformation are still felt in Latin America since its economic growth was mainly induced from the outside." This notation was taken from an unedited work, *Changes Within the Economic Space Structure in Latin America,* prepared by Estevan Strauss, Jan., 1969. We acknowledge, with thanks, Mr. Strauss' permission to use this extract.

11. In this respect see, David Brion Davis, *The Problem of Slavery in Western Culture* (Ithaca: Cornell University Press, 1966).

12. Paulo de Tarso, "Necesidades Educacionales de Una Sociedad en Desarrollo," remarks at Inter-American Forum: The Continuing Impact of Technology and Modernization on Latin American Society (Washington: Division for Latin America, USCC, Jan. 1968), 47. pp.

13. Padre Antonio Vieira, "Sermao de Visitação de Nossa Senhora," Hospital Misericordia, Bahia, *Obras Completas*, Sermoes (Porto: Lelo Irmaos Editores, 1959), vol. III, p. 330.

14. On the reactivation phenomena see Althusser, *op. cit.*

15. Francisco Weffort, *Clases Populares e Politicas* (São Paulo: Universidad de São Paulo, 1968), Introduction, p. 2.

16. Weffort, *op. cit.*, Introduction, p. 1.

17. The masses who support the Populist leader do not possess the subjective and objective conditions necessary to avoid his fall. They were mobilized by him with the purpose of increasing their economic and political participation in the existing system, not for the purpose of conquering it and creating a "new society." Wilson Cantoni, *The Dilemma of Education Before the Partiality of Latin American Development*, International Sociological Association VI World Congress, Agrarian Reform Training and Research Institute, ICIRA, Santiago, Chile, 1966.

FREEDOM OF LABOR UNIONS
IN LATIN AMERICA

ROBERT J. ALEXANDER

It is very difficult to generalize about the freedom of organized labor in Latin America. For one thing, the situation is strikingly different in each country. For another, it is subject to change without notice in any given nation of the region.

To begin with it is best to define just what one means by freedom of labor unions in Latin America. For my purposes I shall mean the basic right of trade unions to exist. Second, I shall mean their right to control their own affairs; third, their right to negotiate freely with those who employ their members.

At the present moment, the basic right of labor unions to exist is not in question in any country of Latin America, with the possible exception of Haiti where, under the dictatorship of "Papa Doc" Duvalier, virtually all of the labor movement has been destroyed. All of the other nations, with the exception of Uruguay, have legislation specifically authorizing the establishment of unions, with some kind. of legal recognition from the government.

The mere existence of laws providing for the right of labor to organize does not by any means assure that the workers will have this right in fact. Frequently in countries which have dictatorial regimes such laws are recognized more in the breach than in the execution. Thus, during the government of Perez Jimenez in Venezuela in the 1950's, the labor movement was decimated and most of the unions which had existed before that time were destroyed. Under Odria in Peru during the same period, unions in many fields were destroyed and the existence of regional and national central labor bodies was forbidden, in spite of the law. The legal recognition of all existing unions was cancelled in Guatemala upon the accession of Castillo Armas to power in 1954, and it was several years before most of them had reorganized and once again secured legal status.

The right of the labor unions to run their own affairs is a more complicated matter. In a certain sense, most of the unions of Latin America don't run their own affairs; to a greater or lesser degree most labor organizations are dominated by one or another political party. The parties not infrequently use the unions under their control for purposes which have much more to do with what is good for the party than they do for what is good for the members of the unions involved.

I think it is fair to say, however, that where circumstances exist in which it is possible for the members of unions to get rid of leaders who are affiliated with a particular party and substitute others if they so desire, to that extent the basic freedom of the unions to run their own affairs can be said to be still intact. It's not for an outsider to say that a particular union should or should not elect its officials in accordance with those leaders' political affiliation.

One cannot place two kinds of limitations on the freedom of the unions to manage their own affairs: legal restrictions, and *de facto* or political ones. Most of the Latin American countries have labor codes which spell out in more or less detail how a union should be organized and how it should conduct its business. In each nation these legal provisions are somewhat different, but certain generalizations can be made with regard to the general nature of such statutory limitations on the functioning of the labor organizations.

Frequently, the labor code of a particular country will define the jurisdiction which a labor union can have. The most extreme case of this is probably in Brazil, where the Consolidation of Labor Laws first promulgated during the Vargas dictatorship in the 1950's is still largely intact. That legal compendium has an appendix covering many pages which spells out in great detail how each industry should be subdivided insofar as unions are concerned. Until recently, it was the official policy of the Ministry of Labor to restrict a union to the narrowest possible jurisdiction, in conformity with the well-known principle of divide and rule.

Chile represents another case in which this jurisdictional problem is a special handicap for the labor movement. The Chilean Labor Code provides for recognition of only two types of unions. One is the so-called "industrial union," which covers the manual workers employed in a single plant. The other is the "professional union," which can be composed of white-collar workers in a single enterprise, a group of workers with a particular skill even in a plant where an industrial union already exists, or workers in several small workshops, none of which has the 25 workers required legally to organize a "sindicato industrial." There is no provision in the Chilean law (with the single exception of the copper miners, who have their own special statute) for the establishment of national unions covering the workers in a particular industry, or for a national labor confederation. The efforts of the government of President Eduardo Frei to bring about a modification of these aspects of the Chilean basic labor law have so far been unsuccessful.

Various other aspects of the internal affairs of unions are often regulated by Latin American labor legislation. The unions are often required to submit to the government either their budgets or an account of how they have spent their funds. The law frequently forbids the unions to spend their resources for such things as strike funds, business enterprises, and political activities. (This last prohibition is lightly enforced.) Sometimes, too, the law does not allow the unions to spend more than a small amount of money without the counter-signature of a government official on a check drawn by a union official.

Latin American labor laws also frequently exercise control over the electoral processes of the unions. They sometimes demand that candidates for office in the labor organizations be screened by Ministry of Labor and other officials before they can run; sometimes representatives of the Ministry must be present at elections; sometimes union officers cannot take their posts until their election has been attested to by government representatives.

Probably more important than such legal restrictions on the right of the labor organizations of Latin America to run their own affairs are the more informal but frequently more damaging informal controls exercised by various governments. One could cite numerous examples of such situations.

During the 31-year dictatorship of Generalissimo Rafael Trujillo in the Dominican Republic, virtually all urban workers, as well as those in the sugar industry, were in unions. However, the labor movement, like the rest of Dominican society, was honeycombed with one or another of the numerous secret police forces which reported their findings directly to the tyrant. It was they, not the workers themselves, who chose the leaders of the unions, while the top officials of the labor movement were selected by the dictator himself. No dissidence or militancy was allowed in the labor unions.

In Argentina under Peron, the independence of the trade unions was undermined over a considerable period. After Peron's election as president, supervision of labor matters was turned over to his wife, Evita, and between 1946 and 1951 she removed virtually all of the union officials who had aided her husband in his rise to power. As early as 1947, a labor attaché of the Argentine government told me that the leadership of the General Confederation of Labor was chosen by the President of the Republic. In subsequent years, the Confederation's leaders were the ones who chose the leadership of its constituent unions.

The Castro regime presents another example of government control over the internal affairs of the labor movement. When the followers of Fidel seized control of the unions during the first two days after Batista's fall, their leaders promised that the labor movement would assume a role independent of both employers and the government, which had not been customary in Cuba.

By the end of the year 1959, however, Castro had decided to take the path of revolutionary dictatorship. One of the first places where the results of this decision became obvious was the labor movement. Early in November the Confederation of Workers of Cuba held its congress. More than 90 per cent of the delegates to that meeting belonged to Castro's 26th of July Movement. However, Castro and other top leaders of the government wanted the confederation to give the 5 per cent of the delegates who were Communist Party members equal representation in the confederation's executive committee with those belonging to the 26th of July Movement. Although Fidel, Raul Castro, and the Minister of Labor all appeared before the congress to urge this upon the delegates, they refused to follow their advice, in spite of the fact that the Army made a show of force inside and outside the convention hall.

Finally, as a result of discussions with Castro, a "compromise" was reached, by which the delegates agreed to allow the provisional executive committee established right after the Castro victory, to choose a new executive for the Confederation of Workers of Cuba. The group chosen consisted only of members of the 26th of July Movement, but with a majority chosen from that relatively small minority of 26th of July trade unionists who favored collaboration with the Communists.

In the following seven months a "purge committee" appointed by the new executive of the Confederation removed the leadership of the national unions, in spite of the fact that the Confederation had no such power according to its own constitution. The excuse for this purge was that those removed were "Batistianos," but the fact was that all Batista followers had been removed during the first two days of the Revolution; those who were purged were those members of the 26th of July Movement who refused to collaborate with the Communists.

During the following two years, the government's control over the Confederation became increasingly tight. Although he held no official position in the organization, the Confederation and the regime referred constantly to Lazaro Pena, an old-time Communist trade unionist who had been secretary-general of the Confederation during the first administration of Batista, as the "leader" of the organization. In another congress in November, 1961, he was once again placed in the post of secretary-general. However, when this old-time Communist fell out of favor with Fidel, he was removed once again from this post, and his place was taken by a virtually unknown young trade unionist who was loyal to Fidel.

Another, not atypical example of the attitude of the dictatorial regimes towards the freedom of the labor movement to run its own affairs has been the behavior of the Stroessner regime in Paraguay. Although the Confederation of Paraguayan Workers was organized under the patronage of Stroessner's own Colorado Party, its leaders began to show some independence of the government several years ago. As a result, the Stroessner government arrested most of the Confederation's top leaders, while those who could escaped into exile, where they maintain a Confederation of Paraguayan Workers in Exile in Montevideo. Meanwhile, the Stroessner government imposed new leadership on the Confederation within the country, headed appropriately enough by one of the top officials of the national police.

The freedom of the labor organizations to negotiate with those who employ their members is also subject to both legal and *de facto* limitations in Latin America. The laws of several of the countries substitute arbitration for collective bargaining in the case of certain groups of workers such as government employees and agricultural workers. In addition, most of the countries provide some limitation on the right to bargain even of those groups to which bargaining is generally permitted. For instance, unions and employers are often required to appear before government conciliation and mediation boards, usually composed of representatives of the unions, employers, and government. These bodies seek to resolve disputes in a peaceful fashion.

One of the severest limitations on the right of collective bargaining was that imposed by the Vargas regime in Brazil during the Estado Novo dictatorship of 1937–1945. A system of labor courts was established under this legislation, and during most of the Estado Novo, those unions which wished to obtain wage increases and other improvements for their members brought their requests to regional labor tribunals. Even the number of such requests was relatively small and there were virtually no collective bargaining agreements signed during this period.

At the present time, collective bargaining is certainly restricted in such countries as Brazil where the limits of wage increases are established by government decree; in Paraguay, where all aspects of organized labor are restricted; and in Nicaragua, where it is possible to organize only the workers of firms in which the Somoza family does not have a major interest. Labor organization and collective bargaining are forbidden in firms which belong to the ruling family.

However, the restrictions on collective bargaining are probably most severe in Cuba. A series of decrees between 1960 and 1962 limited the right of collective negotiation, culminating in the Third Law of Labor Procedures which said that "if the Ministry of Labor observes that a collective labor contract . . . infringes the economic-social juridical order, it can suspend its execution. . . ."

A few months later, in September, 1962, Augusto Martines Sanchez, then Minister of Labor, commented that "the making of collective contracts is converted into . . . a measure directed to guarantee the fulfillment and surpassing of production plans." Thus, in the Cuban regime as in virtually all Communist countries, the role of unions as collective bargainers trying to get additional benefits for their members has been abolished, and in its place, the unions have been converted into a means by which the workers are prodded to meet their production quotas.

In those countries in which a democratic regime is in power, however, the rights of the unions to bargain collectively with the employers of their members are generally preserved. Thus, there are voluminous collective agreements negotiated periodically in Mexico, in present-day Venezuela, in Chile, and in Costa Rica. During the Prado and Belaunde administrations in Peru, this procedure was also common, as it is at present in Uruguay. Here, however, the rapid inflation makes collective contract negotiation a virtually unceasing process.

Fundamental to the right of collective bargaining is the right to strike. There are severe limitations on this in the labor codes of several Latin American countries. In some nations it is merely prohibited for certain categories of workers. However, in most countries in which dictators are in charge strikes are generally forbidden *de facto,* whatever the terms of the law may be. Thus, even in the supposedly pro-labor government of Juan Peron after 1948 there were virtually no strikes which were recognized as legal by the government, except those few which were stimulated by the government itself in order to "punish" some opponent of the regime. Under Trujillo, strikes were in fact forbidden during most of the 31 years in which the dictator ruled over the Dominican Republic. When some did break out in the sugar fields in the middle 1940's, their leaders were killed, jailed, and driven into exile. Today, strikes are virtually impossible in Stroessner's Paraguay and Costa e Silva's Brazil.

The same is true in Castro's Cuba. Although the 1940 constitution specifically provided the right to strike, and it is presumably still in effect at least to some degree, no such right was established in the Law on the Administration of Labor Justice, issued in May, 1962. About the same time, Blas Roca—now one of the members of the Politburo of the Cuban Communist Party—expressed the regime's position on the question, when he commented: "Before, a sector could go out on strike. . . . Now, of course, such procedures are not tolerable."

Generally, the workers of Latin America are aware of the fact that trade union liberty depends on the existence of more general freedom. This has been one of the principal reasons why most of the labor movements of the area are aligned with political groups which support and defend general political democracy. Although the labor unionists of Latin America are strongly in favor of economic and social reform, they also generally believe that this reform should be brought about through the democratic process. So long as the democratic alternative is available to them, it is unlikely that most of the organized workers of Latin America will choose any other.

FREEDOM OF OPINION
IN LATIN AMERICA

HECTOR BORRAT

Before it can be expressed, opinion must be made—in freedom, in a real exchange among free men. But Latin America is a land of illiterate people, alienated groups, and to make their *own* opinion is a very difficult task for most of its people. What responsible opinion could be formulated by the miserable inhabitant of our "suburbia," shocked as he is by posters which propose to him impossible Hiltons with impossible blondes lounging alongside impossible pools? Or by the example set by the son of wealthy parents who learns English or French in a very exclusive school to live as a foreigner among his countrymen and to flee to the cultural metropolis as soon as he can?

Because Latin America has been divided into separated states by others, the Latin American gets his concept of *Patria Grande* (Big Homeland) through the information and deformation of foreigners' views. A German gave us the name "America." Other Europeans intending to concretize added "Latin," others "Hispano," "Ibero." We have not even named ourselves, although

Haya de la Torre attempted "Indoamerica" and Rodó, "Nuestra América" (in contrast with the "Anglosaxon America"). Rarely do we know our own history, and more recent history, that which we are still enduring, doesn't cast us as the main characters. Others are writing or rewriting this history from power centers which are foreign to us. Those powers, however, assault us with a number of opinions about ourselves. They refer to our misery as the "development process." They call the high rate of increase in the populations "demographic explosion." Once and again, they come to conduct research—to give their opinion about us—with an amount of time and resources that we cannot afford. They are taking away not only information but documents and books, not only printed material but men, sometimes our best men, those who could better cooperate in shaping our *own* public opinion. This is a task not only for politicians and writers but is a responsibility to be fulfilled by others engaged in a diversity of areas, from sociology and economics to the natural sciences.

Increasingly, our history and our projects are becoming the initiative, action, decision, *opinion* of others. Whether the cause be from American universities or from agencies for foreign aid, our past and our future are escaping us; we know each other through the structures of encounter arranged by the U.S. metropolis on her own soil.

The others, however, are not always the Americans; cultural and political colonialism do not necessarily coincide. Spain still maintains a compelling influence in some intellectual areas in Central America and the Caribbean, as France and England do in the southern countries. Moscow and Peking are exercising a kind of alternate magisterium among some leftists. Yet United States influence remains the largest, the increasing one, supported as it is by a technological power which pervades the whole world.

It would be too comfortable to stress only the influence of others in this diagnosis. At the same time, we must regret a vacuum in Latin American efforts to make and express our own opinions. "Uncle Tom" could have been a Latin American, and not only a servant but a general-in-chief, a famous sociologist or businessman, the editor of a big paper, even a former president or a president. "Entreguista," "cipayo" are familiar words in leftists' slogans and statements; however, many of these critics don't succeed in articulating their own thoughts. Mere imitators and poor translators are frequent among liberals as well as among conservatives; imagination is often as scarce as intellectual precision. Under such conditions, it appears that the real task of forming Latin American opinion is being carried on by only a few, and among these there are fewer still who face it as a permanent task, a personal vocation.

De Facto and De Jure

Not only do Latin Americans have difficulty formulating responsible personal opinions, but they experience even more frustration when they try to give public expression to their views.

The first difficulty, and the most obvious to foreign observers, usually comes from the political powers themselves. It is the one stressed, for instance, in the *New Survey of Journalism*.[1] In classifying the world's press systems into "free press," "the semifree press," "the communist press" and "the fascist press," the survey includes "most South American countries" in the second group, characterized by "a precarious freedom of expression. . . . The semifree system, exemplified, among many other places, in South America, Turkey, and Greece, affords only sporadically the benefits of freedom of the press. In good times, press liberty may be unrestricted. But in times of crises, when the people need vital information, the government may deny it to them by abolishing or effectively curtailing press freedom."

The curtailment of the freedom of the press doesn't necessarily imply a dictatorship. For example: for the past several months, under the constitutionally elected regime that now rules Uruguay,

press, radio and television were suffering restrictions more strin-
gent than those imposed by the current Argentine military dictatorship. Besides, among the *de facto* governments, restrictions
could reach different levels—stronger, for instance, under General
Costa e Silva and General Stroessner than under Lieutenant General Onganía. These two circumstances indicate that the juridical
or institutional criterion is not enough to make our diagnosis concrete. Still, there is a third case to be remembered, a very special
one—the Cuban revolution. Fidel Castro explicitly explains the
limitations imposed on freedom of opinion because of the greater
significance of revolutionary needs.

Well (he confessed) what is said is true. There is a minimum of criticism. An enemy of socialism cannot write in our papers, but we don't
deny the fact and we don't proclaim a hypothetical freedom of the
press in the way you proclaim it. And you don't have such a freedom
either. Besides, I admit that in our press there is very little criticism.
I don't think that the lack of criticism is a positive fact. Criticism is
rather a useful and very positive instrument and, I believe, all of us
should learn to use it. . . . I am not going to tell you that we could
think, naively, that under the circumstances, journalism has a more
important task than to contribute to the political and revolutionary aims
of our country. Now, how are the aims to be achieved? How develop a
people with broad culture, critical powers? Which are the things con-
tributory to the building of a more complete man? All this is to be
discussed. What is not to be discussed is that the activity of the
intellectual workers must be really submitted to those aims.[2]

The Priority of the Transistor

Thirty-five per cent of all Latin Americans have never had a
single book; 40 per cent of them have never entered a library or
even a reading-room; millions of families have never had a book-
shelf in their homes, not to speak of bookcases.[3] The spoken word
is the one most employed by the mass media. "Hablando se enti-
ende la gente," it is by speaking that we understand people, we
usually say—speaking and not writing. The spoken expression is a

popular fact; the written one, an elite's media. Such is the priority of the speech over the text, of the transistor over the periodical. This fact has created a strange coupling effect between illiterate underdevelopment and popular technology. As Marshal McLuhan pointed out, the electronics world is closer to the oral community of developing countries than is the structural discipline of the printed page and mechanized industrialization.[4] Let us not over-emphasize, however, the sense of community that really exists in societies where the gap between opulent minorities and miserable masses is constantly increasing. And let us not assume that electronics necessarily favors a humanizing expression. This "new media world" is not ours, although it reaches us as a daily pro-posal. It belongs to the same world which created and commer-cialized it, and which now provides the words, the sounds, the images—and at the same time is a remote world, the source of frustration and resentment for Latin American masses.

From Graffiti to Print Media

Much more than the printed word, it is the word directly scrawled with chalk or tar on the walls and in the public facilities of our cities that reaches our people with shocking slogans. It proclaims old loyalties (Haya de la Torre, Peron, Bosch) and young revolutionary celebrities (Fidel, Che), as well as anathe-mas against the current rulers and the United States. Providing a "snack politization," this kind of direct communication, sometimes wise, sometimes very crude, works to counterpoise the sophistica-tion of the big advertising posters.

The more expensive the mass medium, the more difficult it is to use it for making public one's own opinion. A TV minute costs much more than one press centimeter. In some countries we find in the press a relatively large variety of ideological trends which enable us to express our own point of view in the corresponding context. Radio and TV broadcasts are much narrower, if they exist at all.

It is useful to check the role of the founders and current directors of the so-called "big press": ("big" is defined according to the number of pages and the space devoted to advertisement, and not necessarily according to its distribution. According to UNESCO, there were in 1962 1,154 daily newspapers, but only 10 per cent could be considered "big press.") The pattern of ownership seems to reveal that family control is more or less traditional, which makes us suspect a closed defense of the establishment. To give only a few examples: *El Comercio,* Quito, founder Carlos Mantilla 1906, director Carlos Mantilla; *Diario de Noticias,* Rio, founder Orlando Dantas 1930, director O. J. Portelas Dantas; *O Globo,* Rio, founder Irineo Marinho 1925, director Roberto Marinho; *La Nación,* Buenos Aires, founder Bartolomé Mitre 1870, director Bartolomé Mitre; *La Prensa,* Buenos Aires, founder José C. Paz 1869, director Alberto Gainza Paz; *La Mañana,* Montevideo, founder Pedro Manini Ríos 1917, editor Carlos Manini Ríos. And this list is much less than exhaustive.

But it is not only a matter of big families coupled with the big press. In much larger terms, very important limitations to the freedom of opinion in the press, with or without the big families' ownership, emerge from the strong, intimate bonds existing between mass media and big capital. Profit, of course, is the main motivation for investing capital in press, radio, cinema, television. And profit does not usually tend to inspire a critical approach to the regime that in a large measure makes it possible for the enterprise to exist in the first place (Especially is this so when those criticisms are made from the socialist point of view which, with various nuances, is the dominant position among the Latin Americans who intend to change the current situation.)

Besides, to make room for such criticism implies for the owners of the mass media a twofold risk: first in regard to the national government, which many times menaces every critical expression, and second, in regard to big business, which furnishes the main source of income—advertising. According to Eleazar Díaz Rangel

(*Pueblos subinformados,* Caracas, 1967), the daily income from advertisements in the "big press" ranges from $4,000 to $15,000. In radio and TV it is also very high and, furthermore, TV and radio stations are frequently linked to each other and with the big press, as other branches of the same tentacular enterprise.

Three-Quarters U.S.

Speaking about capital, it is easy to realize that in this area we face the strongest among all conditioning factors: American influence.

This influence has three main channels. The first is the direct American ownership of big mass media.

The second is the decisive dependence of local media on the advertising paid by American enterprises. At the last CICOP Conference Marina Bandeira put it this way:

With regard to the administrative and economic aspects of mass media, the international trusts have ample room for maneuver. And on the national, and even local level vested interests are present. On this subject Professor Jean Meynaud, a political scientist from the universities of Montreal and Paris, and a specialist in the study of pressure groups, has described the influence of giant companies on the international level. He gives as a prototype the United Fruit Company, which owns lands, a chain of radio stations, a press service, and railway and shipping facilities in the Caribbean. Another important economic aspect of mass media is publicity. The prosperity of the media is connected with the advertisement contracts obtained from the largest companies of the world.[5]

In connection with the second channel the Argentine sociologist Pablo Franco writes: "There are big American firms such as McCann-Erickson and Walter Thompson against which national firms on occasion cannot contend."[6]

The third channel deals directly with the sources of the news effectively "mediated" by the mass media. Let us take a look at a Latin American daily. What are its sources of information on the world in which we live. The agencies. Which agencies? Mainly the following five: AP, UPI, France Presse, Reuters, ANSA. None of them is Latin American. In contrast, Cuban Prensa Libre only serves a few leftist papers in Mexico, Chile and Uruguay. Interpress (which is Italian but has Latin American correspondents in our main cities and in New York and Washington) embraces more journals than Prensa Latina but has not until now succeeded in reaching the level of circulation of the big five agencies. Most of the news, consequently, comes to us translated from other languages, viewed from different frameworks, serving scales of interests other than our own. The first two agencies mentioned above are American, the third French, the fourth English, and the fifth Italian. May we expect that in spite of the poverty in sources written and directed by Latin Americans, this variety of nationalities preserves us against the danger of receiving nothing but the main world powers' views? Not at all: AP and UPI afford 75 per cent of the teletypes, while AFP only 20 per cent and Reuters and ANSA, together, 3 per cent.

Contemporary history is therefore daily presented in Latin America from an overwhelmingly American viewpoint. The world it brings corresponds to the U.S. geography of interests. This is even true of our more immediate world: Normally, we know about our Latin American neighbors, not from them or from our own correspondents, but from American agencies. Latin America then appears to the largest audiences against a *Pan*-american image—not as the *Patria Grande* she is and should become in a more intrinsic way, but as the divided, poorer part of a system of power extrinsic to her.

It is against this mass distortion of information that we must consider the problem of freedom of opinion in Latin America. The task of informing, then, must be understood as a form of judging this distortion, of influencing counter-opinion. Not necessarily because of the evil aims of those who intentionally mask their opinion—their propaganda—under the guise of news, but because there exists this deeper and more general bias. To make news of one event and not of others already implies an option, a choice— *an opinion*, that is—which accords rank to the former and refuses it to the latter. Every informed event, that is, every event in order to become news, must do so through the media of words, and words always reflect opinion, participating in the ideology and the interests of the one that writes it, even though his care for objectivity and fair play be a personal obsession. (I reject, then, the distinction between "opinion press" and "information press" subscribed to, for instance, by the *New Survey of Journalism* already cited.)

An Often-Total Accord

The Venezuelan writer Díaz Rangel proves that the tremendous scarcity of Latin American correspondents is not to be explained by the supposed poverty of these papers, since *Le Monde*, with less income and fewer pages than our papers, counts thirty correspondents. He also stresses the fact that, when there are correspondents, most of them are working in New York. The same could be said about radio reporters who, from New York or Washington, complete or merely repeat the daily news delivered by American agencies.

All this is the result, not only of the colonialist structures from which Latin America still suffers, but also of the accord, often total, between Latin American businessmen and American interests. It is very easy to observe it in reading the editorials. As a matter of fact, most of them seem to be but apologies for what is published in the wire releases.

Now, let us deal with a very serious page of our press: the comics. Again, we detect there the omnipresent North American influence. Most of the comics are directly imported from the States. Sometimes, they reflect the warmer, more attractive trends of American life: "Donald Duck," "Blondie," "Dennis the

Menace," "Mutt and Jeff," "Katzenjammer Kids." Sometimes
even the most critical: "Lil' Abner," "Peanuts." But as soon as
comics turn to "epic," their heroes appear always as invincible
Anglo-Saxons exercising policy-making in ideas and mores on sin-
ister or servile citizens of the Third World or the Socialist world:
"Terry and the Pirates," "Tarzan," "The Phantom." . . . The few
Latin American cartoonists that work on a professional level in
this field often only parody U.S. models. Sometimes, however,
they are able to use U.S. comics as tools to elaborate their own
characters, in a very communicative mood. So inspired by "Peanuts," "Mafalda" is a typical Buenos Aires creature, and the
figures Ramos draws for *Siempre* under Feiffer's inspiration, are
Mexican. There are also cartoonists who by themselves, without
any foreign dominant models, succeed in creating very local characters, such as the *Rico Tipo* staff (Buenos Aires) or the late
Julio Enrique Sucrez' comments on Uruguayan political life.

Prohibit to Prohibit

American primacy continues with no less intensity if we pass to
other media. In TV programs we face a huge avalanche of "Bat-
man," "Bonanza," "Combat," "Lucy," "Peyton Place." . . . Sometimes it arrives three or four years later, but without attempting
to be acculturated into our societies. (On the contrary, murdering
our language through the slang in which it is dubbed!) The movies lie in American distributors' hands, and they prefer, or course,
American or Western European films, while some serious Latin
American films, for example, the Brazilian *Cinema Novo*, are able
to reach only very small audiences. Northern singers dominate
in the records market even though Latin American fans usually
cannot understand a word of the English lyrics. At the same time,
an increasing number of young Latin American stars copy—even
in English—American and British models, although foreign singers of Europe and the United States try to sing their biggest hits
in Spanish.

Popular song, however, is becoming a Latin American medium through the effort of some pioneers who have rejected the old, individualistic feeling and are reacting against the injustice of the situation we live in. Charming Argentine Maria Elena Walsh satirizes the model of Yankee champions in saying "Ay qué vivos son los ejecutivos, ay qué vivos son!" ("How slick the executives are—How slick!") In the recent Third International Folk Song Festival in Rio de Janeiro, Brazilian Caetano Veloso sang "Prohibit to prohibit": "and I say no / and I say no to no / and I say prohibit to prohibit / prohibit to prohibit / prohibit to prohibit." And some military men were angry at hearing Geraldo Vandré's song which was on the verge of winning the first prize:

"Walking and singing and following the song we are all equal, alienated or not.
In the schools, on the streets, in the fields, in the houses
Walking and singing and following the song.
In the fields there is hunger on the big plantations
Along the streets are walking uncertain demonstrators
The flower still is their strongest refrain
And they believe that with flowers they will overcome the guns
There are armed soldiers, beloved or not
Almost all of them sorrowful for having weapons in their hands
In the barracks they are taught in ancient lessons
to die for the homeland and to die without reasons.

In Montevideo, an Uruguayan composer and musician disputes with the Beatles and Mary Hopkins for first rank with his song saying:

I ask the people present
if they haven't begun to think
that this land is ours, and not of the one who has more.
Breaking down the barriers, breaking down the barriers. Because the land is ours, yours and his,
Pedro and María's, Juan and José's (111)
If by my song
I disturb someone around,

I assure you he's a gringo
or a proprietor of Uruguay.

And in another song: "Where Camilo fell, a cross was born / not
of wood but of light. / They killed him when he went for a gun. /
Camilo Torres died to live. / They say that after the bullet, a
voice was heard / it was God who cried: Revolution."

The Church Becomes News

"It was God who cried: Revolution"? Let Viglietti's verse open
a last (but not least important) question: How do we appear,
we Latin American Christians, in a diagnosis of the freedom of
opinion in Latin America?

As Christians, whether journalists or not, we are all called to
cover a story that reached its climax 20 centuries ago in a distant
corner of the Roman Empire in which we find the main, definite
sense of all the chronicles we can write or read. Although its
leading character, now absent, eludes our cameras and writers,
he goes on being the Lord of all events, actually the "Man of
the Year" in 1968 as in the 1st year A.D.; in 1969, as well as when
He comes back, in His Day.

To continue writing this story doesn't mean simply to return to
the facts revealed through those more or less good reporters who
registered in writing the Good News that first of all was a spoken
word. The Lord is our contemporary. As such, he must be met
and introduced to others within the context of current history. His
cover story must be developed through many other chronicles
dealing with many other men who, in accepting or refusing him,
are both the subjects and the objects of public opinion.

I think that we still haven't written the contemporary Jesus'
cover story. We Roman Catholics go on eluding him, speaking
rather about "the Church" or the "world." If we sometimes mention the leading character, we still don't devote to Him the close-
ups. Perhaps because we get tired of the defeated, mourning

Christ, so far removed from the one of the Gospels. And that is a regrettable consequence of the fact that the Bible is not yet a popular perspective open to public opinion.

All of a sudden the Church becomes news, not only for us, but also for those who are not part of her. The daily press underlines her opinions inasmuch as they coincide with its own, sometimes glaring headlines only vaguely related with the context. For example, if we read many Latin American versions of the Pope's speeches in Bogotá, his only subject would seem to have been a negation of any kind of revolution. On the other hand, it avoids systematically or fights against those other statements of the Church that affect its interests, which may incidentally explain a rather extended silence on the CELAM's documents issued in Medellin.

The press written mainly by Christians, on the contrary, watches very carefully every word and every action of the Church and is giving her opinion on it with a freedom unforeseen five years before. *Mensaje* (Chile), *Criterio* (Argentina), *Paz e Terra* (Brazil), *Comunidad* (Paraguay), *Cristianismo y Sociedad* and *Víspera* (Uruguay, for all Latin America), are some of the magazines where this opinion can be known, beyond the daily press. Among them, the fourth comes from a Protestant movement; the third stresses an ecumenical expression which, occasionally or permanently, is also to be observed in the others.

A Unique Audience

In other mass media, the presence of the Church is neither so frequent nor so evident, excepting perhaps the radio that sometimes has special programs and at other times is organized and directed by the Church, to educate and stimulate awareness among the popular sectors. The high rate of illiterates—and functional illiterates—should call our attention to the most important role that radio should play in the preaching of the Good News.

The ever present transistor—used not only in the cities but particularly among the peasants—should rightfully, therefore, stress the importance that the spoken word had and continues to have in the life of the Church. But we still lack a tradition in sacred oratory, and besides, many existing programs sound like a mere literal translation of evangelical, pietist missions.

Transistors cannot replace pulpits, however. For he who speaks from a pulpit addresses himself to a unique audience: the community of believers, liturgically called and assembled. It is there where the priests' and pastors' voices find their actual, specific locus to form and to express an opinion which could be considered a real mass medium because it is publicly spoken, reaching sometimes huge audiences—including nonbelievers, and zealous guardians of the status quo, whose main purpose is to squelch all criticism. Some sermons have been written down by police spies mingled among the congregation. In Asunción, for example, the Ministry of the Interior warned the participants in a students' mass in which the Gospel was commented upon through a dialogue between the priest and the laymen, saying: "I cannot accept that the Church be identified as a focus of subversion."

Medellín Views

As a matter of fact, priests and laymen are searching, with renewed enthusiasm, for ways to exert their freedom of opinion on the conflicts we are experiencing inside and outside the Church. Shortly before Medellín, a letter was addressed to CELAM by hundreds of priests asking to take into account the "established violence" and the injustices Latin Americans are currently suffering. In Santiago de Chile a group of priests, laymen, and nuns occupied the Cathedral on August 11, with a threefold proposal, asking for a real evangelical spirit in the Eucharistic Congress, denouncing the "unjust social, political and economic system, which forces thousands of men to live in infra-human conditions" and protesting against "the ecclesiastical structure which appears to be compromised with the ruling system."

But the big event in 1968, namely Medellín, was enacted by CELAM in its Second General Conference. When, at the end, Latin American bishops delivered a message, the intended recipient was Latin America—not only the Latin American Church—and explicitly it was intended to express "to the public opinion" the spirit that vivified its sessions.

Medellín speaks of an opinion which is being formed at an increasingly accelerating pace among the popular classes of this continent. This opinion is presented as "a new fact: the swift and massive awareness of the situation, especially by the marginal groups, which are the more numerous." This awareness Medellín defines with a political and therefore polemical term: *"Liberation."* The Conference wants the Church to be "audaciously committed" to this process and points clearly to the two basic obstacles: the "international tensions and external neocolonialism," on the one hand, and the "tensions between the classes and internal colonialism" on the other. Hence her energetic denunciation of "the imperialism of any ideological sign being exercised in Latin America, in an indirect way and even through direct interventions." Medellín prefers the "revolutionary" type of Christian over the "conservatist" and "developmentalist." And devoting an entire report to the mass media, the Latin American episcopate makes a complex diagnosis in which stark criticism of "many of these media" is not excluded. They say:

In Latin America the mass media is one of the big contributing factors to awaken the conscience of great masses to their conditions of life, inspiring expectations and exigencies of radical changes. Although in an incipient way, they are also acting as positive agents of change through basic education, formation, and public opinion programs, and so on, many of these media are however connected with economic and political, national and foreign groups, interested in maintaining the social status quo.

Inter-American vs. Pan-American

Now, let us stress two facts that rarely appear in Latin America, but are evident inside the Roman Catholic Church.

First: the CELAM, which is the major institutional expression of Latin American Catholicism, is a Latin American, not a Pan-American institution. In this way the Church achieves an identity scarcely present in other continental bodies. Most of them, from the OAS to the Interamerican Press Association and the Inter-American Radio Association, were planned and are working at a Pan-American level; therefore they are making and expressing their opinion from a pan-American, not a Latin American, point of view. If we really want an inter-American dialogue, it would seem to me we should understand, first of all, that *inter*-American doesn't mean Pan-American, but precisely the contrary. This is true because dialogue presupposes at least two partners. As history teaches us, Pan-Americanism has worked and is working as a U.S. monologue in which the other America plays a merely dependent, silent role, as a big colony (or neo-colony, if you like), not as a free nation; as a servant, not as a partner.

In contrast, to create Latin America's structures, such as CELAM, there is implied the articulation of Latin America's voice, to form and to express in full, mature responsibility her *opinion*: To become a partner in *inter*-American relationships.

In connection with the Church, the sources of information so important to exert a real freedom of opinion are already, in good part, Latin American in their organization, in the network of their correspondents and sometimes also in the direction: *Noticias Aliadas* (Lima), *CIDOC* (Cuernavaca), *Centro de Documentación de MIEC-JECI* (Montevideo), several *I-DOC* and *Informations Catholiques Internationales* correspondents, *Carta Latinoamericana de ISAL* (an evangelical service).

The effect of these two movements will be to place the Church within the real avant-garde in comparison with other Latin American groups. At the same time this implies an actual achievement and an exciting challenge for the months to come. How will the Church, amid the limitations on freedom of opinion that Latin America is now suffering, accomplish her unique service of preaching the word of God in human words that the lay Latin American often dare not pronounce, nor yet ignore? How will she fulfill her mission as opinion-maker, taking into account simultaneously the diversity of opinion among those within and outside her fold? What word will she offer in behalf of this time of critical inter-American dialogue?

NOTES

1. George Fox Mott *et al.*, *New Survey of Journalism* (New York: Barnes and Noble, 1961). 4th revised edition, College Outline Series.

2. Lee Lockwood, *Castro's Cuba, Cuba's Fidel* (New York: Macmillan, 1967).

3. Edmundo Desnoes, "Las Armas Secretas," in *Casa de las Americas* (La Habana, Cuba: Instituto del Libro Unidad Productora, May–June 1968), no. 48, pp. 32–43.

4. *Understanding Media* (New York: McGraw-Hill, 1964).

5. Samuel Shapiro, ed., *Integration of Man and Society in Latin America* (Notre Dame: University of Notre Dame Press, 1967).

6. *La Influencia de los EE.UU. en America Latina* (Montevideo, 1967).

RELIGIOUS FREEDOM
IN LATIN AMERICA

JORGE MEJIA, S.J.

Religious freedom is the Cinderella of human rights. For a certain time it had the limelight. During, and especially after, World War II, due partly to the genocide of Jews, and partly because of the occupation of the Eastern European nations by the Russians, Catholicism and other Christian religions were suppressed. The situation has since changed.

Freedom of religion came again to the forefront of public opinion during the Second Vatican Council. It was indeed a novelty for the Roman Catholic Church, and it somehow came to be a kind of test of the true ecumenical, and even simply progressive, orientation of the Council. Thus, the Declaration on Religious Freedom was, and will remain, one of the most important achievements of the Council. As a precedent in Catholic official teaching, one could only point to the explicit statement on the same subject made by John the XXIII in his famous *Pacem in Terris.*

Since Vatican II, other rights of the human person, and of the human community, appear to have drawn the attention of those concerned with the welfare of men. These are the so-called social rights, to which most of the CICOP Conference is dedicated. One of the reasons for this is certainly the fact that the CICOP Conference is about Latin America, a place in the world where human rights could be and should be more fully respected.

There is no question about this last point. But the problem of religious freedom immediately brings to mind those social rights just mentioned. What about the right of "all men to be immune from the coercion of individuals, of social groups, or of any human power, in religious matters? No one should be forced to act against his conscience or restrained from acting according to his conscience, whether privately or publicly, whether alone or in association with others, within due limits" (Declaration on Religious Liberty). Is this right respected in Latin America? Is it important that it should be? Why? The answers to these three questions will form the framework of my contribution to the present CICOP Conference.

I

Latin America is a continent of traditional Roman Catholic religious affiliation. Its Catholicism was shaped except for a small part (important but still non-decisive, that stems from pretridentine times) in post-Tridentine molds and past-century antiliberal commitments. One could say that up to the third decade of the present century, to be a Catholic in Latin America meant to be antiliberal, and to a certain extent, also antisemitic. In this climate there was not much hope for religious freedom. In spite of the aggressive liberal orientation of many governments and constitutions during the 19th century in imitation of either the French or the United States' model, religious freedom did not always become a part of the juridical ordination of civil society. It is enough to mention the example of my own country, whose

1853 Constitution is quite liberal to the extent of allowing the diversity of religious profession in Argentine society. But the Catholic, apostolic, and Roman religion is still "maintained" (*sostenida*) by the State; the president and vice-president must be Catholics; and the government takes upon itself the duty of the evangelization of the Indians. Other juridical ordinations go still further, as the famous Colombian Concordat of 1887. It is highly interesting to see in a volume like the *Raccolta di Concordati*, published in 1919 in Rome by Angelo Mercati, the whole series of Concordats with the Latin American republics concluded during the pontificates of Pius IX or Leo XIII (sometimes even twice, as in the case of Guatemala—1852 and 1884). Almost all of them have as their first article the same declaration that the Catholic, apostolic, and Roman religion is or continues to be, the religion of the state in question "with all the rights and prerogatives which belong to it according to the Law of God and the Holy Canons." The Concordat with Ecuador (September 26, 1862) adds, in the selfsame article "the *only* religion" and goes on to say that "in consequence, no other dissident cult, nor sect damned by the Church, can be permitted in Ecuador."

Such texts, however solemn and conclusive, were not always carried out in practice. They reveal two things, first, the main theological trend of the ecclesiastical leadership of the time; and second, a certain response from part of the traditional society. Thus, the presence of Protestant churches and missions, or even of individuals from biblical societies, was regarded as disruptive of the established order and rejected. There remains to be written a long history of discrimination and persecution against Protestant missionaries which partly accounts for the present wariness of many churches and individuals about entering into any kind of dialogue, or cooperation, with the Roman Catholic Church. The same is, of course, true of the Jewish community.

The present situation is much changed, either because most of the concordats have not had a long span of life, or else because they have been superseded by the evolution of history. And one must add, of course, that the great change taking place in the Roman Catholic Church after Medellín has contributed much to the establishment of a true spirit of respect for and collaboration with the non-Roman Churches. I doubt very much that any episcopate in the continent could now stand up and ask for the end, or the limitation, of the activity of the non-Catholic missionaries. The same could be said of relations with the Jews. And I should quote in this connection the conclusions arrived at in the recent (August 1968) meeting in Bogota. Bishops and prelates indicated that they would prefer to enter into conversation with those missionaries to see what they are doing, learn their motives, and even, if possible, to arrive at a certain formula of collaboration. Some still complain about the activities of the so-called "sects," for want of a better name, which are sometimes aggressive and anti-Catholic, or proselytic. But I don't think the civil government would be asked to intervene anywhere in order to check them. This time has passed.

Does this mean that we have presently no problems at all with regard to the exercise of religious freedom in the Latin American continent? Such a statement would be very rash indeed. I will point out at least four spheres in which religious freedom is still to be worked out, or restored.

One such sphere regards the juridical ordination which in some places is still valid—although it is in the process of being left behind by public opinion—changes in the Roman Church and in society, and other factors. Where this is still a valid issue, as in Colombia, there remain reasons for saying that non-Catholic citizens can in some respects appear to be second-rate citizens. Non-Roman ministers have their passports stamped with a special stamp indicating their denomination; marriage creates special difficulties because of the necessity of dispensations for non-Catholics, and even getting buried can bring problems, cemeteries being to a certain extent religious and of course Catholic. We have here a sphere of human rights the implementation of which yet requires much effort.

Secondly, the present transformation of the continent has brought about a new and rather unexpected development in the matter of religious freedom which affects this time the Roman Catholic Church, but is indeed potentially dangerous for any church. This is the recognizable intolerance on the part of certain governments toward public interventions of the Church into anything that may seem to them to be "political." Such an opposition does not always take the form of an open or basic resistance, but it is, nonetheless, at least in its projections, incompatible with a true conception of religious liberty. An episcopate cannot simply be submitted to pressure because it promulgates the documents of Medellín, nor can priests or laymen be persecuted because they feel they must express their religious opinions about local human conditions: social, economic or political. Having said this, it is only fair to acknowledge that the dividing line can be very thin at times between voicing the legitimate concern of one's own conscience, religiously informed, and constituting political opposition, not to speak of the cases of real agitation. But this belongs to another aspect of human rights and human freedom, and it is known by Christians that persecution is part of their distinctive vocation. Only it must be suffered in the name of Christ.

Thirdly, there is Cuba, where undoubtedly practicing Catholics are discriminated against and not permitted any kind of public expression of their concern for the way things are going. Religion is limited to the cultic profession and very little more. This is a situation that ought not to be forgotten when an appraisal of the Cuban problem is in order.

To this, I will now add a fourth sphere of religious liberty which badly needs recognition and commitment. This is the area of coexistence and relations with Jews. Antisemitism is as anti-Catholic as segregationism of any kind can be.

The question then arises: Is this freedom really important to

defend in the present human plight, especially in Latin America?
Does it really matter that people have the freedom to worship
their God when they scarcely have the freedom to dispose of their
lives? Is this not a kind of cultural luxury which underdeveloped
people cannot afford? Let them *first* build their future and *then*
worship God and practice their religion.

I must say squarely that I cannot accept this position, although
it seems to be implicit at least in some recent presentations from
different quarters. My reasons are manifold, of which I shall
select only three:

Freedom is indivisible, like light or life. Either you have it or
you have it not. You cannot say: let us have this freedom, and
then avoid some other one. When one freedom is curtailed, all are
hurt. In other words, the respect for religious freedom belongs
to a conception of the dignity of man, as the Second Vatican
Council rightly pointed out (No. 2), with which all other liberties
stand or fall. It is, therefore, not only because of the "social benefit" of religion that a civic order has to acknowledge the need for
its members to worship, but because they are men, whatever
their religion may be. Then, of course, religious freedom will be
acknowledged even if it happens to be socially unproductive, as
certain religious groups can be.

To work out his destiny, man needs a motivation. In fact, this
motivation is a religious one in many people, especially the
underdeveloped people of our continent. The content of this religion may be, to a certain extent, superstitious, although this
rather rash judgment is at once submitted to a radical revision. It
may also be alienating. But the potentialities of religion for the
interpretation of human life and work in history are tremendous.
He who cuts down religious freedom may be closing one of the
wellsprings of human transformation in the continent. The proof
for this assertion was given in Medellín.

Finally, "man cannot live by bread alone." This is, to my understanding, the deepest reason for the concern about religious free-

dom. It is not, I fear, accepted, or even understood by everybody. It implies the acknowledgment of the transcendent dimension of man, without which he cannot live. I will turn to Sweden to make my point. There you have a society where there is no need, no poverty, no want, no unjust division of property. There is also religious freedom, although this has come about rather recently. But, as it exists, it is a "freedom for nothing." And the question is raised: Were this religious freedom to be suppressed, would something change deeply and radically? The question may seem invidious. It haunts my mind all the same. Because the question is: When we will have done all that is needed to make man happy and free, what will he do with his freedom? At least in a Christian view of liberation, as was expressed in Bishop Pironio's keynote speech in Medellín, man must be liberated from oppression and alienation because he has been redeemed from sin and death, of which all human miseries are consequences. So there is a transcendent side to the fight for liberation, and here is where the positive aspect of religious freedom comes in. It is certainly a freedom *from* something, but is much more a freedom *for* something. And this is the ultimate reason for being concerned at all with this kind of freedom. It finally gives man his true human stature. Let Christians not forget this lesson. Theirs is the witness and the service to this ideal of freedom.

PART FOUR

TOMORROW'S HOPE:
NEW INITIATIVES FOR
CHANGE IN THE AMERICAS:
CHALLENGES AND RISKS
IN THE LIBERATION
OF MAN

PRESENT AND FUTURE
COMMUNICATIONS AND
STRATIFICATION PROFILES IN
LATIN AMERICA

NEIL P. HURLEY, S.J.

Social stratification is a *given* of world society in terms of a *de facto* differential distribution of prestige, privilege, power, and economic opportunity. There is an entire school of social theorists who regard this fundamental phenomenon of class, caste, and status as a necessary, inevitable consequence of motivation patterns in staffing the variety of positions in any society. We know, however, that inherited social positions and lack of social mobility can result in a dysfunctional system of rewards, services, and opportunities. E. Digby Baltzell has stressed how institutionalized social inequality has come about in American life in two well-documented books: *The Philadelphia Gentleman: The Making of a National Upper Class* and *The Protestant Establishment*. In Latin America the problem of differential prestige, power, mobility, and opportunity is acute even though there has been a progressive multiplication of power bases, such as the military, unions, government corporations, student groups, technocrats, bureaucrats and the entrepreneur.[1]

215

We accept that in this hemisphere there is a clear case of "institutionalized" social stratification with dysfunctional links with kinship system and social closure in terms of upward mobility. However, unless this becomes a "mind-binding" assumption in future planning, there is strong evidence that today there exists new technological, organizational, and information influence in terms of resource-regenerating capabilities that has never existed hitherto. Professor Melvin Tumin has warned against freezing sociological theory in terms of precarious historical social arrangements.[2] Robert Bierstedt has called this "temporocentrism," the tendency to exclude from cultural consideration any item or pattern which had not already been developed.[3]

We must understand that mankind is in a state of transition between two types of societies with totally different assumptions regarding resource production and allocation. The dominant concept among planners, economists, and political rulers, from the ancient hydraulic economies down to the present free-market systems based on investments in manufacture and service industries, has been that of resource scarcity. The idea that technology is resource-regenerating is a recent one. The economist Eric Zimmerman developed the notion that resources become and are not static; Wesley, Mitchell, Buckminster Fuller, John McHale and Nigel Calder are among those who see resources as a growth process nurtured by education, research and development, and comprehensive anticipatory planning. In societies which have been the object of social science observation, stratification has tended to rest on the assumption of constant technology, and differential statuses, rewards, and opportunities have been considered natural consequences of a "conservationist attitude." This attitude is basically what strategists call a "zero-sum" game: One gains at the expense of the other. The kinship arrangements naturally gave preferential treatment to relatives in this competitive struggle for access to the limited political, social, and economic fruits of a nation's toil. The stress on marriage ties, kinsmen, *compadres, cunas* and *amigos* establishes a pattern of reciprocal obligations. This is particularly true of the upper class where there prevail sets of preferred interaction. In Latin America, kinship ties play an important role in industrial, commercial, and government activities. In Latin America there is much evidence to show that family-centredness still remains a condition of industrialization and an obstacle to dividend redistribution.[4] Since the white-collar worker is a conservative, trying to survive in the lower strata of the upper class or perhaps in the middle class, he does not agitate for change.

What we see then is the persistence of certain historical patterns of social equilibrium based on kin, functional differentiation, and a psychological attitude of resource scarcity. I wish to suggest in this paper that there is evidence that the three classical bases for social stratification will be transformed by the rapid advance in technology as a resource-regenerating process which will erode the "zero-sum" attitude of planners and decision-makers. To the extent that this occurs, the kinship preferences will play a progressively decreasing role and this, in turn, will loosen up the patterns of social mobility and economic opportunity. In other words, hierarchy, division of labor, and incentive systems of reward and status will not disappear, but the ethically undesirable and sociologically dysfunctional conjugates of social stratification as historically realized in Latin America will be acted on by technical and organizational pressures. This means a decline of factors such as the social inheritance of opportunity through blood and school ties. Even in the United States, these social status factors (rather than economic or political power factors) have created social immobility.[5] Intimate friendships, clique solidarity, association and club membership, and intermarriage have been ways of integrating, maintaining, and augmenting exclusive participation in the higher-priority levels of opportunity.[6] Granted a change in the technological and productive infrastructure of Latin American society, there will be corresponding changes in the mental maps.

Unfortunately, there is a time lag between the creation of a new physical environment and the redrawing of our mental maps. This paper wishes to redraw one mental map which, if accepted widely enough, could help relax the classic "mind-binder" of a resource-scarcity psychology and thus promote a less dysfunctional structure of social stratification.

Our example will be taken from new advances in communications technology, and our basic postulate will be that the most fruitful kind of resource regeneration is through education. Whereas physical resources are subject to the law of diminishing returns under certain conditions, the same principle of economic performance enters as a human capital. Knowledge is the basis of organization. Chester Barnard in his classic work on *The Functions of the Executive* has stressed this.[7] The notion of human capital is one that has become accepted in the contemporary literature of economics.[8] This expansion of the traditional notion of capital to include education, broadly conceived, is due largely to new, more effective and economic means of transmitting knowledge, particularly through electronic media. The exponential increase of knowledge is the result of the change in the "mindbinding" assumption that education through schoolhouses, libraries, equipment and trained personnel—all scarce resources—must be limited necessarily to a few. Man's knowledge stocks doubled in the 100,000 years of the Paleolithic Age; then they doubled again in 5,000 years in the Neolithic Age, and then doubled every thousand years until the rise of science in the late Middle Ages. Today in the era of Teilhard de Chardin's Noosphere, our capital stocks of knowledge are doubling every fifteen years.[9]

Just what the abundance of information resources implies for a change in attitude regarding the inevitability of resource scarcity and, consequently, differential access to work, education, and a higher standard of living is shown by the fact that in ten years the communications capability in the world will be doubled. This means that a revolution in mass education is possible by shaping

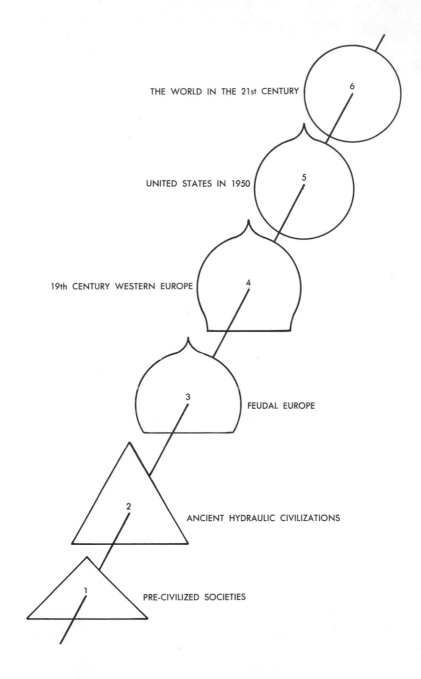

THE WORLD IN THE 21st CENTURY

UNITED STATES IN 1950

19th CENTURY WESTERN EUROPE

FEUDAL EUROPE

ANCIENT HYDRAULIC CIVILIZATIONS

PRE-CIVILIZED SOCIETIES

a world which does not yet exist, instead of the arduous, uphill, often-frustrating if not impossible task of redistributing existing resources, be they wealth, positions, or educational opportunities.

This study, far from proclaiming the disappearance of social stratification, merely suggests the possibility that hierarchical social orders (and all organized states have them) can bring rapidly into their expanding organizational structures new blood which previously did not qualify because of lack of investment in human capital. Population profiles of societies down through the ages demonstrate the effect of social stratification on increments in knowledge stocks.[10]

These diagrams show that the authority structure does not disappear, nor does the social system of classes based on income, residence, status, and peer-group relations. What changes is the profile of the society, so that more people escape misery, deprivation, and frustration. What we are saying is that there is an elevation of the axis with reference to social and economic development, as the diagram on the opposite page shows.

There seems little doubt that if we can attain a planetary social system whose contours resemble that of our sixth diagram, we will be closer to stability, order, and peace: that is, a world-wide arrangement of interdependence which Marshall McLuhan has called the "global village." Without ignoring other factors such as research and development, scientific discovery, organizational innovations, and new regional and hemispheric forms of cooperation, we wish to stress the note of hope which new media technologies bring to about 15 billion persons in the world and about 100 million Latin Americans. Tempted to revolution and social protest, these persons—the submerged two thirds of the world population—are amenable to the psychological law of human expectation which says that the degree of willingness to revolt varies inversely with the curve of benefits to be achieved for one's family.[11] This hope is implicit in the present "knowledge book" and "communications revolution."[12] Let us now make this hope explicit by showing how the dysfunctional aspects of stratification in terms of differential opportunities can be counteracted.

Relatively few persons doubt that a mass system of electronic education designed for a billion persons in the world would result in huge economies of scale. Prime Minister Indira Ghandi approved last April an All-India Direct Broadcasting Satellite Plan which some experts estimate will cost about $1.00 a student per year for 300 million Indians.[13] This figure is confirmed by an interdisciplinary study conducted by the Electronics Laboratory of Stanford University regarding satellite coverage for Indonesia and Brazil as well.[14]

In a still more recent study by the Stanford Research Institute, it was suggested: "If full geographical coverage is sought, the direct broadcast satellite system becomes the least cost mode for the population residing beyond the range of transmitters located in principal cities."[15] Two Peruvian students at Stanford University have elaborated the technical requirements for a satellite educational TV system for Latin America.[16] To blanket the hemisphere with "sight-sound" satellite-relayed signals would mean a per capita cost of five cents per year or a $50 million investment for five years to reach 200 million people in Canada, the United States, Mexico, the Caribbean and South America. When we recall that Brazil alone is doubling its 80 million inhabitants every 35 years then we can see that huge economics of scale are technically within reach. Politically, there are serious barriers to achieving these economies of scale which might educate the hemisphere for a yearly charge of five cents a person. It is—to return to our theme—the preconception of resource scarcity: that life is a "zero-sum" game. (I would remind the reader that neither he nor the author lose in any information-sharing situation such as we are now engaged in.)

We have talked of satellites. However, equally as revolutionary as satellites in both effectiveness and cost is the Electronic Video Recorder of the CBS Laboratories, a device which is eminently suited for self-pacing methods of instruction.[17] The inventor of the EVR, Mr. Peter Goldmark, foresees that to a single spool of tape there could be added animation, sound, and print techniques. In five years his special 8.75 mm. film could be as cheap as an LP record and could give an hour of sport events, movies, ballet, drama, debates, or classroom instruction. These are only two of the revolutionary electronic techniques which are available to contemporary mankind. Developed in an advanced industrial society, such information-transfer devices meet with considerable problems of entry since they compete vigorously with conventional techniques.

Three proposals suggest themselves if we wish to share with the "know-nots" of the world the growing reservoir of information being amassed. First, there must be demonstrations of new technologies in those areas where vested interests are at a minimum. In the rural areas of Asia, Africa, and Latin America, not only do technical deficits exist, but there are as well acute shortages of teachers, reading materials, and information. It would seem that, as in the case of the All-India Satellite TV Plan, such underdeveloped regions would be logical sites for experimentation. There are plans for multinational projects, especially satellite educational TV, which will be realized by the Inter-American Cultural Council of the Organization of American States.[18]

Secondly, those active in the formal educational establishment should seek to extend their influence beyond classroom walls and the confines of the campus. As Marshall McLuhan has pointed out, the traditional means of information-transfer have ceased to be oral for almost 500 years in the West. The blackboard, the notebook, and the library will always have a unique role in education, to be sure. However, electronics enables the teacher, the researcher, and the student to expand their sphere of influence. The recent student protest movements are due in no small measure to the broader horizons opened to students through communications, especially film, radio, and TV. Far from threatening educators, electronics presents a challenge to reach the great pool of uneducated, economically and effectively.

Thirdly, commercially-motivated groups in the field of communications should understand the real scope of their influence on illiterates, the poor, the young and, in general, the impressionable. They are the world's educators today, if not *de jure,* then in a very real sense, *de facto.* They are shaping souls as much as the clergy; they are forming personalities as much as parents; they are inculcating values and imparting life-style as much as teachers; they are disseminating an ideology as much as politicians and orators. The negative aspects of *concientisacion* in Latin America due to commercial communications "fallout" merits greater research.[19] The cultural agencies such as UNESCO, the foundations, the educators and churchmen must invent new ways of commercial participation in multinational programs which can serve educational, cultural, and development purposes as well as the legitimate objectives of entertainment, newscasting, and marketing.

We are entering a new world of civilization in the singular, a global society united by telecommunications arteries such as frontier-transcending satellite capable of economically transmitting sight, sound, and data to any part of the world. Psychologically speaking, there will be no social stratification because all members of the planet will be in involuntary contact with each other, providing a single "attention frame." No longer, as Robert Burns the poet said, will the tragedy of the poor consist in their poverty of desires. The poor will have towering aspirations to match those of our wealthiest families. But will they have the means to attain these newly inculcated desires? If not, violent revolution and its counterpart, military dictatorship, will ensue. This paper suggests immediate comprehensive anticipatory planning to shape the second world of communications which will exist in ten years, thus flattening out the traditional, often unjust, profiles of social stratification both within countries and among nations.[20]

NOTES

1. Richard N. Adams, *Political Power and Social Structures* (Austin: University of Texas, no. 49).

2. Melvin Tumin, "Some Principles of Stratification: A Critical Analysis," *American Sociological Review*, XVIII (August, 1953), 387–394.

3. Robert Bierstedt, "The Limitations of Anthropological Methods in Sociology," *American Journal of Sociology*, LIV (July, 1948), 22–30.

4. Adams, *op. cit.*, pp. 27–28.

5. Milton Gordon, *Social Class in American Sociology* (New York: McGraw-Hill, 1958), pp. 248 ff.

6. R. M. Mac Iver and Charles M. Page, *Society: An Introductory Analysis* (New York: Rinehart and Co., 1949).

7. Chester Barnard, *The Functions of the Executive* (Cambridge: Harvard University Press, 1962), pp. 106, 113, 175.

8. P. J. D. Wiles, "The Nation's Intellectual Investment," *Bulletin of the Oxford University Institute of Statistics (XVIII)* (August 1956), 285 ff.; Theodore Schultz, "Capital Formation by Education," *Journal of Political Economy*, LXVIII (December, 1960), 571–583; Investment in Human Capital," *American Economic Review*, LI (March, 1961); Fritz Machlup, *The Production and Distribution of Knowledge in the United States* (Princeton, N. J.: Princeton University Press, 1962) pp. 188 ff.; *Economics of Higher Education* (Washington, D. C.: Office of Education, 1962); "Investment in Human Beings," *The Journal of Political Economy* (October, 1962); Gary Becker, *Human Capital* (New York: Columbia University Press, 1964).

9. Neil P. Hurley, "The First Decade of the Noosphere," *America* (August 19, 1967), p. 172.

10. Rene Koenig (ed.), "Schichtung," *Soziologie* (Frankfurt-am-Main: Fischer Verlag, 1959), pp. 249 ff.

11. This principle is an adaptation of a similar behavioral law regarding the diffusion of innovation, namely "the gradient of potential diffusion varies directly with the cure of favorable expectations." Harold D. Lasswell, "Communication and the Mind," in S. M. Farber and R. H. L. Wilson (eds.), *Control of the Mind* (New York: McGraw-Hill, 1961), p. 253.

12. Kenneth Boulding, "The Knowledge Boom," *Challenge* (July–August, 1966), pp. 5–7; Neil Hurley, "Communications Revolution,"

Special Issue on the Year 2000 in Architectural Design (February, 1967), pp. 100–101.

13. Howard Taubman, "Mrs. Ghandi Backs All-India TV Plan," *The New York Times* (April 23, 1968).

14. *Advanced Systems for Communications and Education in National Development* (Palo Alto: Stanford University School of Engineering, June, 1967); cf. Harold Rosen, "A Satellite System for Educational Television," *Astronautics & Aeronautics* (April, 1968), pp. 58 ff.

15. *Satellite Distribution Educational TV For Developing Countries: Case of Latin America*, vol. III (Menlo Park: Stanford Research Institute, 1968), pp. 8–17.

16. Jorge Heraud and Jose Pomaloza, *Educational Television and Communications System for Latin America* (Palo Alto: Stanford University Electronic Laboratories, 1968).

17. Frederick Klein, "The Innovators," *Wall Street Journal* (May 17, 1968), p. 1; Lee Edson, "His Invention May Make You Your Own TV Producer," *Popular Mechanics* (May, 1968), pp. 88 ff.

18. *Alliance for Progress Weekly Newsletter*, vol. VI, no. 47 (November 18, 1968), p. 1.

19. Paul Lazarsfeld and Robert Merton, "Mass Communication, Popular Taste and Organized Social Action," in Wilbur Schramm (ed.), *Mass Communications* (Urbana: University of Illinois Press, 1960), pp. 470 ff.; Oscar Lewis, *Five Families* (New York: Science Editions, 1962), pp. 82–83; Wilson Dizard, *Television: A World View* (Syracuse: University Press, 1966), pp. 51–55, 133–140; Ernest Blum, "Brazil's Yankee Network," *The Nation* (March 29, 1967), pp. 678–681; "Television is the Message Down in Rio," *Business Week* (June 17, 1967), pp. 86–88; Malcolm Browne, "Television Is Opening a New World to Many Dwellers in the Slums of Buenos Aires," *The New York Times* (January 28, 1968), p. 7; Neil Hurley, "Tele-culture and the Third World," *The Commonweal* (April 19, 1968), pp. 131–133.

20. Gustavo Lagos, *International Stratification and Underdeveloped Countries* (Chapel Hill: University of North Carolina Press, 1963), pp. 246–258.

ECONOMIC INTEGRATION AND LATIN AMERICAN DEVELOPMENT

CARLOS SANZ DE SANTAMARÍA

One of my colleagues once observed that if the United States writer, Vance Packard, were doing a book on a Latin American executive, he would call it "The Disorganization Man." He meant that our peoples in generations past have spent much energy in building barriers instead of bridges between countries. The fact is, of course, that after the struggles for independence the new countries of our region had a difficult time in consolidating their boundaries and achieving their national identities and that the economic structures of our countries were based on trade with the United States and Europe rather than trade within the region itself. We can also note that factors of geography and climate have had some influence in isolating countries from each other. In fact, perhaps we can best begin our discussion by taking a very brief look at the Latin American region.

When we speak of integration in Latin America, we should understand first of all that we are talking about an area that is in no practical respect similar to the area embraced by the European Common Market.

Our region sprawls over more than 7.7 million square miles of territory.

Geographically, climatically, geologically, culturally, and ethnically the region is one of great contrasts: vast, unpopulated territories in the Amazon basin; towering mountain ranges that work strongly against physical integration within countries and between countries; expanses of desert interspersed with fertile pampas, llanos, valleys, and coastal plains; rich reserves of petroleum, iron ore, copper, and other minerals; populations of preponderantly Indian origin in some countries, others with populations of preponderantly European origin, and some with peoples of African, Middle Eastern, and Asian ancestry.

We have sharp contrasts in the degree to which agricultural and other natural resources have been developed—contrasts in the size of countries. Barbados, the newest and smallest member-nation of the Organization of American States has an area of less than 200 square miles, while Brazil is larger than the United States. We have great differences in per capita income from country to country and within countries.

But we also find similarities: economic structures that have long been based primarily on the production for export of a few agricultural or mineral products; low per capita output and productivity and hence low income for the masses of the people; widespread lack of education and poor conditions of housing and health; a relatively high rate of population growth and a steady migration from rural areas to a few urban centers that are already hard pressed to create employment opportunities and to provide essential social services.

Since 1959, when the member nations of the OAS subscribed to the Charter of Punta del Este and set in motion the Alliance for Progress, economic integration on the national level and on the regional level has been a major goal, along with modernization of industry and agriculture; tax, agrarian, and other kinds of reform; improvement of Latin America's terms of international trade; expansion of education, health, and housing services. And in 1967, when the presidents of the OAS nations met in Punta del Este, Uruguay, they gave primary emphasis to a series of agreements to promote integration with the aim of bringing a Latin American Common Market into being by 1985.

National Integration

The way that our economies developed over the past century gave us a few highly developed urban centers and left vast areas little developed. For example, a former member of CIAP from Brazil, Celso Furtado, made a study of his country's industrial development. He found that in the 30-year period from 1920 to 1950, São Paulo's share of Brazil's industrial workers rose from 29 to 39 per cent while that of the depressed Northeast declined from 27 to 17 per cent. In recent years, Brazil has given a very high priority to development in the Northeast, with some very encouraging results, but this has not prevented still further growth in the traditional centers of São Paulo and Rio de Janeiro. Even more recently, the Government of Brazil has been offering attractive incentives for development in the Amazon region, also with encouraging results.

In other countries various kinds of steps have been taken to promote national integration, for example: the great programs of irrigation and transportation development that Mexico has been carrying out in its northwest region; the programs of road building that have opened up new areas for development in Peru; broad-scale agrarian reform programs in Colombia and Venezuela.

Hoping to contribute to the process of national integration, CIAP has drawn up a national market strategy. It takes account of differing needs and conditions in each country, but in general it suggests programs to improve land tenure (a basic problem), to increase agricultural productivity, to improve marketing of farm products in urban areas, to produce manufactures of high utility in rural areas at the lowest possible cost, to develop credit structures for rural consumers, and to undertake new initiatives in the development of export products.

While some countries have been carrying out this strategy, at least in part, there is still a vast need for cooperative action by governments and the private sector.

Regional Integration

I need not go into great detail, I am sure, about the history of regional integration movements in Latin America. We now have four such entities: The Latin American Free Trade Association, composed of Mexico and the 10 OAS member nations of South America: the Central American Common Market, composed of the five Central American republics; the relatively new Andean Group, composed of six LAFTA members, Bolivia, Chile, Colombia, Ecuador, Peru and Venezuela, which are working to create a subregional movement; and the relatively new Caribbean Free Trade Association (CARIFTA), which includes two OAS member states, Barbados and Trinidad and Tobago, and three non-member nations, Antigua, Guyana, and Jamaica.

The regional integration movements are striving to liberalize trade, to work out agreements on industrial complementation, to carry out multinational projects, to establish systems for the settlement of trade balances, and to meet other needs and wants.

The LAFTA treaty provides for negotiation of tariff concessions on a product by product basis and also for the negotiation every three years of a 25 per cent reduction on tariffs on all products traded within the region. The second 25 per cent reduction was the subject of negotiations in 1967 and 1968 but no agreement was reached. This does not mean that the LAFTA countries have given up on integration; it is simply a reflection of how difficult the integration process is for so diverse and far-flung a group

of countries. LAFTA has comparative industrial giants such as
Argentina, Brazil, and Mexico; countries of intermediate development such as Chile, Colombia, and Venezuela; and relatively less
developed countries such as Bolivia and Paraguay. LAFTA has
continued to be very active. There were a substantial number of
tariff concessions negotiated last year on individual products; the
total number of concessions agreed to since 1961 runs to 10,000.
The countries have begun to work out a schedule for a common
external tariff. They adopted their fifth industrial complementation agreement last year, covering certain chemical products.
They had their first meeting with the Central American Common
Market to discuss convergence of the two movements, as called
for by the meeting of the presidents in 1967.

The Central American Common Market has made impressive
progress. Tariffs have been eliminated on 98 per cent of the trade
within the region. In the seven years since the Central American
movement began, trade within the region has increased nearly
sevenfold. Central America now has a common external tariff covering about 82 per cent of its imports from the rest of the world.

The countries of the Andean Subregional Group have been
busy during the past year establishing the basic framework for
their promising movement. The Andean Group has signed its first
agreement, covering the petrochemicals industry, and it has been
approved by LAFTA.

In the field of multinational projects, a number of important
developments have occurred. Work is going forward on an Inter-American telecommunications network. The five nations of
the River Plate Basin—Argentina, Bolivia, Brazil, Paraguay and
Uruguay—have established an intergovernmental coordinating
committee. In cooperation with this group, the Inter-American
Development Bank is working on a number of feasibility studies
and the Organization of American States is conducting natural
resources and hydrologic surveys in the River Plate area. Last
July, CIAP and the Central American Economic Council jointly

sponsored a meeting on the financial implications of Central American economic integration. As a result of that meeting international financing agencies agreed to work with regional institutions on a number of major multinational projects, including transportation, telecommunications, and river and harbor development. The Andean Group has approved statutes of a new Andean Development Corporation which will undertake certain types of multinational projects, and neighboring countries of the group are working on programs for joint action in power, highway and telecommunications development.

There is a great deal of activity in regional integration, but the process is difficult and slow, partly because of internal problems, partly because of factors beyond the control of the countries.

One point deserves emphasis. Economic integration, like development in the broadest sense, is not an event but a process. The failure of a particular group of governments to agree on a particular aspect of integration at a particular moment may well be regrettable, because it means that the process will go more slowly. But it does not mean the weakening of the process as long as discussion and dialogue continue. I would say that *dialogue is one of the most powerful and important elements in the whole integration process*, and I am encouraged that it continues throughout the Latin American region.

There is full agreement among governments that the integration process must move forward. The question is, how fast? Governments, industrial leaders, and workers know that integration will require some major adjustments. Industrialists will need assurances of financial assistance; workers, of retraining and relocation assistance. The countries concerned have been carrying on studies and holding meetings to consider these questions; and CIAP, along with the Inter-American Bank and other regional entities, have also helped, always in accord with the respective countries' desires and instructions. But we do not have full answers to all the questions.

Even without all the answers, however, integration would probably be somewhat easier if certain external problems could be solved. Our economists have calculated that if our countries could achieve a sustained rate of economic growth of six per cent a year, the process of integration could move along fairly evenly. That does not mean that there would be no hitches; when you are talking about a region composed of more than a score of nations and an aggregate population of 250 million that is increasing year by year, you have to expect many kinds of crises, somewhere, most of the time. But there are two factors that militate against the ability of our countries to achieve a sustained economic growth rate of six per cent or more. One factor is the hardening of terms of development financing from international agencies and industrialized countries. In recent years, the United States Congress has been steadily reducing the volume of long-term financing provided through the Agency for International Development. In his budget message in January 1969 President Johnson asked for a substantial increase in development loan funds. We of CIAP hope that President Nixon supports the request. It is one that CICOP could also well support because the Latin American countries will not be able to service loans at higher and higher rates of interest—seven and eight per cent. In other words they will be unable to finance urgently needed programs of education, health, and housing in addition to highways, power, and other infrastructure investments. The International Bank for Reconstruction and Development has also had some difficulty in increasing its funds for long-term, low-interest loans; the efforts of President McNamara in recent months give us hope that that institution will be able to increase its "soft loan" resources.

The second factor impeding Latin American development and the integration process is the problem of the unfavorable terms of international trade that face our countries. Latin America's share of the world trade has been declining for two decades. Before and after World War II, Latin America shipped 10 per

cent of world exports. Now, with a much larger population to support, our share of world exports is barely six per cent. Our traditional agricultural and mineral exports will continue for some
time to be our principal earners of foreign exchange. All of our
countries are working to develop new products for export and a
new Inter-American Export Promotion Center is beginning operations in Bogota. But the development of new exports takes time.
Furthermore, we find strong efforts being made in the United
States to erect barriers against the kinds of products we can now
export and that we should be able to export in the coming years.
Our exports are also subject to various types of discriminatory
treatment in Europe so that our access to another major market
of the world is limited. Latin America has supported the idea that
the industrialized countries could offer generalized, temporary,
non-discriminatory, non-reciprocal preferences for manufactures
and semimanufactures from developing countries and this is still
under consideration in UNCTAD.

While we are on the subject of world trade, I might mention
that it seems to me that the future growth of the economies of
the industrialized countries will come largely as a result of efforts
to upgrade the skills of labor and the use of advanced technology.
This should make it possible for the developing countries to
export not only agricultural and other primary products but also
manufactures and semimanufactures of many kinds that do not
require the very high technical level of labor skills called for by
the so-called post-industrial era. From this pattern of the labor
distribution throughout the world should come benefits for both
the industrialized and the developing countries.

Now, just a few words by way of summary. National and
regional integration are major goals of the Latin American countries. Integration was the principal topic of the agreements
reached at the meeting of presidents in 1967 and it is a major
point in the new Charter of the OAS which should come into
force this year. Activities designed to advance integration are

going forward within countries and on regional and subregional levels. Our aim should be to improve the conditions of international trade and external financing so that Latin America by its own efforts can accelerate its development and its national and regional integration. This is in the interest of the United States for at least two very good reasons: first, a rapidly developing, better integrated Latin American region should provide the United Stated with an increasingly large market; second, a prospering Latin America will be a powerful partner for peace in the world, and peace, above all, is important to the continued security and prosperity of the United States.

HOPE: MAN'S POTENTIAL
FOR RESPONSIBLE FREEDOM

GLENN SMILEY

Hope is the disquieting difference between what is and what is not yet.

Hope tends toward the future to fulfill the insufficiency of the present.

Hope stresses the dynamism of being over against any static conception.

. . . . . *excerpts from Karl Lenkersdorf's address, "Signs of Hope"*

But what of the millions without hope?

Without the power to change the circumstances, then hope is dead except for that vague spiritual exercise expressed by the Psalmist when he talks in terms of "hoping in God and waiting patiently for Him." In modern times this philosophy is often interpreted as "suffer quietly and with resignation, for your reward will be greater in Heaven." This is a kind of hope, but of little value when children are already starving.

We should have learned by now that revolution does not arise out of intolerable circumstances. For the majority of Latin America the situation of the poor has been intolerable for all of the memory of living man—and his father before him, and his father before him. Nevertheless, all of the countries remain with unfinished revolutions: with the rich getting richer and the poor getting poorer. Studies in revolution would seem to indicate that intolerable circumstances do not breed revolutions of any sort, much less authentic revolution. Apparently it is only when things become suddenly worse that men are driven by their desperation to revolt. This sudden reminder of how things were better creates bitterness and then rebellion. But even this rebellion is not without hope. Is it not better that men should rebel than supinely to acquiesce to every known evil? And as in other parts of the world, so in Latin America, there has been rebellion—frequently and at great cost. Some rebel from the madness of despair and others from a type of hope. This hope arises from a fairly well known fact: that man for the first time in history is capable of feeding himself, thereby making starvation a cruel mockery for those who cannot eat.

Precisely because "hope tends towards the future to fulfill the insufficiency of the present," and precisely because the sister of hope is frustration, or the knowledge of alternatives, it would seem that ours is a promising age in history in which the possibility of change is very great.

I would like to posit four points concerning hope and change, followed by two reminders to keep us within the realm of reality.

1. Hope can awaken or conscienticise.
2. Hope can create the will to resist which is really but another definition of conscientization.
3. Hope can activate and set in motion.
4. Hope as awakened resistance set in motion can transform the individual and the situation, making for more dignity and humanity.

These are all conditionals, conditioned upon action—not just any action, but right action. One hears much talk about how hard it is to conscienticize the poor, and it must be so. Possibly one of the reasons is that we have tried to conscienticize by words and not by a holy example of dedicated action. Being without a method of our own, and mindful of the futility of violence, we have too often sounded an uncertain note in seeking to rally the poor. In the meantime, since "hope long deferred maketh the heart sick" it is understandable that the Marxist would say, "You could not expect me to trust a priest." And in passing, it would seem that the time is long overdue for North Americans to question themselves as to how their attitudes and practices have helped to defer the hopes of the poor in Latin America. At any rate—hope is the conscienticizer, the motivator, and the activator offering the people some alternative to the bitterness and despair of hopelessness.

Certain events have conspired to make it appear that we have been given a second chance—if God has granted us the gift of time.

"Hope stresses the dynamism of being over against any static conception" says Karl Lenkersdorf. Latin America cannot be called a static society. There is a movement all across the pattern of society. Students, by virtue of the economics of the situation, are largely rich or middle class, but many of them are not now committed to the ways of the privileged; others in smaller numbers have chosen to fight in the hills or they have dedicated themselves to the service of the poor in the barrios. Intellectuals increasingly object to the paternalism of the ruling elites and of foreigners, primarily the United States. Labor unions are developing their own plans for the integration and development of Latin America, plans that are at odds with the plans from the North. They seek Latin American solutions to Latin American problems. They seek to free their lands from imperialism of whatever stripe, and they seek an economic system that is neither capitalism nor communism. The vast winds of change sweeping the Church throughout the world are in some way magnified in Latin America as clergy and laity seek greater relevance in a world gone astray. These movements within the society, painful as they are, nevertheless represent movements in which there is hope. To remain unchanged in the sort of world in which we live is to crucify Christ afresh every day of our lives.

Most of all, and probably most hopeful of all, is the movement of the poor. In one of the greatest migrations in history, the people move from the rural sections to sit in silent, sullen protest around the major cities. This increasing tide of urban poor cannot be ignored by the Church nor by the dominant groups in society, for they do indeed represent a threat to the establishment and its stability. From a 35 per cent urban population in 1950, the figures for Latin America now approach an incredible 55 per cent. With at least a small degree of conscientization, these millions have moved from boredom and irritation of life in the country to the barrios encircling the cities, for that is where the action is. Squatting there by their millions, literally looking in the windows of relative affluence, they cannot accept things remaining always as they are. Someone will lead, or attempt to lead, these people out of their slavery into the promised land of relative plenty and technological gadgetry. They can see it, they want it, and the very fact that they are locked out merely increases their frustration, and they may well take it in time. This movement of the poor is a response to hope, notwithstanding all of the misery that is involved. The very question of who identifies with and attempts to lead these masses may decide for them and for us whether the future is one of hope or hopelessness.

Furthermore, it seems to me that there is hope because the centuries-old reliance upon violence as a means of achieving authentic social change has been seriously called into question for a growing number by the events of the last few years. Not long ago there was great expectation among many Latin Americans that *La Revolución* could be brought about by violence. It had been true in the past in some parts of the world—why not now and here? Some had their doubts due to the fact that revolution remained unfinished in spite of the losses in men and material. There were reasons for many of these failures, it is argued, such as foreign intervention (mostly on the part of the U.S., we must admit). But in a world of the superpowers the one constant factor in the face of authentic social change is the possibility, even probability, of intervention: armed or otherwise.

At any rate, guerrilla groups were fighting in the hills of half a dozen countries, some aided by foreigners, both Cuban and North American. It is true that a few people complained of the "el error de Fidel" in assuming that every Latin American country was the same, but few would actually criticize the Cuban Revolution, which was a living and breathing example of a successful revolt against the imperialism of the United States.

But with the death of "Pobre Che" in Bolivia, something began to happen among the people that I came to know. Even the most outspoken defenders of violence began to admit that the possibility of successful violent revolution was remote at the present time. The men fighting in the hills were often forgotten, and sometimes betrayed by the people they sought to help. And along with the death of Che was another and more surprising event— the assassination of Dr. Martin Luther King in faraway Memphis, Tennessee.

My first 1968 visit to Latin America was 11 days after the assassination of Dr. King. Because I had worked intimately with him in the early years of the non-violent movement in the South, and because I was working for him in Washington, D.C. at the time of his death, I went to Caracas filled with my own grief and sense of loss. I was completely unprepared for what I found. Three men were talked about more than others in the circles in which I moved—Camilo Torres, Che Guevara, and Martin Luther King. Caracas papers were still filled with news about King's assassination, his picture occupied the cover of almost all magazines, (even that of a "nudie" magazine that in addition gave six pages to a straight article with pictures of this man). *El Nacional,* the leading daily, gave pages to the teachings of Dr. King. In subsequent trips to the Dominican Republic and most of South America the reaction was the same. Students held huge memorial services, and even governments stopped their work to pay tribute to this beloved leader in North America. Some came to understand that he was really "revolucionario" as a result of the publicity in the press and on radio and TV.

The intensity of this interest in Dr. King's work spurred my own hope for a non-violent movement in Latin America. I would be far from honest if I did not indicate that the prospects were, and remain, bleak indeed, viewed with only the natural eye, and without that hope founded in Christ. Non-violence has little place in the minds of the average Latin American, who (if he has heard of it) looks upon it as an admonition to "be good" and not rock the boat. He sees no history and no philosophy of non-violence as compared to the well developed history and experience of violence. Non-violence has practically no literature in Spanish or Portuguese, and what it has is largely pietistic and other-worldly. Possibly what is even worse is that some who have taken the greatest interest in non-violence look upon it as phase one in a process in which phase two is violence. Nevertheless, I recognized hope in the lively curiosity about this method of warfare that had at one time given promise of creating a true revolution in the United States.

There has even been some small experimentation in non-violence in Latin America, though much of it has been without training and without philosophical base. Often, confronted by the institutionalized violence of this system, it has been beaten down and the experimenters have been forced to flee in panic. Sometimes the non-violent march or demonstration has become violent in the face of provocation.

Moreover, in the schools of non-violence in which I have participated, students and workers have indicated that they tried non-violence and that it did not work, because of the violence of the police or army. As an example, in at least two Latin American cities students have moved their classes 'into the streets, and seated themselves with the professor at the head of the class. The police reaction was to line up four squad cars and bear down upon the students at a high rate of speed. Under these circumstances the students fled, and well they might, for upon investigation it appears that there had been no preparation for the project, no training, no contact with government or police, and no effort to interpret their project to the general public. Having violated all of the rules of non-violent warfare, these students could hardly claim that this was a defeat for non-violence. Non-violence requires more than to say, "Here now, we shall have a non-violent demonstration next Sunday."

Demonstrations and marches are not programs in themselves. In fact, their primary purpose is twofold: they are a means of communication with a larger public, and they are a means of training for the participants. In the beginning stages, the latter looms much more importantly than the former. And even this must be preceded by training both of mind and body. In the schools of non-violence in Latin America, as in the United States, we must use the socio-drama, or role-playing, as a training technique. In Mexico we prepared a confrontation between "students" and "police." Priests and pastors were assigned the roles of the "police." Students played "priests," while everybody left were "students." Each group talked over their reactions, and the "students" marched against the "police." In the first encounter the police fell upon these students with such vigor that I had to pull the combatants apart to keep them from doing each other physical harm. In subsequent encounters the student groups tried to develop approaches that would avoid suffering and allow non-violence to "mature," which in fact means stalling for time while sympathy is developing.

Then comes planning for specific projects. Let me describe one of the schools to illustrate my point. (It is really irrelevant to report that this project has not yet been carried out.) In a certain barrio of a large city the poor are without water except between 3 and 4 a.m., and then only from certain spigots located among the hovels of the 10,000 people living there. This barrio, like many of the poor, is unconscienticized, and movement has been impossible in the past.

What could be done under these circumstances to bring dignity and a sense of expectancy to the people? Get the people into the streets? Create a confrontation with the established violence of the state? We didn't think so, and the people seemed to agree with us. Instead we began to think of small projects that would train a few people and create a sense of movement that would lead more and more to believe that they could in some measure control their own destiny. In other words, a movement that would enlist support at the level of the barrio's willingness to participate, as well as make an appeal to the community at large.

PROJECT NO. 1

This was an endeavor that involved only one woman, her child—an infant—and five or six nuns in the school. This woman was to go with her baby to the municipal building, in front of which there was a fountain. With the sisters around her she would proceed to bathe her baby in the fountain. It was such a simple act, but it was agreed that this would create curiosity, attract a crowd, and make a small incident. Since it would be slightly and harmlessly illegal, it might even bring about a small confrontation with the police. At this point the sisters would enter the scene to interpret this symbolic act of bathing the baby in the fountain. This mother is from a poor barrio. Where else is there to bathe the baby? There is no water in the barrio except under the conditions mentioned above. And so on.

PROJECT No. 2

The water company is privately owned, although it receives
government assistance and cooperation. Therefore, the people
organized a "haunting." (These have been used very effectively
in India.) Shifts of five people, working three hours per shift,
were to be organized to visit the manager of the water company.
Each person would carry in his hand an empty water pail to sym-
bolize the absence of water in the barrio. If the men refused their
request for a water system, or refused to see them, they would
"haunt" him, shadowing him wherever he went, with their empty
pails. If he went to lunch they would be there. If he went home
they would be there. Since project #2 would no doubt be attended by a good bit of publicity, it is possible that it would
create quite a stir both in the barrio and in the city as a whole.

PROJECT No. 3

Building gradually, and giving non-violent methods a chance
to mature through training, a larger group of from 500–1,000
people would eventually be organized to march, each with a
symbolic empty pail, back and forth through the rich barrios of
the city. They would stop occasionally in a particular barrio to call
upon each house and explain the plight of their own barrio.

Useless? Infantile? Attacking only the symptoms? Perhaps, but
in the meantime something would be happening to the people in
the poor barrio, and hopefully to the people in the rich barrios as
well. There is moral power in truth and love, and it is not loving
to allow the rich to continue in ignorance of the suffering of the
poor. Instead of permitting the rich to rest gently on their consciences, the poor would be attacking the rich by goading their
consciences. (A method twice blessed), said Gandhi, "Blessing
both him who uses it and him against whom it is used." In other
such projects in India and in the United States, freshly conscien-
ticized people have deserted the ranks of the privileged and

joined in the suffering of the non-violent people. Because one of the first principles of non-violence is to keep one's demands simple and uncomplicated, such a project described has every promise of success.

The non-violence I mentioned is not vapid and flabby, but vigorous and militant, and does not fear the realities, "resistance" and "power." True, non-violence refrains from violence in the sense of "hurt," but it looks upon itself as coercive good will. It does not acquiesce in evil, for to do so is neither love of self nor of enemy. Non-violence could become that alternative weaponry system that could effect changes so badly needed, for it is a method in keeping with the highest aspirations of man and consonant with true religion.

In a South American country restive under the heels of dictatorship a group was discussing the age-old question: "What can we do?" The discussion revolved around a number of suggestions, among them being the possibility of a house strike, in which working people would refuse to leave their houses for a period of time. "How long could the dictator hold on in the face of a house strike?" The answer that they gave me after an hour of discussion was: "In six days we could bring him down." Such a strike would be, or at least could be, within the tradition of non-violence, and the fact that the soldiery might come and drag the people out of their homes in some instances would not invalidate the non-violent nature of the strike. Only the strikers can brake the logic of their violence. It should be understood that even as violence has its prize, so does non-violence. But non-violent suffering is redemptive in nature. Only non-violence has the capacity to convert, to influence, and eventually to conquer in such a way as to keep the fabric of the community intact. And eventually love is capable of conquering, although it seeks to conquer the evil and not the evil-doer.

Another reason for hope is the fact that there is new spirit of adventure which influences the loyalty of both clergy and laity to the demands of the Good News. Men and women who have found it difficult to accept the moral implication of violence, have until recently felt powerless in a world of violence. To repeat, not having a method of our own, we feel at the mercy of the system. And with a penitent heart, I guess it must be admitted that we have been only half-hearted in our condemnation of violence when it has been used by the state to protect our interests—even when it was aimed at the poor. In the invasion barrio of Santo Domingo Savio in Medillin, Padre Gabriel Diaz is waging a stout battle for its 7,000 people. The city provides no schooling for the children, no security for the residents, and not even electricity for the houses. At the same time in the plaza in front of the new cathedral a beautifully illumined fountain has been erected at a cost estimated at $130,000. Until plans were made recently for *La Batalla de las Velas* (in which the people of the barrio would march to the fountain, each with a candle in his hand), no one had sought to protest either the erection of the fountain, nor the lack of electricity in the barrios. It may be a coincidence, but it is significant that two days after the "battle of the candles" was announced, the papers carried a statement from the government that electricity would be provided to the barrios. But the people will not rest until promises have been transformed into light poles, wires, and light for the people of Santo Domingo. Will it happen? Who knows? But a little hope arises when people begin to think in terms of their own social good.

If there is hope for America, part of that hope lies in a change of attitude within the United States. At this point I find a glimmer of hope in the fact of a small but rising tide of opinion in the U.S. opposing the adventurist approach of our country in the other half of the hemisphere.

More people are agreeing that there must be change—radical, authentic change. A larger number are willing to accept the consequences of such change even though it may mean loss of trade and even face. In our arrogance it may be very hard to accept expropriation without compensation, "Latin America for Latin Americans," and distinctly Latin American solutions to Latin American problems, but in some instances these will be the price we pay for justice and equality.

In the final analysis, in the face of the imponderables hanging over Latin America and this other half of the hemisphere, it is hard to find hope unless one has that larger conception of the will of God for His children, and of His power, freely extended but so seldom accepted by the church. We have lain too long with the State, and too often our power has been reflected by the State. Our methods have too often been those of the State, and seldom have we really attempted to find a methodology of our own. Could it be that in this day we are being called to militant, aggressive non-violence, which Gandhi defined as a combination of Love and Truth? He also said, "non-violence without the spirit of non-violence is a dangerous thing." Living this kind of life, he accepted and died a martyr's death, assassinated by one of his own religionists. Martin Luther King died by the bullet of an assassin. Can we in the church ask for less when we call into the court of conscience the dearest possessions of modern life—profit and power? But if we can bring ourselves to this point, if we can accept our destiny as unworthy sharers in the fellowship of His suffering and His Cross—then power will come to the church.

Ignazio Silone grasped this truth more clearly than some in his novel *Bread and Wine*. In that familiar section, a girl goes to a would-be priest to ask him why it was that when someone said something bad about the Dictator his police would be sent into the village to kill a dozen or a hundred innocent people? The priest, groping for an answer said, "I think that it is because in the land of unanimity it is dangerous for even one man to say 'No'." "And what if the man who says 'No' is a sick man?" asked the girl. "I think it would be the same," answered the priest. "And what if he is a good man who was lying in his bed one night thinking about these things? Suddenly he can stand it no longer, so he rushes out into the street to write 'No' on the wall, after which he jumps back in bed? What then?" "It would still be the same," insisted the priest. And the girl, with tears in her eyes, whispers, "And what if they should kill him? What then?" Silone goes on to say, "The priest, suddenly made glad, replied to the girl, 'It would always be the same for it is specially dangerous to kill a good man, for even the corpse might continue to say "No" with an insistency that only certain corpses are able to achieve. And how do you silence a corpse?' "

It has been so, with Socrates, the saints, Martin Luther King and more than all others, in case of our Lord. May it not be repeated in our day? If other men gird their loins to go out to do battle with principalities and powers, armed only with the weapons of the spirit—which are the weapons of non-violence—are we able in humbleness and hope, although in fear and trembling, to begin that long road that by way of Memphis and even the Cross might lead to the City of God? How long, O Lord, how long?

MAN IN QUEST OF
LIBERATION IN COMMUNITY

BERNARD HÄRING, C.Ss.R.

The greatest liberating power is that of love: love in its fullness as social and interpersonal relationships, love growing in articulation with justice, wisdom, valor, and temperance. Man imprisoned in his own ego remains underdeveloped, a slave to narrowness and pettiness. The human person finds himself in an encounter with the Thou, in genuine human relationships anticipating and fostering the freedom of all.

Love itself is threatened by the desire to dominate the other person. Love in freedom is possible only in mutual respect, in mutual giving and receiving on all human levels.

In its very first stages, the Bible describes sin as disregard for God—loss of the communion of love with God—and disregard for the other person. The immediate result of sin is domination of man over woman.

Historically, the disturbed balance of liberty between man and woman seems to have moved first in the direction of matriarchy.

When woman invented horticulture, she often took advantage of her position and tried to possess man (the husband, the children) as she possessed the garden and cottage. Of course, she took care of man as she took care of herbs and trees. She "ate of the fruit" of domination and thus she contaminated man, who was at least as eager as woman to take advantage of his economic and cultural adventures. He began to exert his authority through organized hunting in the totem cultures, and in the more highly organized agriculture once man had domesticated the animals. "Your husband will lord it over you" (Gen. 3:16).

Wherever the relationships between husband and wife are disturbed by a system of inequality and domination, there the relationship between parents and children will also be disturbed. In such circumstances, education consists more in training for obedience than in training for the good use of freedom. Every system of domination manifests immaturity—a lack of capacity to love in mutual respect; such a system keeps others in immaturity.

Paternalism as Alienation

A family system in which domination is accepted almost as a "natural right" (cf *Casti Connubii!*) taints all other social relationships. A male-centered society can neither truly appreciate nor fully realize human respect and freedom. There is an inherent interdependence between the family structure and all other social relationships and structures.

Where a strong patriarchy is a well-established and unquestionably-accepted family pattern, the whole human person will reflect the same basic structure. It is then that God appears as the worst of situations; the image of God intimidates man (scrupulosity) when the father as authority-figure intimidates the wife and the children. In the best of situations, where the forceful and unquestioned father-authority grants a certain security, religiosity and morality, the authority will focus chiefly on security and on the maintenance of the status quo.

The great proprietors in many Latin American societies—in the modern agricultural and industrial economy—are characterized by the same brand of paternalism as corresponds to the male-centered, strongly patriarchal family structure. The paternalist expects gratitude and submission since he fulfills the needs of the people. He is convinced that he knows what is best for those under his control. He promises security and defends the status quo for security's sake. The whole system, of course, is based on the conviction that the paternalistic mode of domination is good, but it soon degenerates into a brutal exploitation marked by no evident concern for those exploited.

Patriarchy, Paternalism, Centralism and Individualism

A strongly developed patriarchy which spreads paternalism over the cultural, economic and social life will necessarily exert influence in the direction of centralism. A despotic patriarchy overemphasizes the dependent relationship of all family members to the head of the family. The overtone is that of obedience to the one who issues all orders. The other intrafamily relationships of necessity remain in the embryonic stage of development, or also atrophy. The paternalist in the cultural and socio-economic realm fails to encourage the well developed forms of sharing and mutual responsibility, save for those forms promoting the observance of existing regulations or his own precepts. It follows that under a paternalistic regime a certain individualism develops naturally. Individualistic behavior will be ever-better sustained by a system of strict laws and controls.

Paternalism and centralism readily recognize that preservation of the existing order and power will be easier if small groups and individuals seek their own security and advantages independently, without association with others, without subsidiarity, and in total dependence on the protecting authority.

The typical paternalist, for example, has always been opposed to any form of trade or labor union.

Another example would be the centralism of the Latin Church
which, for centuries, reflected the prevailing centralism of the
larger civil society. The bishop in one diocese had little if any
direct relationship with other bishops and dioceses. Security
emanated from the central government. The same held true concerning the relationship of parish to diocese, with a consequent
marked group egotism at both levels, a group egotism corresponding closely to the basic individualism. Legalism is the accepted
media of any such system, which promotes this kind of individualism while protecting the status quo through centralism.

Interaction of Social Structure and the Community of Faith

Christ enriches the world with the liberating power of love that
is humble. This love is devoid of all types of domineering, and the
exercise of authority is characterized by service, the fostering of
maturity, initiative, and brotherhood. "In the world kings lord it
over their subjects; and those in authority are called their country's 'Benefactors.' Not so with you; on the contrary, the highest
among you must bear himself like the youngest, the chief of you
like a servant. . . . Yet here am I among you like a servant" (Luke
22:25–27). Christ does not want a bare system of external rules
and blind obedience; He wants mature Christians who act with
deep insight and in a spirit of solidarity. "I call you servants no
longer; a servant does not know what his master is about. I have
called you friends because I disclosed to you everything I have
heard from my Father" (John 15:15).

Since that time, the gospel of redeeming love and the new
concept and form of authority in the community of the disciples
of Christ is a ferment in the society. The Church as a social institution is also exposed to the "old leaven" of a patriarchal, paternalistic, and domineering society. As the Church of the Word
Incarnate, she must somehow adjust herself and her structures to
the existing society, guarding herself always against the danger
of contagion. Her being in the world must be dynamic and pro-

phetic, forever questioning the status quo and striving ever towards conversion on all levels. Should the Church be self-complacent and cling rigidly to inherited structures, she would dangerously alienate herself from her mission. The danger is all the greater if she gets entangled in "sacred alliances" with the dominating powers of paternalism and dictatorship whose chief concern is the maintenance of an unjust status quo. Especially at a time when our whole society and culture is undergoing a transformation, it becomes more and more unjust for any social unit to cling to the status quo.

Only to the extent that the Church gratefully and humbly accepts the prophetic context and protests against outmoded and immobile structures and attitudes, can she be the leaven for a humanity longing for greater freedom. The Church must herself yearn for the liberty of the sons and daughters of God in the totality of her life. To think that the freedom of God's children can exist in man's innermost being, without committing itself to the whole of man's life, is already a sign of alienation, of being enslaved in an establishment thinking according to status quo structures.

Such an attitude is reflected typically by movements (immobile "movements" indeed!) for "family, tradition and property," if understood in this context: preserving the patriarchal tradition of family and society and the present distribution of property. Of course, such organizations as "Pro familia, tradicao, propriedade," as well as the "John Birch Society," can have a healthy function insofar as they serve to unmask to all the connections between family patriarchalism, traditionalism and concern for the status quo as regards the distribution of wealth and power.

Only then, to the extent that the Church purifies herself by perhaps painful processes of trial, self-criticism, self-denial, and reform will her voice be credible to a society yearning for liberation. The community of faith is more influential through its presence and its witness to an unmistakable interdependence (where the stronger and more authentic self-manifestation speaks for itself) than through a social doctrine which does not reflect the Church's own life.

In this sense, the implementation of the doctrinal development of collegiality within the whole life of the Church is a condition for the effective teaching of the basic principle of subsidiarity in the modern world.

Subsidiarity and Solidarity

Two key attributes of a free society of free persons are subsidiarity and solidarity. In a modern society especially, subsidiarity is the very opposite of paternalism and centralism, and solidarity represents the victory over individualism and group egotism. As a dynamic process of liberating efforts, subsidiarity starts "from below" and encourages, fosters, and, where needed, coordinates "from above," while gradually blurring the lines of "below" and "above," at least as regards useless privileges. Freedom exists in the concert of responsible persons and communities, who encourage the maximum of initiative with the maximum of responsibility for the whole society. Subsidiarity means shared responsibility and to some extent, shared authority. The higher authority and the larger group should respect, foster, and protect the functions which are properly those of the individual person or smaller group. Both the personal initiative and group initiative should be encouraged in view of the common good. When extraordinary difficulties forcibly curtail the exercise of the normal function and rights of persons or groups, these functions and rights "should be restored as quickly as possible after the emergency passes" (*Gaudium et spes,* art. 75). All the relationships among the various communities and authorities should be marked by the readiness to contribute to the greatest possible liberty and the best possible discharge of responsibility on all levels. Individuals and small groups should only accept (and be offered) assistance which does not suffocate, but rather stimulates and liberates initiative and responsibility.

Modern Means of Communication, Progress of Freedom and Culture

In a society where only a few had access to higher learning, paternalism was appreciated, insofar as it expressed concern and service for the weaker members. Family patriarchalism was also characterized by an education gap between man and woman. The wife who was only trained for household duties and child-rearing willingly accepted the moderate patriarchial authority of the husband, renouncing gladly the representation by her of the family's rights outside the family.

Our highly scientific, technological age, characterized by the mass communications media and the general desire to share in learning and culture, can not be reconciled with the older forms of paternalism and centralism. Where there exists new and evident possibilities of equal sharing in the goods of cultural progress and in social responsibilities, the older forms of inequality become ever more strikingly unjust and are severely judged as obstacles to liberation.

If society wants to avoid unnecessary tensions and conflicts, liberation has to begin simultaneously on all levels. I would greatly favor equal opportunities for women and men. This would quickly come to bear on family structures. An effort to curb prostitution and similar forms of exploitation of women must be organized and coordinated simultaneously with positive efforts to foster and promote the new and equal dignity of woman. The partnership family is posited as a basic condition for the liberation of man and woman from the base desire to dominate others. Human life can be described as a system of interdependencies. The most decisive are the interdependence of family and the other social realities, the community of faith (religion), and social life (including family and marriage). It is imperative, therefore, that close attention be given to the overcoming of all forms of alienation and domination in the realm of family and religion. To this end, the modern means of communication and education are most important instruments. There is no doubt that they can be used for new forms of slavery, but they offer themselves as instruments of liberation. For instance, if all believers have a high level of education and share in culture, and at the same time possess a good knowledge of faith, the relationships between clergy and laity can change in the direction of greater sharing of learning and responsibility. As a consequence, the relationships between "higher" and "lower" clergy will also change.

I-Thou-Personalism but No Romantic I-Thou-Island

In the past, man spent better than 80 per cent of his time within the patriarchal family and in life structures modeled on that of the family. Today, modern man spends better than 80 per cent of his waking hours outside of the family circle, in a highly organized and "impersonal" social and economic role. A necessary reaction to this depersonalizing environment is the human person's greater need for intimate relationships in marriage, in family life, in friendship. Modern personalism's emphasis on the I-Thou relationship reflects this new psychological and sociological reality. Society will also lose its "soul," its human qualities, if man does not cultivate genuine personal relationships in marriage, in the family, in friendship, and in small communities. The profound transformation of the whole society calls for a totally new balance between intimate personal relationships and life in the socio-economic realm; it is an absolute prerequisite for man's liberation.

In this respect, two different "romantic" temptations are likely to arise. The first lies in building a romantic "I-Thou-Island" without a liberating commitment to the economic, social, and cultural life. The freezing cold relationships of the socio-economic world drive the human person to seek life and fulfillment almost exclusively in friendship or marriage and family. The I-Thou relationship becomes the island on which he wants to dwell if he is to find a personal life style and happiness. The socio-economic life is then the "other world" into which he penetrates solely for the purpose of obtaining the necessities of his "real life" in marriage and family. Psychologically, there is a dichotomy between the world of love and the world of justice. The warmth and respect which characterize the personal relationships in the small world do not irradiate the social and economic realm. Interest and commitment are almost totally exhausted or limited to the intimate group life. It follows that this kind of friendship can degenerate into a small group egotism of two or three. At any rate, the world would not be humanized if all the dyads and triads acted that way. And so the family and all these inhabitants of the "I-Thou-Island" would be creating stifling, suffocating social environments to which their backs are turned. Are not the powers behind our backs the most dangerous to our freedom?

The other form of "romanticism" is the archaic concept of economy and society as an "extension" of the patriarchal family. This unrealistic concept underlies the many forms of paternalism adopted by great landowners and the other so-called family enterprises representative of the early stages of capitalism. Their concept of property is linked to the immediate family. In the name of "Family, tradition and property" all forms of shared property and shared responsibility are suspect and declared communistic or marxistic. Some Catholic moralists of the traditional school (e.g., B. Ermecke) even went to the extreme of proposing an ethics of socio-economic life under the heading of "familiarism."

In a religious vocabulary we can refer to mankind as "the family of God," since we all have God as our Creator, Redeemer and Father, but we must seek the profound differences in the personal relationships in the family in modern organizations, both on the organizational and psychological levels. I am not playing down the transitional elements of intermediate types of community. There are definitely similarities between a family-community and cultural, socio-economic relationships and structures. But woe to the people who plan their family life on a bank model or who want the same kind of relationships in banking matters as in the intimate family circle.

The I-Thou relationships must not be confused with an institutional structure or contractual obligations. Despite Joseph Fletcher, in view of our modern life and more so because of it, we must distinguish love from justice. Love and justice are interrelated but they are not identical. Love has differing wavelengths, starting from the most intimate relationships in marriage, family life or a religious community, and extending to big corporations and international bodies.

A realistic approach distinguishes sharply between love and justice, but one's perspective should be integrative. For a healthy development of persons and interpersonal relationships, for a wholesome reciprocation of love, there can be no dichotomy between the I-Thou community and the broader social life. The human person is molded by the totality of his environment and above all, by his attitude toward this whole environment. For man to remain truly a person he must be open to the other and to the world in which he lives. Unless man continually tries to shape and reshape his world, his relationships, and the structures which condition or change them, he will never attain the full dimensions of freedom.

The good of freedom expresses itself in many forms and on many levels, but in the final analysis it is the good of undivided freedom. Mankind has to strive toward that ever greater freedom befitting man's nature, with both personal initiative and common efforts. Man contributes to the undivided freedom of all by a wise commitment to his neighbor and to all human conditions of life. At the same time, the human person constantly experiences the extent to which he is indebted to the community and society or is threatened by it.

Solidarity and Non-Violence

In the last analysis, liberation means the full development of all the energies of love and justice and of a human environment in which these energies of love find an ever better "investment." Such development gives encouragement to the world around us and fosters the free commitment, the constant effort to liberate the energies of love.

Freedom of the human person, of communities and of society is not something gained once and for all. Freedom is to be achieved and deepened through a constant struggle against the radiations of frustration and slavery that come from an unfree world around us, for persons who do not know what constitutes genuine freedom fail to commit themselves to the undivided good.

Genuine freedom cannot be enforced by means diametrically opposed to true freedom, namely, the freedom to develop all the energies of love and justice. Freedom and liberation for freedom can only be acquired by the right use of freedom, expressed in love and solidarity.

Non-violence, understood as an act of commitment to freedom and as the art of gathering together one's love energies for the sake of freedom and justice, is an expression of solidarity. Non-violence arises from the deep conviction of human solidarity. We are truly becoming free if we evince concern for the freedom of all and justice for all.

Non-violence does not imply passivity or lack of fortitude. Neither is it a cowardly acceptance of the status quo with its attendant impediments to freedom. Non-violence is an active and wise commitment to freedom in love and justice.

The Christian conviction of the solidarity of all before the God, Creator, and Redeemer of all men, enables the Christian to love his enemies, to show concern for the "liberation" of oppressors and tyrants as well as the oppressed. Since the ultimate role lies in the liberation of all energies of love for the full realization of human persons in all their dimensions, the means and methods to this end must be such as to express this love and contribute in shaping the world into a hospitable place for the liberating power of genuine love. Of course, opinions will differ in extreme cases: how much force can and must be used to offset or overcome the unjust violence of those who oppose rightful freedom and justice? But the fundamental question remains: "How much of our energies of non-violence and love can we really set free and coordinate in view of the gradual liberation of all?"

HUMAN RIGHTS
AND THE LIBERATION OF MAN
IN THE AMERICAS:
REFLECTIONS AND RESPONSES

HELDER CAMARA

I. Extremes Meet

All of us at the 1969 CICOP annual conference—who have come from the most diverse milieux, fields of influence, organizations and denominations—are studying the situations of the world and, more precisely, of our own countries, 20 years after the Declaration of the Rights of Man by the United Nations. The subject is of great importance because, as we see it, the liberation of man, threatened as it is by slavery, by a misery that sub-humanizes, and by a selfishness that de-humanizes, depends upon the respect that is shown towards human rights.

Let us plunge into this meditation trying to avoid, at least, two stumbling blocks:

— the risk of falling into unproductive and sterile mutual inter-personal aggressions capable of generating nothing but bitterness and resentment;

— the risk of remaining in the field of vagaries without coming to some brave and practical indicators and directions.

If it is true that we cannot, in any way, forget the roots which bind us to the countries where we were born, let us also remember that chance does not exist; it is Divine Providence that links us to a given spot in the world, to a given culture, to a given period of history. Let us have in mind then, that at all times we must make an effort to realize that we are inserted into one great human family. Let us mediate, let us talk, and let us prepare ourselves to act as Latin Americans, or as North Americans, but also as Citizens of the World!

II. Sub-Humanization and De-Humanization

THE MISERY THAT SUB-HUMANIZES

For someone who was born and has spent his whole life in a developed country, it is not, perhaps, easy to understand fully the meaning of article 1 of the Declaration of Human Rights, although I am sure that after all these days of work, you know it by heart:

All men are born free and equal in dignity and rights. All have a mind and a conscience, and all must act, in their relationship with others, in a spirit of fraternity.

Whoever lives in an underdeveloped country knows that there are millions of human creatures who are born and vegetate in an infra-human situation. Of course, they are sons of God endowed with a conscience and with the capacity to think and reason. But, as it is, their intelligence and liberty are slumbering and must be awakened.

Thence arises the impassioned task of *conscientization,* which in no way should be confused with mere *alphabetization.* To "conscientize" consists in the awakening of conscience, in the awakening of initiative within a spirit of team work. . . . Thence, comes the thrilling mission of fostering the enhancement of human beings, of fostering "human promotion"; that is, fraternal aid aimed at overcoming a state of affairs in which sub-men, dragging a sub-life, are tied to a sub-work.

Religion has a most relevant role with regard to "conscientization" and its consequence: human promotion and the organization of the community.

When the religious mystique renders man capable of really feeling himself a *son* of God, created in the image and likeness of God, the Lord and Father, entrusted with the mission of dominating nature and completing creation—when the religious mystique urges man to act as co-creator, religion transforms itself into a powerful force towards integral development.

It is almost unbelievable that in the 20th century the United Nations has deemed it important to proclaim the following in article 4 of the Declaration of Human Rights: "No one will be kept in a situation of slavery or servitude; slavery and the traffic of slaves are prohibited in all their forms."

In our underdeveloped countries, this is most precious. It allows us to ask: Is slavery prohibited in all its forms? In this case, it is up to us to denounce national forms of slavery and all forms of internal colonialism; that is, the system by which small groups, in all Latin America, build their own wealth upon the misery—I am not talking about poverty, but I do mean misery—of millions of their countrymen.

Of course, with regard to slavery, it all occurs without official character. The abolition of slavery in Brazil was proclaimed in 1888. It usually happens without a very distinct consciousness on the part of the enslavers. Many of them would feel offended if they were told that they still had slaves. They would only open their eyes and realize what they are doing if they exchanged places for a few moments with their own workers, to whom—they imagine—they assure human conditions as well as human work and a human standard of living.

It would be easy to multiply the articles on the Rights of Men. We can group the full measure of their implications only in the underdeveloped world. May I draw you to one very significant article. Article 5: "No one will be submitted to torture, nor to cruel punishments, un-human and degrading."

Although it is true that it was not in underdeveloped countries that "brainwashing" was invented, we must admit that in our countries it is disgraceful to see what happens to prisoners, from the humblest chicken thief to a political offender. Refinements of moral and physical torture are practiced in the name of scientific processes intended to find the truth.

After 48 hours of uninterrupted interrogations, in which the interrogators succeed one another, but the interrogated remains the same—after 48 hours of dizzying hypnotizing under spotlights —after 48 hours intermingled with promises and threats, of false information and hunger—what value should be attributed to the declarations that have been extorted? And what about the "ice-box treatment" and the sterilizing electric shocks? . . .

It is urgent to discredit these processes of obtaining so-called evidence, which very often are given "respectability" by the presence of law and psychology graduates.

THE SELFISHNESS THAT DE-HUMANIZES

As set forth in the Declaration of Human Rights, in article 22 and onward, we learn that social, economic, and cultural rights are considered and recognized as fundamental rights of man.

The world must surely believe that this is so because, since 1948 (and each year it becomes clearer) we have recognized that, besides the proletarization of persons and of groups, there exists the very serious phenomenon of the proletariat nations. And we see the resulting scandal in the existence of the underdeveloped world, which comprises almost three whole continents and includes the overwhelming majority of the world population!

It was easy for the United Nations to see that personal rights would be useless if the whole context of social, political and economic structures were crushing the human being. Therefore, article 22, for instance says:

All men, as members of a society, have the right to social security and to the accomplishment, by national effort, by international cooperation and in accordance with organization of resources of each State, of the economic, social and cultural rights, indispensable to his dignity and to the development of his personality.

If we look more closely into this article we will see that:

— the United Nations recognizes that there are economic, social, and cultural rights essential to the dignity and the free development of the human person;

— the United Nations proclaims that in order to assure that economic, social and cultural rights do not remain as mere words (and it is never enough to stress that these rights are indispensable for the dignity and the free development of the human person) and become a reality, all men are entitled to rely upon a national effort and upon international cooperation.

If one should ask the United Nations which are the rights without which the human person is injured in dignity and mutilated in enhancement, the United Nations would answer with article 23, analyzing the right to work; with article 24, referring to the rights of rest and leisure; with article 25, which refers to the right of each man to have a standard of living capable of assuring health and welfare for himself and his family; with article 26, referring to the right of instruction; and with article 27, the right to participate freely in the cultural life of the community.

In other words, we have the whole problem of integral development outlined in the Declaration of 1948. Twenty years later it would be well to speak still more clearly, after having gained experience from the painful failure of the first decade of development and the failure of the two attempts made by UNCTAD (United Nations Conference for Trade and Development).

Article 23 places all hope of integral development—considered as a basic element to avoid the crushing of the human person—in a national effort and in international cooperation. And is there any one so naive who does not know that, under the appearance of international cooperation, there are international injustices that annul all and any national efforts to reverse underdevelopment?

With all due respect towards the United Nations, may I ask you how the United Nations expects to be respected while saying "All men are born free and equal in dignity and in rights," when within the United Nations itself the member-states are not equal in dignity and in rights? As long as there are strong states and weak states within the United Nations itself, as long as there are some members with the veto power:

— the Declaration of Human Rights will be no more than beautiful, ringing words, capable only of creating illusions;

— the Declaration will not be brought up to date with regard to assuring the effective integral development of man and the development of the solidarity of mankind;

— the Declaration will not include anything that may stop the abuses of the super-powers, which will continue to promote the armaments race on a special scale with strategic aims, wars always-more-inhuman, economic blockades, make-believe aids and proletarizations on a world scale.

III. To What Practical Conclusions May We Come?

If we want CICOP to be more, and much more, than just a friendly meeting which brings together leaders from the U.S.A. and from Latin America to study serious problems and even to issue some solemn and beautiful declarations—in order that CICOP, as all of us want, may bring about concrete conclusions that bind us all—may I suggest some common tasks that could be attempted before the next CICOP meeting? I suggest the following points:

THE INTEGRATION OF CUBA INTO THE AMERICAN COMMUNITY

Let us try to organize and conduct (with the necessary precautions), in the United States and in Latin American countries, an effort having as its main object the reintegration of Cuba within the Latin American community. Our sister Cuba must be integrated into our community, with due respect for her political option and the acceptance of her autonomy as a sovereign nation.

To whoever is shocked and irritated, protesting in the name of the Cuban exiles and recalling the dangers of the guerrillas trained in Havana, let us recall that:

— the more the economic blockade is pursued and the continental excommunication encouraged, the more we will be forcibly confining a people who have given sufficient proof of heroism and capacity to suffer; the more the situation persists, the more we will be strengthening the barriers against a better relationship with all peoples and nourishing an attitude of sterile hate.

After all, let us not forget that the Cubans are also sons of God. We cannot condemn a whole nation to live in a ghetto.

THE ADMISSION OF RED CHINA TO THE UNITED NATIONS

Let us organize and conduct (with all due precautions) in the United States and in Latin America countries an effort aiming at the integration of Red China into the human community.

Two arguments seem enough to convince us:

— this was one of the appeals brought to the United Nations by one of the greatest visitors it ever had, the "pilgrim of peace," Paul VI;

— how can we leave out of the United Nations a country that is a real continent, whose population is a ponderable fraction of the population of the world?

A UNIVERSITY DEBATE ABOUT THE REPORT OF UNCTAD

Let us suggest and stimulate a meeting of four or five great North American universities with four or five Latin American universities with the object of examining the material of the two UNCTAD conferences. Such a group might question the scientific value of these reports or, on the contrary might use them as a starting point towards a complex but indispensable change in international trade policy.

If development is the new name for peace, and if without justice there will be no development, it is impossible to think about peace without examining deeply the accusations of large-scale injustice presented twice by the underdeveloped world, at Geneva and again at New Delhi.

A STUDY WITH REGARD TO THE NEW CONCEPT OF WAR AND OF THE NEW OBJECTIVE FOR THE ARMED FORCES

It is important—it is most urgent—for mankind that the average American convince himself of the absurdity and the foolishness of a new world war (which, to say the least, would mean the collective suicide of the whole earth). But the average American must also convince himself of the incredible price in human lives, in money as well as in prestige, of local wars like the Vietnam war.

This will not be easy because vast economic interests are sometimes very involved in the waging of war, and often these interests control the mass communications media and exert immense impact on the forging of public opinion.

However, the religions, and I say "religions" in the plural, could arouse mankind by using all of their resources to prove that war is always most absurd, inhuman, and immoral. We could take on ourselves the responsibility of proving that if the super-powers would spend for development what they are now spending for war—be it a cold or hot war—it would become evident that man, who is capable today of sweeping life from the face of the earth, is also capable of assuring for all human beings a standard of life compatible with human dignity.

The religions, all religions, could and should combine their forces to complete the beautiful statement that "development" is the new word for peace, by proclaiming that the only justifiable war must be the war against human misery.

Who knows but that some day the Pentagon may not give an example to the armed forces of the whole world by organizing a global strategy to liquidate misery from the face of the earth? And do not tell me that such a strategy would deliver the free world into the hands of the Communists and of the enslaving east!

When will we be able to show everybody that the number one problem facing mankind is not the clash between East and West, but between the North and the South—that is, between the developed world and the underdeveloped world? When will we be able to help everybody understand that misery is the enslaver, the assassin *par excellence,* and that it is the war against misery which should be the number one and only war, that war upon which we must focus our energy and resources.

A LIFE REVISION ON A WORLD SCALE

And now may I ask: What is the mystery that exists with regard to human rights? In theory all men should agree about human rights, and all governments should respect human rights in their totality. In practice, no government, no people can have a good conscience with regard to the Charter proclaimed 20 years ago by the United Nations.

It is curious to note how, in defense of liberty, one often denies the rights of an individual.

The United States, at least, admits the right to criticize and to dissent, which is not easy to find in many other countries.

I suggest that, as a result of this meeting, a documentary film be prepared by North Americans about the sins of the United States against the Rights of Man. I could make this same suggestion to other countries, but you still retain the freedom to do this. And I propose that this documentary film should be objective, without half-truths; but that it be also a dossier which would be an invitation to other countries to carry out similar examinations and revisions of life with regard to the rights of man. The more courageous the dossier of the United States, the more valuable will be the contribution to the whole world.

And now my brothers and sisters, permit me to say a final word at the hour in which the astronauts take off from the gravitational security of the world and move courageously towards the stars. Could it be that man is now capable of learning how to take off from selfishness and move courageously once and for all, towards love for his neighbors and love for God?

PART FIVE
AFTERWORD

THE LONGEST NIGHT

LOUIS M. COLONNESE

The liberation of man in the Americas is far from being achieved. The generally accepted guidelines to achieve that liberation, namely, the Declaration of Human Rights, have been articulated, but have not been implemented in any significant degree in Latin America today. Most countries in Latin America are enduring what one prominent labor leader calls "la noche mas larga," the longest night. It is a night in which military dictatorships suppress by national security acts even the hope to be free. It is a night in which university students, popular leaders, indigenous labor leaders, and conscience-stricken Church leaders are exiled, persecuted, or murdered for their belief that their people have the human dignity to be free to shape their own destiny. Not even Castro's revolution in Cuba against an oppressive governmental structure was as vicious or oppressive as what we are now witnessing most obviously under military regimes and elsewhere, less visibly, in Latin America.

Our authors have spoken of the obstacles to human rights in Latin America, both in their historical and current contexts. Possible approaches to the liberation of man have been delineated. But the fact remains that militarism is being encouraged, economic livelihood inhibited, education deprived, public assemblies prohibited, and human dignity crushed, in large measure due to American ambivalence toward the liberation of man in the Americas. If the United States discontinued its military aid, encouraged indigenous industry and labor movements instead of imposing foreign aid monies to be spent on purchases from American manufacturers or organizations, advocated mass education, instead of indoctrination, and promoted vital self-determination, self-dignity, and conscientization in our own hemisphere, oppressive regimes could not persist. But the United States appears to choose collusion instead of collision with the fragile status-quo centers of power that psychologically if not physically enslave most of Latin America.

Thus our commitment to liberating men in the Americas must be focused on accessible American institutions that inhibit liberation: the Department of Defense, the State Department, certain American business interests, and other nerve-centers of real and potential oppression currently espousing "a Pax Panamericana instead of Inter-American justice." The accepted roads to action in our democracy are through Congress, popular university, professional, and labor constituencies, communication media, the churches, and cooperative businessmen.

The obvious first step is a personal commitment to put one's self on the line for change in the Americas. Consider the fact that the student leaders, priests, ministers, and popular leaders jailed or slain these last months are real people whom you may have encountered at CICOP or elsewhere. Consider Monsignor Fox's admonition: "*I do not know how much I can afford to be free. The question of the liberation of others is the liberation of me.*" What are we willing to contribute to eliminate the grave inadequacies we confront in our common effort to realize human rights?

There are those who ask why the Church is engaged in these socio-economic issues, all of which affect the human condition. To paraphrase the late Senator Robert F. Kennedy, I would raise the following consideration: Some ask why the Church has not used its moral teaching authority to awaken a sense of human dignity, social justice, and social action among the masses and leadership in the Americas in the past. I dream dreams of the Church's potential for popular "conscientization" and Christian social action now and in the future and ask why not?

"La noche mas larga" is upon Latin America. Or as Juan Luis Segundo states, "neither revolution nor evolution but endurance" characterizes this transitory historical epoch in Latin America.

For those of us in the United States, these times must be marked with achievement beyond commitment. For all men of good will the United Nations Declaration of Human Rights can certainly provide a standard of progress or failure in human development in the Americas. Individual options beyond this universal norm must be the decision of each of us. The Catholic Inter-American Cooperation Program is an instrument of Christian commitment available as a channel of education, information, and communication on the urgent issues we have raised herein. This and other instruments for change in the Americas must be utilized more deliberately to achieve and sustain every aspect of human dignity in the Americas. As citizens of a country still permitting free speech and other freedoms, we are called upon by Latin Americans to use our situation as a springboard to "free up" the Inter-American system of increasingly oppressive and inhuman change: As Christians can we do less? As men of good will is there anything more urgent? Will we complete our work while *our* own daylight remains?

Index